Georges Feydeau
and the Aesthetics of Farce

Theater and Dramatic Studies, No. 9

Bernard Beckerman, Series Editor

Brander Matthews Professor of Dramatic Literature
Columbia University in the City of New York

Other Titles in This Series

No. 1	*The Original Casting of Molière's Plays*	Roger W. Herzel
No. 2	*Richard Foreman and the Ontological-Hysteric Theatre*	Kate Davy
No. 3	*The History and Theory of Environmental Scenography*	Arnold Aronson
No. 4	*The Meininger Theater: 1776-1926*	Steven DeHart
No. 5	*Shakespeare Refashioned: Elizabethan Plays on Edwardian Stages*	Cary M. Mazer
No. 6	*The Public and Performance: Essays in the History of French and German Theater, 1871-1900*	Michael Hays
No. 7	*Richard Boleslavsky: His Life and Work in the Theatre*	J.W. Roberts
No. 8	*Andrea Palladio's Teatro Olimpico*	J. Thomas Oosting
No. 10	*The Theatre Director Otto Brahm*	Horst Claus

Georges Feydeau

and the Aesthetics of Farce

by
Stuart E. Baker

UMI RESEARCH PRESS
Ann Arbor, Michigan

Copyright © 1981, 1976
Stuart E. Baker
All rights reserved

Produced and distributed by
UMI Research Press
an imprint of
University Microfilms International
Ann Arbor, Michigan 48106

Library of Congress Cataloging in Publication Data

Baker, Stuart E.
  Georges Feydeau and the aesthetics of farce.

  (Theater and dramatic studies,, no. 9)
  Revision of thesis (Ph. D.)–City University of
New York, 1976.
    Bibliography: p.
    Includes index.
    1. Feydeau, Georges, 1862-1921–Criticism and
interpretation. 2. Farce. I. Title. II. Series.

PQ2611.E86Z55   1981   842'.8   81-16410
ISBN 0-8357-1265-6   AACR2

Contents

Note on Titles   *ix*

Acknowledgments   *xi*

1 Introduction: The Aesthetics of Farce   *1*
   The Missing Standards of Farce
   Literary Bias and Scornful Laughter
   Philosophical Laughter
   Reality and Unreality
   Farce and Games
   Rules of the Game
   Modes of Farce: Who Is the *Farceur?*
   The Independent and Constant Clown
   Players and Playthings
   Form and Pattern
   The Manipulating Playwright
   Clowns and the Mechanized World

2 Plot and Action: The Mechanics of Misunderstanding   *25*
   Consistency and Conventionality
   The Deception Formula
   Evolution of His Style
   The Comedy of Misapprehension
   The Logic of *Vaudeville*
   Tools of Manipulation: Objects and
      Appearances
   The Inverted Pyramid
   Order and Chaos
   Variations on the Theme
   New Directions
   Wisdom and Folly

3 The Inner Structure   45
   Probabilities and Progressive Madness
   Exaggeration and Truth
   Fatalism and Farce
   Conflicts, Contradictions, and
      Transformations
   The Playwright as Magician
   The Familiar and the Exotic
   The Two Sides of Sexual Fantasy
   The Role of Violence
   The Integration of Conflicts in Farce

4 Character: Disrupters and Victims   75
   The Community of Fools
   The Disabled in Body and Soul
   Money and Appearances: The Basic Values
   The Role of the Physically Impaired
   Orbits around the Bourgeois Household
   The Ingénue as Trickster, Clown, and Fool
   Husbands, Wives, and the Sanctity of the
      Hearth
   Puppets and Pawns
   Servants and Masters
   Foreigners and the Assault on Civilization
   The *Cocotte*, Queen of Fools

5 Conclusion: Thoughts on the Significance of
   Feydeau and the Value of Farce   *107*
   Limitations of Serious Criticism
   Je m'en foutisme: The Philosophy of
      Frivolous Disenchantment
   Feydeau and the Absurdists
   The Value of Frivolous Objectivity
   Feydeau and Shaw
   Limitations to the "Absolutely Comic"
   For the Love of Foolish Things

Appendix A.   On Performing Feydeau   *117*

Appendix B.   Feydeau and the French Theatre: A Chronology   *123*

Notes   *133*

Bibliography   *151*

Index   *159*

Note on Titles

There is no standard English version of the titles of most of Feydeau's plays. The titles of the majority of translations bear little or no resemblance to the French originals. In order to avoid confusing those familiar with Feydeau in his native language, the original titles are used in the text. As an aid to those not familiar with French, literal translations are provided when the plays are introduced. A complete list of titles with their English equivalents is given below:

Affaire Edouard, L' (The Edward Affair)
Age d'or, L' (The Golden Age)
Amour et piano (Love and Piano)
Bain de ménage, Un (Household Bath)
Bourgeon, Le (The Sprout)
Cent millions qui tombent (One Hundred Million Windfall)
C'est une femme du monde (She's a Respectable Woman)
Champignol malgré lui (Champignol in Spite of Himself)
Chat en poche (Pig in a Poke)
Circuit, Le (The Road Race)
Dame de chez Maxim, La (The Lady from Maxim's)
Dindon, Le (The Sucker)
Dormez, je le veux! (Sleep! I Command You!)
Duchesse des Folies-Bergère, La (The Duchess from the Folies-Bergère)
Feu la mère de Madame (Madam's Late Mother)
Fiancés de Loches, Les (The Fiancés from Loches)
Fiancés en herbe (Budding Fiancés)
Fil à la patte, Un (Tied by a String)
Gibier de potence (Gallows-Bird)
Hortense a dit: "Je m'en fous! (Hortense Said: "I Don't Give a Damn!")
Hôtel du Libre-Echange, L' (Hotel Paradiso)
Je ne trompe pas mon mari (I Don't Cheat on My Husband)
Léonie est en avance (Léonie is Premature)

Lycéenne, La (The Schoolgirl)
Main passe!, La (Pass the Deal!)
"Mais n'te promène donc pas toute nue!" ("Do Not Parade around Stark Naked!")
Mariage de Barillon, Le (Barillon's Marriage)
Monsieur chasse! (Monsieur Has Gone Hunting!)
Notre futur (Our Intended)
Occupe-toi d'Amélie (Keep an Eye on Amélie)
On purge Bébé (Junior Gets a Laxative)
On va faire la cocotte (Going to Play the Courtesan)
Par la fenêtre (Through the Window)
Pavés de l'ours, Les (The Bear's Embrace)
Puce à l'oreille, La (A Flea in Her Ear)
Ruban, Le (The Decoration)
Séance de nuit (Night Session)
Système Ribadier, Le (The Ribadier System)
Tailleur pour dames (Ladies' Dressmaker)

Acknowledgments

I wish to express my deepest gratitude to the many people without whom this book could not have been written. I especially want to thank Professor Daniel Gerould, who first taught me the joy of scholarship, gave me both the courage and the encouragement I needed to begin and complete the work, and who continues to be an inspiration; Professor Albert Bermel for his thorough and meticulous comments on the manuscript; Professor Marvin Seiger for his careful reading and comments; Professor Edwin Wilson for his encouragement and support; my mother, Mary Charlotte Baker, for her moral and monetary assistance; and finally, Shirley Chipman and Jalma Shaffer for their help in preparing the manuscript.

1
Introduction: The Aesthetics of Farce

God hath chosen the foolish things of the world to confound the wise.
I Corinthians 1:27

Every more general principle of aesthetics founders on the farce.
Kierkegaard[1]

The Missing Standards of Farce

Before one can begin to examine the plays of Feydeau *as farces* it is necessary to discuss the nature and purpose of farce. Such a theoretical introduction would be unnecessary, if not tediously pedantic, were tragedies or comedies under consideration. The more respectable dramatic genres have already been thoroughly discussed and analyzed. There is disagreement among theoreticians, but the major premises and arguments are familiar. Farce, on the other hand, has rarely been subjected to theoretical analysis. The scarcity of farce theories alone would not make a new one necessary. One could cite L.C. Knight's contention that such theories are lazy generalizations that serve only to hinder the criticism of individual plays and conclude that the lack of farce theories should be a boon to farce criticism.[2] But traditional farce, with its frivolous devotion to amusement and its apparent irrationality, is less susceptible to the tools of literary criticism than is the more respected genre of comedy. The criticism of individual plays may not require the formulas of the comic theorists, but it does depend upon at least a general agreement as to the purpose of this form of dramatic literature and the standards by which it should be evaluated. Such an understanding does not exist with respect to farce. It is judged by the standards of literary comedy and, not surprisingly, is usually found wanting. Before farce can be judged on its own terms, there must be some agreement as to its particular aims and the means by which it achieves them.

Kierkegaard, in support of the statement quoted at the head of this chapter, said that farce "is totally incapable of producing a uniform mood in the more cultured audience."[3] Traditionally a popular entertainment, farce has had difficulty gaining appreciation or understanding from the "more cultured audience" which includes its self-appointed judges. The critics have usually seen farce in a negative light, describing what it lacks by comparison with literary comedy. Such assessments often lead, not illogically, to an attack on farce as undisciplined, vulgar, grotesque, or irrational. The attacks are frequently accompanied by some expression of bewilderment that their target, so obviously deplorable and unpleasant, should be so popular. Farce's ability to please is commonly assumed to spring from the ignorance, folly, or viciousness of the public. Dryden's comparison of comedy and farce is an excellent illustration of the literary point of view:

> Comedy presents us with the imperfections of human nature: Farce entertains us with what is monstrous and chimerical. The one causes laughter in those who can judge of men and manners, by the lively representation of their folly or corruption: The other produces the same effect in those who can judge of neither, and that only by its extravagances.... But, how it happens, that an impossible adventure should cause our mirth, I cannot so easily imagine. Something there may be in the oddness of it, because on the stage it is the common effect of things unexpected, to surprise us into a delight: and that is to be ascribed to the strange appetite, as I may call it, of fancy.[4]

Even many of those more sympathetic to farce see it as debased and undisciplined comedy. According to Lea, "when we care for neither character nor motives, but are content to be amused by whatever absurdity may be trumped up, it is farce."[5] Like Lea, Hughes sees farce as devoted to exciting laughter at any cost, and concludes that neither plot nor any other form of overall, unifying structure is important to farce:

> Clearly enough, the structure of farce is readily divisible into two phases or levels: the framework and the details or, an even better figure, the thread and the separate beads. Of the two the former has little interest for us. Almost any form of intrigue or chain of incidents will serve to link the *lazzi* which are the real stuff of farce.[6]

The negative, reductive approach is carried further by Stephenson, who claims that farce has so little which really belongs to it that it is only a "method" and cannot properly be called a genre at all. His argument is circular, since it starts with the assumption that early farce was "inchoate *vis comica* in search of a body," and concludes that farce, being formless and protean, "indifferently assumes the shape of its materials."[7] Despite his own faulty logic, his description of farce as "inchoate *vis comica*" represents the logical result of describing farce only in terms of what it is not.

Farce presents difficulties beyond its indulgence in apparent irrationality and formlessness. There is much in both the subject matter and the treatment of farce that many find disturbing. Farce is not gentle. "One of the hallmarks of farce," as Albert Bermel writes, "has been its pitilessness."[8] Although

Bermel writes of farce in sympathetic and positive terms, many of the qualities he describes have caused others to see farce as even worse than irresponsible and frivolous. It is destructive; "it strives to reduce the pillars of society to ruins." It frequently employs physical violence: "Some or all of the characters in farce undergo physical damage." It is indiscriminate in its violence; the innocent suffer equally with the guilty. It does not confine itself to ridiculing correctible faults and vices, but invites us to laugh at "blindness, deafness, speech defects, goiters, and sundry other disfigurements and deficiencies." The characters themselves often seem less than human, or at least subnormal. "They are not equipped for reflection; they do not appear to lead self-conscious, independent lives nor think interesting thoughts." Bermel points out that it is unreasonable to object to the limited characterizations in farce, for if they "seemed more like human beings, we would be less able to laugh at their misfortunes."[9] But this may not be justification enough for some, particularly those who, in the tradition of Hobbes, assume laughter is always derisive. Shaw, who attempted to "humanize" both melodrama and farce, argued that conventional farces produced "base laughter" by turning "human beings on to the stage as rats are turned into a pit, that they may be worried for the entertainment of the spectators." Such laughter, he felt, meant the "deliberate indulgence of that horrible, derisive joy in humiliation and suffering which is the beastliest element in human nature."[10] Even Eric Bentley, who strongly defends farce, finds its basic appeal in the enjoyment of violence and aggression, which he justifies as a harmless outlet for hostile, anti-social feelings.[11] But by itself this is a weak defense, for it puts farce in a class with pornography. It is properly an argument against censorship, but it cannot justify calling farce an art, however humble. One may instinctively feel that there is a great difference between the violence in farce and the dehumanized sex and sadism of pornography, but to understand farce and to defend it as an art, one must define the nature of that difference.

Literary Bias and Scornful Laughter

Surely the key to the difference is in laughter. But to discover the nature and meaning of farce laughter, it is necessary to dispel a long-established prejudice regarding the function of laughter in art. Of the numerous and varied theories of laughter which have been offered since the time of Plato, one theory, or group of theories, has found especial favor with literary critics: those formulas that see the source of laughter in derision or a sense of superiority. Such theories offer them something the others do not provide: a rational basis for comedy. Corrective comedy, founded on derisive laughter, not only has a useful social function, it puts laughter firmly on the side of reason. To the advocates of superior or derisive mirth, the person laughing always maintains a view consistent with his rational or serious perception of the thing laughed at. He shares the judgmental bias of the critic. Comedy can then be defended as fundamentally serious, with laughter serving to reinforce its rational content. The theory of scornful laughter provides comedy with an admirable defense against the charge of triviality, but this defense has certain disadvantages. It effectively limits the scope of comedy in two important ways. First, to the extent that it elicits laughter, comedy must be a representation of reality. Comedy must direct laughter beyond itself and focus on the abuses of the world. If it presents objects or events that cannot reasonably be said to represent absurdities in the real world, then comedy itself becomes the target of laughter, and the comedian is open to the charge that he is debasing himself for the derisive pleasure of the spectators. Moreover, such laughter would be pointless. Feeling superior to imaginary and impossible absurdities can hardly be an edifying or artistic experience. The spectator is in the absurd position of priding himself on his superiority to nothing. Second, comedy must be limited in the kinds of reality it represents, avoiding all objects unworthy of derision. The physical deformities and violent abuse characteristic of farce must be shunned, for the comic portrayal of such things invites the audience to mock that which they should pity. The theory of scornful laughter, by the same criteria with which it affirms the value of comedy, must condemn farce as either worthless or harmful.

Modern critics, less defensive about the value of comic art than those of earlier periods, are also less insistent that comedy be corrective. They may even be embarrassed by the idea, perhaps fearing that if comedy were judged on its effectiveness in mending the ways of men, it could logically be dismissed as a waste of effort. Nevertheless, the underlying assumption of corrective comedy, that laughter implies censure, is still the basis of most literary discussions of comedy. If today's critics are hesitant to affirm the moral usefulness of comedy, they still cling to the idea of laughter as a rational judgment of worth. It is a notion that greatly simplifies their task. To discover the meaning of a comedy, one need ask only who or what is being mocked. Nonrealistic comedies present a greater challenge and a wider selection of interpretations, but the aim of the critic is the same: to disclose the target of the author's scorn.

Even if false, the assumption that laughter is always derisive probably causes little serious misinterpretation in the case of literary comedy. Most plays of this type can be properly regarded as portrayals of the absurdities of life, whether they are presented realistically, symbolically, or in exaggerated form. More importantly, there is much in literary comedy that is not directly related to provoking laughter. The vision of a critic biased toward scornful laughter may be limited by his prejudice, but it need not be distorted. In farce, the opportunity for misunderstanding is much greater. When farce is noticed by the critics, it is apt to be treated, like comedy, as a critical commentary on the real world. The early French farce *Pierre Pathelin* is praised for its portrayal of the roguery of lawyers, the plays of Eugène Labiche admired for their exposure of bourgeois pompousness. Georges Feydeau is esteemed for his observation of the foibles of his time or for anticipating the Absurdist vision of the universe.[12] Specifically farcical elements may be mentioned, often by way of apology, but are rarely discussed or analyzed. The assumption of most is that laughter, whether in comedy or farce, must be critical in order to be defensible.

Philosophical Laughter

That assumption, however, is not necessary to an appreciation of the significant role laughter can play in literature, even in acknowledged classics. The spirit of festive or carnival laughter found by Barber in the comedies of Shakespeare, by Segal in the plays of Plautus, and by Bakhtin in the works of Rabelais, more than being simply a matter of gaiety and lightness of tone, forms part of the philosophy or view of the world contained in those works.[13] According to Bakhtin, Rabelais embodies a Renaissance concept that saw laughter as "one of the essential forms of truth concerning the world as a whole."[14] One of the principal sources of this view was the popular tradition of carnival laughter, laughter that is universal in scope, taking the entire world as its object. It is ambivalent, not wholly negative. "It asserts and denies, it buries and revives."[15] It celebrates all that is relative, incomplete, and changing.

Modern psychological investigations have developed insights which are sometimes similar to the earlier, nonscientific views of laughter described by Bakhtin. Central to the Renaissance concept of laughter is Aristotle's observation that laughter is unique to human beings.[16] To the Renaissance, "laughter was seen as man's highest spiritual privilege, inaccessible to other creatures."[17] In this century, several psychologists have seen a relationship between the processes involved in humor and those characteristic of productive thinking.[18] They see laughter as a sign, not of animal aggression or hostility, but of that which distinguishes us as human beings: our creative imaginations. While some eminent literary critics continue to see laughter as the expression of sexuality and aggression, motivational psychologists—who study sex and aggression—are beginning to view laughter and play as aspects of those mental processes which have freed us from the tyranny of primitive drives and made us the most flexible and adaptive of animals.[19] Play and humor are manifestations of the process by which old patterns of behavior, thought, and feeling are broken down and new ones established. Bakhtin's description of the medieval carnival, whose vital principle was laughter, seems even more appropriate in this light. It was, he says, "the feast of becoming, change, and renewal. It was hostile to all that was immortalized and completed."[20] Laughter is a sign of our freedom from automatic, unchanging responses to the world. Henri Bergson may have been right in thinking that laughter is the enemy of rigidity, but it is our own inflexibility that is attacked when we laugh, not that of others.

To say that laughter is somehow related to creativity, that the mirthful delight in novelty, incongruity, and complexity is much like that which leads to discovery and invention, is to acknowledge that humor often has an important intellectual component, that the "fancy" Dryden saw as a mental aberration has a positive aspect. But what of the emotional element in laughter? The laughter in farce often originates in images usually associated with strong, often unpleasant, emotions. What is the relationship between laughter and emotion? The obvious answer, supplied by common experience, is that laughter is the enemy of emotion. Even Freud, famous for his views on "tendency wit," acknowledged that the function of some forms of laughter is to reduce, rather than to express, emotion.[21] It is obvious that hostility and feelings of aggression play a part in many jokes and witticisms, but such expressions of ill-will are of a different order than direct expressions of the same emotions. An insult in jest is not the same as an insult in earnest, although the motivation for each may be identical. Even when hostility is clearly present, laughter is less an expression of strong emotion than a release from it. There is at least some truth to Koestler's assertion that laughter represents "emotion cast off by the intellect," making it one of the most valuable of human possessions. "Laughter rings the bells of man's departure from the rails of instinct. He has emancipated himself from the humourless laws of the biological urge, from the fanaticism of purposeful singlemindedness."[22] Laughter and a sense of humor have endowed humans with a degree of objectivity and control even over their own passions, something which no other animal possesses.

One wonders why so many have attempted to associate laughter with the worst in human nature, why they have sought to find the source of all wit and humor, as did one theorist, in the *"roar of triumph in an ancient jungle duel."*[23] Rather than speculating about our anthropoid ancestors, they would do well to look at a study done at Yale University on laughter in babies. The researchers found that the most consistently successful "joke" was "swinging the subject out as if to throw him to his mother and then rapidly withdrawing him again."[24] If a single, archetypal image of laughter is wanted, it is here in the laughter of babies, not the victory howl of a jungle primate.

There is no need to find excuses for the "cruelty" found in farce. The unpleasant aspects of farce are there in order to be annihilated by laughter. If there is triumph in farce laughter, it is the elation of victory over pain, disgust, anger, and humiliation. The characters in farce are often quite ordinary;

which is to say, very like ourselves. The pain and humiliation they endure could be ours. But in one way they are strangely unlike us, for they are seemingly impervious to suffering. Eric Bentley has noted that one of the characteristics of farce violence is its abstractness.[25] The violence is robbed of its consequences, and therefore of its pain. Farce characters are enormously resilient; they are always bouncing back from situations that would destroy real people. They may be bruised, battered, kicked, and humiliated, but they always emerge whole. The pleasure they give the audience is not derived from the enjoyment of the suffering of others, but lies in the freedom from pain and defiance of fear that laughter provides. It is not a quibble to say that this laughter is pitiless but not cruel. Farce may still be too strong for some, not because it asks them to feel aggressive or hostile emotions, but because of the feelings of pity and compassion it asks them *not* to feel.

Reality and Unreality

This is not to say that farce is never satirical, or that it never provides an outlet for aggression and hostility, or is never even deliberately cruel. At times it may be all of these things. But satire, aggression, and cruelty are not its essence. The mistaken impression that these things are at the heart of farce stems from a literary prejudice which has been conditioned by centuries of analyzing only comedy. Farce, as Bermel points out, deliberately seeks an "unreality of mood," while comedy "remains grounded in reality."[26] Comedy is founded on the convention that its characters and events have, at some level, a counterpart in reality. The audience is encouraged to think of the characters as they would of real people, and of their problems as real problems. In this sense, comedy is always serious. But farce dissociates itself from the real world. Its situations are no longer bound to real people outside ourselves, whom we might hate, fear, love, or pity. They are wrenched free of reality to become detached and somewhat abstract.

Farce does not avoid reality altogether or confine itself to fantasy alone. In order to achieve a mood of unreality

> ... playwright will generally begin his farce in commonplace, credible circumstances and surroundings. Then by means of theatrical logic he will shift it gradually into improbability and beyond that into the realm of nonsense.[27]

It might be said that comedy both begins and ends in reality, even if it employs nonrealistic means along the way, while farce begins in reality and ends in unreality. Ian Maxwell concludes his examination of medieval French farce with this observation:

> The genius of farce lies in two rival virtues. The one is a keen sense of fact, which includes awareness of the normal background of life as well as an eye for its humours. The other is that light-hearted fancy which delights to stretch its credit with the audience, to touch the limits of conceivable absurdity, to crack the wind of a phrase and caper a yard above the highway of meaning.[28]

The best farces, he goes on to say, contain a balance of the two qualities. Walter Kerr, examining silent film farce, finds that an inherent combination of fact and fantasy had much to do with the success of that form. The medium itself contains an "interior tension" between those two "contending forces [which] have to be kept in balance or the form breaks apart."[29]

Both reality and fantasy are necessary to farce. But if farce does not, like comedy, refer back to reality, then how is it to be understood and evaluated? Comedy can be judged by how well, how profoundly, or how cleverly it portrays the real world. In comedy, unreality may be a means, but in farce it is an end, a necessary part of the final result. Farce may even, as Bermel says, enter "the realm of nonsense." By what rules or principles is this world of nonsense to be judged, and what is the nature of its relation to reality?

Farce and Games

A partial answer to these questions is provided by the earlier discussion of violence in farce. Farce presents unpleasant or violent images of reality, then uses improbability, absurdity, and nonsense to demolish them with explosions of laughter. But the reality of farce is not limited to unpleasantness and violence, and its absurdities, however nonsensical, are not without form. Nonsense itself need not be without order or meaning, as Elizabeth Sewell has shown in her study of the works of Edward Lear and Lewis Carroll. Her use of the term "Nonsense" is limited to the imaginative works of those two men, but her findings are relevant to farce. Nonsense, she says, can be understood as a game involving two contending forces of the mind. One of these is a force toward disorder, represented by the dream and the nightmare, and the other is the mind's tendency to order and logic. Sewell emphasizes the latter, for "true Nonsense...sides with order against disorder," but both are necessary. "Nonsense is a game which requires opposition between the two forces, not the reconciliation of the two nor the complete suppression of one or other."[30] If farce can also be seen as a game, the "interior tension" between fact and fantasy might involve a similar opposition of contending forces.

The idea of farce as a game is especially apt for the farcical tradition of the *vaudeville* in which Feydeau wrote. Successful writers of *vaudevilles* were often likened to jugglers or to chess players.[31] Sarcey wrote of the *vaudeville* as a game that grew in sophistication as the audience became more familiar with the rules.[32] Bergson begins his discussion of the comic in situations by drawing analogies from the playthings of children, and he concludes the section by saying that the *vaudeville,* like such toys, is nothing but a game.[33] Games, like farce, can be engaged in for their own sakes, not for their usefulness or possible relevance to serious endeavors. They may bear resemblance to situations arising in real life (as chess resembles the strategies of battle), but once established, they operate according to rules and conditions which isolate them from outside considerations. Like farce, they may originate in reality, but in the end refer to nothing but themselves.

There are other characteristics of the game which should apply if it is to provide a useful comparison. Games imply not only an opposition of contending sides, but also some degree of manipulation or conscious control. The clash of blind forces does not constitute a game. This element of games is the principal reason Sewell maintains that Nonsense takes the side of order against disorder. The orderly side of the mind (numbers, logic) is subject to conscious manipulation. It can be played with. The disorderly side (dreams, nightmares) cannot, at least not directly.

> Dream vision is essentially fluid; nothing is reliable, anything may change into anything else.... The result is that dreams cannot be controlled and so cannot be played with. From this something rather alarming seems to follow: that dreams play with the dreamer, who is our self. Perhaps this holds good of all the things in experience which we cannot break down and control and play with. They may play with us.[34]

The dream element of the mind can be played with only as an opponent, an antagonist whose moves cannot be predicted. It can be countered through the manipulation of logic and number, but not directly controlled. If farce is considered as a game, reality and fantasy differ in the same way. Reality corresponds to the "dream" of Nonsense, and fantasy to the "logic," insofar as the one cannot be controlled while the other can. The game of farce, like that of Nonsense, pits "the things in experience which we cannot break down and control and play with" against those we can.

There is another level to the game of farce that is even closer to that of Nonsense. In order to sustain the game, its fantasy side must always be under control. Fantasy is like Nonsense in that it is made up of order and disorder, of logic and dreams. Many of the techniques used by farce to defeat reality are themselves disorderly and must in turn be countered by logic and order.

> The plots of farces generally appear to be anarchic. Everything gets out of the characters' control, although, in French farces especially, this effect can be realized only because the dramatist has maintained a tight control over the sequence of events.[35]

Feydeau, for example, is noted both for a sense of madness and for the geometric precision of his plots. Some forms of farce may emphasize the dialectic of order and disorder over that of fact and fantasy. The plays of N.F. Simpson are less firmly rooted in reality than those of Feydeau, and concentrate instead on the opposition of apparent chaos to underlying logic. Simpson is sometimes called a disciple of Ionesco, but logic is important to the English writer, while Ionesco defies it. From the point of view of farce as a game, the difference is crucial. The loss of clearly defined order or logic (and therefore of control) provides a purely technical reason that a farce such as *Les Chaises* must be qualified as "tragic." For when we lose control of the fantastic in farce, it deserts us to side with reality, where it becomes an even more formidable, because less predictable, opponent than reality alone. When this happens, the game ceases. Until the final moments, the action of *Les Chaises* is much like that of a game. Only then is control completely lost, through the finality of death and the incoherence of the speaker. While a traditional farce, like *Pathelin,* might use the lack of speech to prolong the game, here it signals that play is no longer possible. When the players have died, the playthings die also.

The obdurate world of reality, of which the inanimate realm of things is a part, cannot be said to play with us unless we make it do so. The same is true of fantasy out of control. Like the playthings Bergson offers as comic paradigms, these forces outside ourselves cannot come alive and join in the game unless we are capable of playing with them. Their playfulness is an illusion that disappears when we lose control. Because they are not conscious and rational they cannot be thought of as playing even when they control and manipulate us. The analogy of the game becomes less relevant. For this reason it is not as useful in dealing with Ionesco and many other modern writers of farce. But when farce loses its playfulness, it is in danger of becoming something else. *Les Chaises* is labeled a *tragic* farce, and many of the plays of Pinter might be seen with equal validity as either farce or melodrama. There may be other ways as well in which farce can become momentarily serious, but the spirit of play cannot be abandoned for long.

Rules of the Game

The object of the game of farce is not to defeat reality, but to play with it and perhaps force it to play back. To defeat reality would be either an impossible or a trivial and shallow victory. It would be impossible in the case of actual physical reality: the flesh and blood of the actors and the physical conditions of the stage. And to destroy completely the reality represented on the stage by creating pure fantasy would be trivial.[36] Farce is capable of playing with both the imitated and actual reality, sometimes simultaneously. It often acknowledges both levels of reality through a device called "breaking the dramatic illusion," although the term "illusion" is misleading to the extent that the convention it refers to is not limited to realistic or representational drama.[37] Serious drama may employ conventions such as narrators or choral addresses which acknowledge the presence of the audience, but it usually expects the audience to regard the performance *as if it were* real. The integrity of the presentation, however conventional or nonrealistic, is not violated. But the actors in farce speak to the audience in order to expose their own performance as a sham. They may break character, referring to themselves as actors, or make jokes about the artifice of the stage and its machinery. Yet while they call attention to the fact that they are "only playing," they do not usually step entirely out of character. They will continue playing their roles in apparent earnest, even as they admit the pretense of the performance. They simultaneously inhabit two worlds: a world of actuality and a world of imagination. The point is not that they may alternately occupy each realm (an actor in a serious drama may easily speak to the audience *ex persona* between the acts), but that they can do both at the same time, playing with both levels of reality by balancing them against each other.[38]

Not all creators of farce make use of this device. Those most intensely concerned with developing their form's potential often deliberately avoid it. They do so not out of respect for realism for its own sake, but because the device is too easy. For the game to be meaningful it must not be so effortlessly won. They respect the representational reality of the performance in order to increase the challenge, to avoid easy victories. Buster Keaton, for example, carefully maintained the integrity of his performance and the world he created on film. According to Kerr, Keaton regarded the camera lens as an absolute barrier between himself and the public and avoided the device of referring to the audience which other comedians employed.[39] He played the game by strict rules. He insisted, for example, that stunts be shot whenever possible in a single, uninterrupted sequence. The stunt would have to be performed as it would for a live audience. The camera was thought of as an objective recorder of actual events, and Keaton did not wish to undercut that reality with simple cuts. It was not the realism of the result that he respected, for there is much that is impossible in his films. He respected the conditions of reality imposed by the nature of film. He wanted to play the game honestly.

Feydeau was another who respected the barrier between audience and performer, but he worked in a medium which imposed different rules. Norman Shapiro, writing of the film version of *L'Hôtel du Libre-Echange (Hotel Paradiso)*, said

> Feydeau's comedy does not, I fear, translate well into the film medium. It thrives on the restrictions of a proscenium stage, where the very limitations of space impart a focus and an intensity that the camera destroys with its limitless virtuosity.... A thousand things happen in a Feydeau play. Much of their comic strength lies precisely in the fact that, on stage, they all have to happen in the same place.[40]

An extreme example of this occurs in *La Puce à l'oreille (A Flea in her Ear)*, in which an actor must play two roles. Part of the comic effect results from the difficulty the actor must overcome in appearing to be in two places at once. In film the difficulty disappears and the effect is lost. Each game must be played according to its own rules. Feydeau was fastidious about complying with the rules of realism, but when those rules permitted, he was willing to play with the obstacles presented by the physical nature of the stage.[41]

There are many different types of farce and consequently many sets of rules. One way to begin categorizing types of farce would be to look at the conditions imposed by the medium and the conventions of the form. There is another way of grouping farces, however, one that helps to explain the great diversity of style and method found in farce.

Modes of Farce: Who Is the *Farceur*?

Farce is often said to turn its characters into puppets, helpless marionettes subject only to the will of their creator. It might be objected, first, that the playwright never has quite as much freedom as is implied by that metaphor. Furthermore, there are many farces in which it is totally inappropriate. Harlequin and Pantelone may not be precisely like real people, but they are certainly not puppets in the hands of a playwright. Another generalization made about farce is that it is unconcerned with form or structure. Yet one of the chief complaints made about the French farces of the nineteenth century is that they are dominated by their structure—they are "all plot."[42] That these generalizations appear valid in some cases but flatly inappropriate in others suggests the possibility of different categories of farce, the nature of which can be seen by turning once again to the game. If farce can usefully be regarded as a game, there is one important question yet to be asked: Who are the players? The world of reality has been described as in some way the antagonist, but it is a "player" only to the extent that it is played with by a human agent. That agent cannot be the audience, which participates only passively. There are only two real possibilities: the actors or the playwright. Which of these it is makes considerable difference to the nature of farce, because the player must have autonomy. The player must be free to manipulate, and cannot be wholly subject to the will of another. Thus there are two possible modes of farce, depending on whether actors or playwrights are the principal players in the game. Which of these modes is employed determines the organizing principle of the farce and the basis of its unity. When controlled by the actor, farce is organized around the special nature of its principal characters; while in the mode where the playwright prevails, farce is dominated by "plot," "structure," or the ordering of the incidents, for it is by these that the dramatist shows his manipulating hand. In practice, the two methods are not mutually exclusive.

Farce generally employs both modes, but to the extent that one prevails, the other becomes much less conspicuous, so that the more farce is dominated by "character," the more formless it appears. Likewise, the more important structure becomes, the less important are the characters.

The first of these two modes is that which is dominated by the special theatrical nature of the clown: the world of Harlequin, Pantelone, Gros-Guillaume, Hanswurst, and the Marx Brothers. Where such characters reign the text is diminished in importance, sometimes to the point of disappearing, because the clowns shape their materials to suit themselves. The second mode or method of farce subjects its characters to the whims of a theatrical, mechanized universe and converts the world into a kind of plaything controlled by the playwright. Here structure becomes increasingly evident, but it is not an organic structure generated by the wills and conflicts of the characters; rather, it is imposed upon them by the hand of the playwright, who juggles them as he pleases in the theatrical world he has created. The aim of both modes is the same: the interplay of reality and fantasy and the metamorphosis of the world of existence into the world of theatre. Both forms can be destructive, and love to turn the world of reality into chaos, but both also oppose disorder with their own kind of theatrical order. In the first mode, order is represented by the enduring personality of the clown, in the second by the ever present and controlling hand of the playwright.

The Independent and Constant Clown

The oldest and perhaps most primitive of these modes has the figure of the masked clown at its center. He is more real than the clown of the modern circus, who is in some ways a parody of the primitive clown, yet he is always essentially theatrical. His mask is the badge of his theatricality, but it is not simply an artificial symbol or convention. It lies at the heart of his essence and is a vital part of his nature. Because it is essential and not superficial, it need not always be literally a mask. The clown's mask may take many forms, but in all of its forms it retains the function and the special symbolic significance contained in the masks worn by the actors of the *Commedia dell'arte,* whose characters are often referred to as "masks." The term acknowledges that what would be superficial and external to a real person is essential to the clown. In this sense the word "mask" can refer not just to a face or head covering, but to all the trademarks of costume, gesture, or mannerism that define the clown's existence. His mask is a combination of external signs that give him identity. He cannot change these signs with the fashion, or in order to suit a new image of himself, as a real person might. For him they are vital, without them he does not exist, for he is a creature of the theatre.[43] The masks are symbols of the characters' permanence and immutability. The fixed nature of their characters, their imperviousness to change, is not simply a reflection of their comic limitations (although that is partly true); it is what enables them to transcend normal limitations, to defy the impermanence of the world and the inevitable decay of all real things. Citizens of a special theatrical world, they are not bound by the limits of an individual play, but often move from one to the other, taking on new roles while always maintaining the integrity of their innate personalities.

The world of farce is made up of contrasts and contradictions. Beneath the mask, the symbol of permanence and freedom from the restraints of reality, is a body which epitomizes the eternal decay and intransigence of corporeal substance. Age, impotence, senility, obesity, deformity, ugliness, incontinence, constipation, poverty, hunger, pain, greed, fear, gluttony, stupidity, lust, madness: these are the realities with which the mask is fused. It is not a simple opposition between the reality of the body and the fantasy of the mask which is at the heart of the clown's existence. If so, the two could be separated, the mask removed to reveal the body in all its distressing reality. Both mask and reality must be bonded together in every aspect of the clown's dress, behavior, and personality. Without the mask of fantasy, the gross body would revert to what it is in fact: a heavy and oppressive weight, depressing and unpleasant. The fantasy, too, would lose its force, because it is empowered by the grotesque reality from which it is inseparable. It is the genius of the clown to transform pain into pleasure, discord into harmony, and to find order in chaos and gaiety in the grotesque. Contradiction is essential to his nature, for it is the means by which he plays with reality and transforms it into his own theatrical substance.

There are many kinds of clowns: cowards, old men, pompous professionals, knaves, beggars, and slaves. But the quintessential clown is the motley-clad fool, and all clowns (perhaps even all comic characters) share in the ambiguous character of the fool, described by Enid Welsford in her book *The Fool*:

> Fundamentally the clown depends... upon a certain inner contradiction in the soul of every man. In the first place we are creatures of the earth, propagating our species like other animals, in need of food, clothing and shelter and of the money that procures them. Yet if we need money, are we so wholly creatures of the earth? If we need to cover our nakedness by material clothes or spiritual ideals, are we so like the other animals? This incongruity is exploited by the Fool. The Fool is an unabashed glutton and coward and knave, he is—as we say—a natural; we laugh at him and enjoy a pleasant sense of superiority; he looks at us oddly and we suspect that he is our *alter ego;* he winks at us and we are delighted at the discovery that we also are gluttons and cowards and knaves. The rogue has freed us from shame. More than that, he has persuaded us that wasted affection, thwarted ambition, latent guilt are mere delusions to be laughed away. For how can we feel spiritual pain, if we are only animals? But even the primitive joke about the human body has its complexity. We laugh to find that we are as natural as the fool, but we laugh also because we are normal enough to know how very unnatural it is to be as natural as all that.[44]

As Welsford goes on to say, the Fool exploits our ambivalence toward those products of our own creation which distinguish us from our fellow animals: our laws, machines, and social systems. When the clown defies and defeats these restraints of our own making we feel "a sudden sense of pressure relieved, ... a birth of new joy and freedom."[45]

The fool is, as it were, a natural clown, but the fool also has his limitations, and these the professional clown can transcend. There are forms of human folly of which the real fool is incapable, but the clown can transform even villainy into folly and endow it with the same ambivalence the fool brings to his more simple and universal forms of folly. The traits of a clown, including his vices, are fixed and permanent. He cannot renounce them because they are at the core of his existence. They define him and give him his life. His characteristics have the abstract and essential quality which Lionel Abel refers to in saying of Tartuffe that "he is hypocritical in order to be himself: when he is most hypocritical, then he is most Tartuffe."[46] The world of the clown, existing between reality and fantasy, does not obey the same laws as our own. The qualities which, when seen from our own realistic point of view, would seem to deprive him of life and make of him a mere puppet, are the very characteristics which ensure his theatrical life and give him freedom from the restraints and responsibilities of reality. The clown, like the fool, can transform his liabilities into advantages. His limitations provide him with a life that is in some ways more free and permanent than our own. And like the fool, he is often blissfully unaware of his moral defects. His amorality is not accidental. To judge himself by the standards of the real world would be to risk slipping back into it, and that would mean the end of the game. To maintain control he must be able to make playthings of everything he encounters, including the real world's criteria of morality and decency.

Players and Playthings

The need to make a toy of the world determines the special nature of everything within the clown's sphere. Something curious can happen when one plays with things. They may appear to play back. Inanimate objects may suddenly seem endowed with life. Play with unresponsive objects is limited, which is why so many children's toys, be they as simple as a rubber ball, have properties that let them come alive in the child's hand. In demonstrating his ability to play with the world, the clown acquires the magic capability of bringing dead things to life. Precisely the opposite occurs when the objects of play are other living beings. The clown does not always play with others as equals. He prefers, if he can, to treat them as toys. He delights in making others behave like mechanical dolls.[47] As playthings, the animate and the inanimate meet on common ground in the clown's world.

The clown's preference for treating others as playthings rather than playmates does not stem from arrogance. He is not quite like the child, who can play with friends on equal footing. Endeavoring to make a toy of the entire world, the clown begins with himself. He is himself a kind of living marionette, who is paradoxically both puppet and puppeteer. His is a toy world, and everything in it, himself included, must be given the status of toys. The most important reality in one's existence is one's own body, and the clown continually demonstrates that he can make a plaything of his own substance. The fat clown dances with incredible grace; the skinny one performs amazing feats of skill and strength. The bond between the exterior mask and the real body results from his need to make a toy of himself, which in turn gives more reality and permanence to the mask than to the corporeal substance. "We cannot *see* Chaplin," writes Kerr, "... without the trademarks [eyebrows and mustache]. They are birthmarks." When temporarily deprived of them in a Sennett film, "the comedian's face simply vanishes."[48] In order to escape the weight and decay of flesh, the clown's soul takes residence in his mask, transforming itself into the soul of a toy. To become more than human the clown must first become less.

Although farce may play with either actual physical reality or the reality imitated on stage, the nature of the clown inclines him to the former. As a creator of farce, he begins with his own physical being, which he opposes with a fantastic mask, as if to expose his own reality as a sham. His *lazzi*, his conjuring and acrobatic tricks, serve to demonstrate his power over both things and events. His magic touch converts falls into somersaults and iron into rubber. The hard intransigence of reality is an illusion, he seems to be saying; it is nothing but an infinitely pliable toy. Represented reality may be too fragile for such techniques, for it is obviously unreal in the first place. To expose it is again a case of victory too easily won. But in order to maintain his own theatrical life, the clown is apt to demolish any form of reality imposed on him from outside. Clowns prefer to destroy and re-create in their own image. The improvisation of the *Commedia dell'arte* illustrates the autonomy and skill of the clown as supreme player in the game of farce, for it allows him to spontaneously create his own world of imagination as he goes along. Much of our delight in improvisation springs from the knowledge that theatrical illusion is a fragile thing, usually supported by careful preparation and weeks of rehearsal. Improvisation turns the very act of artistic creation into a game through which the clown demonstrates his independence of any text. His life is his own creation; his special theatrical existence is rooted in his own nature. It is he who gives form to his materials, not the other way around.

The special nature of the clown may be used in different ways; it need not always destroy the conventions on which represented reality depends. The cinema provides many examples of the clown's versatility. Much of the quality

Introduction: The Aesthetics of Farce   17

which sets Chaplin's films apart results from his calling attention to the separateness of the clown. His inability to join or fully participate in the real world has a positive as well as negative side, for it is the source of the clown's endurance. The "little man," whom Chaplin's Tramp symbolizes, will go on in spite of the myriad disasters and humiliations he experiences. Yet Chaplin also creates pathos by having his clown envy the real world which he can never be a part of. He is excluded from the cycle of renewal which includes birth, reproduction, and death by virtue of the very qualities that give him his resiliency and permanence. He cannot "get the girl" because he is a clown, yet because he is a clown he can ride over whatever troubles he encounters.

Keaton, on the other hand, achieves a high degree of integration with the world in which he exists. Walter Kerr calls him the "most silent, as well as the most cinematic, of silent screen comedians" because he most fully exploits the inherent contrast of fact and fantasy that stems from the documentary objectivity of the camera and its unreal silence.[49] This characteristic of Keaton's begins with the simple "mask" he has chosen: his deadpan face. The mask has the reality of a photograph; it is the face that stares out from a thousand family portraits. Yet it is strangely "silent" and unreal, refusing to reflect the infinite variations of emotional life, treating joy and sorrow, disaster and good fortune alike. The subtlety of Keaton's mask harmonizes with the world he has created, a world which combines reality and fantasy in the precise measure established by the clown.

Less subtle than Chaplin and Keaton, the Marx Brothers use the destructive qualities of the clown, his tendency to subvert all he encounters to his own purposes, as a kind of principle of farce construction. Like parasites, the Marx Brothers invade the body of a conventional comedy, graft themselves onto a stereotypical comic plot, and systematically convert it into an elaborate plaything. They remain apart from the characters who surround them. Like creatures from a strange planet, they are aliens beside the more realistically conceived characters with whom they share the plot. The contrast is deliberate and pointed because it reveals that the others are really the aliens. This is not the real world, it is the theatrical and fantastic world of film farce, the world which gives clowns their breath and being, and in this world all but clowns become cardboard stereotypes. Genuinely realistic and honestly observed characters could not exist in a Marx Brothers film because such characters depend on the convention that the theatrical world is a reflection of the real world and is in this way controlled by reality. It is the business of the clowns to destroy that pretense and expose it as a sham. The ease with which Groucho, Chico, and Harpo dismantle the affluent, upper-class worlds they invade is based on the fact that they are in their own theatrical element. The outcome of the battle is foreseeable as soon as the clowns walk in, the moment the roles they are playing are accepted at face value. By accepting Groucho as a genuine doctor or impresario, his rich and pompous adversaries expose as a fraud their own claim to reality and seriousness.

The technique of the Marx Brothers is very similar to that of the *Commedia dell'arte* and helps to explain why the *Commedia*, although it did not exclude any genre—even tragedy—from its province, is associated so closely with farce. Lea comments on the *Commedia's* affinity to farce:

> Farce was its element, farce kept fresh only by the continual absorption of alien dramatic material. The action of the farcical spirit upon these acquisitions constitutes the history of improvised comedy. The new wine bursts the old skins. The Commedia dell'arte begins with Zanni and virtually it ends with Pulcinella. Farce it is and to farce it must return.[50]

When the clowns take over another dramatic genre, they convert it, like all else they encounter, into a toy, and cause it to lose its own life and autonomy. Once organic forms lose their original function they become lifeless structures which the clowns can transform into temporary dwellings, much as a hermit crab inhabits the dead shell of another creature.

Form and Pattern

It is not true, however, that farce has no structure of its own. While it sometimes acts as a parasite, wearing the shell of another dramatic form while it feeds on the contents, it may as easily develop its own characteristic forms. When the importance of the clown is diminished in farce, a special kind of structure becomes correspondingly prominent. This structure preserves the playful farce aesthetic of the clown, but wrests control of the dramatic situation from him and returns it to the playwright. There is evidence of this particular sense of form in the popular drama of medieval France which gave farce its name. The attempts of medieval farce to develop its own form were tentative and not always successful; the search for form did not mean that the influence of the clown was absent. The farce developed side by side with the *sottie,* which was essentially a comedy played by "fools" in their traditional costumes.[51] Sometimes the characters were simply listed as "le premier sot," "le second," etc., or sometimes they were given fantastic names, but as Maxwell says, "they never become real men in a real story."[52] The exact boundary between farce and *sottie* is hazy, partly because the *sotties* gradually acquired many of the characteristics of farce, and partly because the companies of fools who specialized in the *sottie* did not restrict themselves to a particular repertory. They might transform even the most pretentious farces to suit their style.[53] In spite of this area where the two forms overlap, there were definite characteristics which served to distinguish the two. The *sottie* was always distinguished by the presence of the uniformed fool, and the farce usually had a strong structural unity which was lacking in the *sottie.*[54]

The importance of form in French farce has been thoroughly discussed by Ian Maxwell. In spite of considerable variety in the plays, he finds that there are two common traits: a tendency toward symmetry and structural balance, and a strong "sense of point" which seeks unity by weaving the action around a single object, theme, or repeated phrase.[55] There is often a marked symmetry in the major phases of action, and a similar sense of balance in the pairing of characters, in dialogue, and in the arrangement of the incidents. The "point" around which the farce is organized may be a commonsense moral, but it may as often be simply an object.[56] The use of verse also displays this feeling for form. A rhythmic pattern of dialogue, maintained by short speeches and an inventive use of variety in meter and rhyme, often exhibits a marked "sense of rhythm and arrangement."[57] The importance of verse in these plays is often overlooked. It is a common assumption that verse is appropriate only to the more serious forms of drama, and that when verse is used in farce, as it is in medieval farce, it is of little consequence—merely an unnecessary convention. But in truth, much of the vigor and life of these plays is a result of their lively use of verse.

Verse is not intrinsically more "elevated" than prose. It is simply more artificial, patterned, and abstract. These are qualities which can be as important to farce as they are to the tragedies of Racine. Stark Young saw just such a bond between farce and poetic tragedy:

> In a sense, all drama moves toward a condition of farce. This is because the theatre's very essence consists in the heightening of its material. Heightening that is free, fluent, almost abstract, unless it has the restrictions of character and rational measure, floats off into farce; which is closer to poetic drama and serious tragedy than to plain everyday prose realism.[58]

The subject matter of farce is often drab and unpleasant, material which might as easily serve the needs of the starkest naturalism; its farcical character is derived from the treatment of these materials. It is not enough to say that farce is unrealistic; any distortion of reality must obey some set of rules, have some meaning or rationale, or it would be merely chaotic and pointless. It must, in short, have form, and farce sustains its flights into unreality with a positive affirmation of form and pattern. Far from being formless, many farces are dominated by their structure. Rather than being dictated by meaning or character motivation, development in farce often acquires a logic which is pursued for its own sake and to which character and meaning are forced to submit. Organic structure is replaced by mere pattern, and the logic of reality gives way to a more abstract logic which controls events and destroys reality. The formal structure of tragedy, no matter how rigid, must express in some way the inner life of the play in order to remain valid. In Racine, for example, the strict and unyielding form echoes and reinforces the rigidity of the society in which the characters are trapped and thus helps to focus on their humanity and their attempts to resist their fate. But the pattern of action in a farce, although it may originally be derived from reality, soon achieves a life of its own; and the characters, unable or unwilling to resist, abandon themselves to the logic of events and seem in the process little more than puppets.

The reduction of characters to puppets in farce goes hand in hand with its fondness for rhythmic but often artificial patterns. This is reflected even in the titles of the farces of J.M. Morton. Titles such as *Box and Cox; Grimshaw, Bagshaw, and Bradshaw;* and *Slasher and Crasher* announce the fact that their principal characters are nearly interchangeable marionettes before they ever appear on the stage. There is often logic in farce, but it may be a logic of theatrical convention which operates free from the restraints of reality and which overwhelms the characters who are subjected to it. Charlton finds that *The Comedy of Errors* is successful as a farce because it demonstrates almost mathematically the logical possibilities inherent in the confusion of two sets of twins.[59] But this is logic pursued abstractly, for its own sake. It has nothing to do with the demands of reality or the wills of the characters. Or rather, it is like a game in which reality—including human will—is manipulated into a logical but abstract pattern. The demands of reality are relevant, but only as the initial conditions of the game, the rules by which it must be played.

The imposition of artificial patterns—whether with verse forms, interchangeable names, or an exercise in mathematics and logic—has the effect of making a toy of the world and marionettes of its living inhabitants. The reduction of human beings to the status of puppets by subordinating them to the logic of situation and form has never been carried further than by the French farce writers of the nineteenth century. Before them farces tended to be short, centering in a single situation.[60] The dominance of situation over character had undoubtedly limited the length of farces. The usual basis of full-length plays—the attempt of characters to overcome obstacles and attain certain ends—calls attention to the characters as human beings endowed with free will and the capacity to influence their own fates. The formula of the well-made play gave farce the means to expand into the longer form.

The Manipulating Playwright

Gerould has shown that the qualities of the well-made play that make it so ill-suited to serious drama (including serious comedy) are distinctly appropriate to farce:

> The farce writers adopted from the well-made formula the drama of things in which objects dominate and become the organizing principle of life.... Already in the well-made play, a human being *qua* human being is nothing, is in fact non-existent; it is only his class, his clothes, his money, his social world that count and make a person what he is....

Introduction: The Aesthetics of Farce 21

> In Labiche's play [*The Italian Straw-Hat*] this process of exteriorization through clothes is carried one step further; the straw-hat becomes the center of attention, the principal character, and the source of all motion. The disorder to respectability threatened by the loss of the hat is almost forgotten in the pursuit of an object which has taken on an absolute meaning and importance of its own. Labiche develops the pursuit of the hat for its own sake, almost abstractly...[61]

Like medieval farce, the well-made farce assigned great importance to physical objects. Even more than the older farce, it subordinated human beings to a theatrical logic of things and circumstances developed into abstract patterns and rhythms which virtually become their own justification. The well-made play offered to farce a means of organization which was not dependent on human will and gave the playwright an essentially external and mechanical method of linking situations.[62] The playwright becomes a manipulator of circumstances and the play is seen as a kind of game in which the object is to overcome material difficulties.[63] Like the chess problems in which one side is expected to win in a designated number of moves, the play is valued for the ingenuity of its solution and for the clever way in which all of the pieces on the board are made to play a role—preferably several roles—in the problem.

The serious "well-made" playwrights insisted on pretending that their elaborate constructions were actually a reflection of reality, and criticized the writers of farce for their frivolity even though they admired their "technique."[64] The writers of farce were simply being honest in treating the theatre as a game and the playwright as a manipulator of events. In the hands of the farce writers this manipulation was enjoyed openly for its own sake.[65] As a juggler of events the playwright assumes a function analogous to that of the acrobatic clown, for he is endowed with the ability to transform reality into a game or demonstration of skill. Just as the clown is capable of transforming the awkwardness and humiliation of a fall into a complex and strangely graceful acrobatic stunt, the well-made farce turns the world into a complex toy, full of surprises, but always under the control of the master juggler.

In both cases some spring or initial impetus is required to set the game in motion. Usually it is a threatening image or symbol of disorder in the normal pattern of events. The clown often takes off from a springboard of physical buffoonery and violence, but the "well-made" playwrights preferred images of sexual impropriety and threats to the stability of bourgeois decorum. Like the straw-hat in Labiche's play, such symbols are often concrete things which once let loose in the world seem to acquire a life of their own and spread disorder about them in widening circles. The increase in disorder is accompanied by a concomitant movement from the world of reality into the fantastic world of theatrical logic where the increasingly obvious hand of the playwright manipulates all. The spreading disorder goes hand in hand with a special kind of theatrical order which transforms the original threat into a plaything. This is not to say that the threat disappears, for then the game would lose its excitement and the source of its appeal. The images of disorder and violence are kept alive by means of new complications and surprising twists which provide the game's source of energy and verve. The well-made farces—particularly those of Feydeau—are often likened to complex and ingenious machines. The continual addition of fresh images of sex and violence helps to keep the machine running.

Clowns and the Mechanized World

Farce may have begun with the masked clown, alone on a stage, demonstrating in his fantastic way that everything solid and oppressive can be made to dissolve, that everything enduring and unalterable can be twisted, changed, and played with. When the playwright takes over, the techniques change and the rules are altered. But the spirit of the clown cannot long be excluded from the world of farce. It is possible for farce to create a mechanized universe—the films of Mack Sennett are examples—in which the characters are soulless objects, so many bowling pins to be knocked down at the will of their creator. But such farce has a limited range, rarely moving beyond the most obvious images of speed and violence. It is a world of things which finally excludes people entirely. Only the clown has the power to transform our lives as well as the universe in which we live. Yet when the clown is in command, he may leave our world behind and enter his own realm of theatrical fantasy. In either case, farce moves further from the reality which initiates its flight into fantasy and supplies the energy for its theatrical games. Thus most farce—probably its best examples—seeks not only to combine fact and fancy, but to blend the two farcical modes—that of the irrepressible clown and that of the mechanized, toy-like universe. At its best, the world of farce, no matter how fantastic and mad, is always recognizably our own, and in its fools we can always see ourselves. Its dedication to laughter and its insistence on making a game of life do not mean that it is unobservant. Feydeau is in the best tradition of farce because he derives his fantasy from shrewd observation of life. He creates characters that have many of the fantastic qualities of the masked clown, yet are drawn from the society in which he lived. His frivolity could at times be more trenchant and honest than the observations of his more serious contemporaries. He excelled in making a game of reality by first demanding that it be as real as possible.

If correct, the observation that farce makes a game of reality has implications that go well beyond the study of Feydeau. It provides tools for the understanding, analysis, and evaluation of all forms of farce, and possibly even of forms beyond farce. As a theory of farce its greatest significance lies in the fact that it provides a combination of qualities most genre theories lack: *both* a universal principle that links together the diverse forms of the genre, *and* a means of analyzing specific techniques and elements within individual farces. In other words, it answers, at least with respect to farce, L.C. Knight's complaint that theories of comedy do little or nothing to promote our understanding of specific plays. These two qualities, so rare in combination, are worth summarizing individually.

First, the theory supplies a common *structural principle* capable of generating individual structures that may appear quite different from each other. The fact that phenomena as diverse as *The Importance of Being Earnest, Pierre Pathelin,* and the scenarios of the *Commedia dell'arte* have all been termed farces suggests such a common bond. Hitherto, the general consensus seems to have been that the common element is merely an irresponsible commitment to provoking laughter at any cost—combined with a basic indifference to structure. The theory of farce as a game sees the devotion to laughter not as an invitation to anarchy, but as the key to a unifying principle. Without being tied down to any specific theory of laughter, it accepts the observation (present in many modern theories) that there is a parallel relationship between laughter, play, and creative thinking: that they result from similar patterns of cognitive behavior. The construction of a farce (at least a good farce) does not simply entail finding a convenient means to string together a series of gags and *lazzi*. The individual gags and the overall structure are informed by the same principle. Jokes and sight gags are a way of playing with words, ideas, and images; the structure as a whole is a way of playing with some larger aspect of reality; and one should expect to find a harmonious relationship between the two in a successful farce. The *lazzi,* masks, and improvisation of the *Commedia* appear not as chance products of historical accident, but the result of a single basic principle. Moreover, this same principle, operating through different means, has produced the elaborate structures and mechanized world of Georges Feydeau.

Second, and most important for the practicing critic, this theory is more than a vague assertion that the "essence" of farce is "the spirit of play." It has practical applications in both analysis and evaluation because the analogy of the game does more than suggest a common playfulness; it proves valid even in concrete and specific instances. There are identifiable rules and players in the game of farce, and the discovery of these provides a key to understanding both the unifying themes of individual farces and the nature of specific differences between them. Such applications have been hinted at in the preceding discussion and will become clearer in the following chapters. Feydeau, of course, is the supreme player in his own plays, although he does allow his principal clowns a degree of *apparent* autonomy. The rules by which he plays are provided by the conventions of the well-made play and the demand by audiences—rapidly growing in the late nineteenth century—for the accurate appearance of reality. His challenge was to observe scrupulously the conventions of realism, yet to transform that conventionally real world into a realm of fantasy.

Games may be frivolous, but they need not be trivial. This is true also of farce, a game of laughter directed at the entire world, like that of the medieval carnival. Farce can simply be appreciated and judged as are other games: on the difficulty of the challenges and the skill of the performer in overcoming them. Farce may have another value, however, stemming directly from its refusal to be serious. Its very frivolity permits it to remove the moral blinders of its age, to accept and explore aspects of reality obscured to seriousness by fear and bias. By calling all into question, including prejudice, hate, anger, and fear, laughter opens a door to renewal and understanding. To laugh at the world as at a game may even allow a clearer view of it than a serious vision could permit.

2
Plot and Action: The Mechanics of Misunderstanding

Consistency and Conventionality

Not all of the thirty-nine plays included in the nine volumes of Feydeau's *Théâtre complet* can properly be called farces, but the exceptions are few, and most of these contain farcical elements. The great majority of the plays are remarkably consistent in the tone, subject matter, and methods which have caused Feydeau's name to be linked so firmly to the expression "French farce." His consistency and rarely faltering devotion to farcical laughter provide an excellent opportunity to study the nature and methods of one particular variety of farce in its pure form.

Feydeau was neither an experimenter nor an innovator; his talent lay not in originality—whether in subject matter, dramaturgy, or psychological insight—but in his ability to exploit fully the farcical possibilities inherent in the dramatic conventions which he adopted. He took standard themes, methods, and situations, and pushed them to their comic extremes. His originality lay in the wealth of his comic invention and in the comic tricks and devices with which his plays abound, but this is precisely the area in which a *vaudeville* was expected to be original. When Feydeau complained of plagiarism by others he was thinking of such gimmicks and devices. Accused of using a standard device to deceive his wife, one of Feydeau's erring husbands declares indignantly, "I'm no farce writer! I don't need other people's ideas in order to invent new plays!"[1]

Even if this represents Feydeau's own indignation, many of his ideas were simply new twists given to previously employed comic devices. For example, the method used by the gentleman above to deceive his wife—hypnotism—may have been an original way to be unfaithful, but it had been used as the central device of at least one other *vaudeville* four years earlier.[2] Feydeau himself was to use the same trick, with yet another twist, several years later in *Dormez, je le veux! (Sleep! I command you!)*

The course of Feydeau's career and the evolution of his style reflect his inclination (and that of his audience) toward the familiar. The same situations, character types, and problems recur again and again in different combinations and in different variations. His plays were often constructed according to standard plot formulas or patterns which allow them to be grouped into simple and logical categories. The largest and most important of these groups consists of eleven three-act plays which involve some form of deception practiced upon a husband, wife, lover, or mistress. In many ways these plays form the core of Feydeau's work. They include nearly all of his most successful and enduring full-length plays, while the plays which stray furthest from this pattern are usually those which were least successful originally and those least often revived.

The Deception Formula

Because of its importance to Feydeau's work, a brief outline of the basic plot formula should be useful. In the first act one or more deceptions are planned, started, or revealed. Events are then arranged by the playwright so as to bring all the characters together in the second act in a manner designed to produce the most embarrassing situations and the maximum threat of exposure. The threat of exposure throughout the second act results in a desperate series of lies, evasions, and frantic attempts to hide or escape. A bewildering profusion of *quiproquos* develops, producing such confusion and misunderstanding among the characters that the misunderstandings continue even after the real or apparent exposure which typically ends the act. A variety of means is used to continue the complications in the third act until the problems are more or less settled. Occasionally an erring husband is forced to admit guilt and is forgiven, as in *Le Dindon (The Sucker)*. More often the lies and deceptions continue; new excuses are contrived which, though usually more or less improbable, are accepted; and when the play ends, at least some of the characters continue to be ignorant of the true situation. The situation is not so much unraveled as it is stabilized, the threat of exposure is eliminated and there is an apparent return to stasis.[3]

The eleven plays in this group are: *Tailleur pour dames (Ladies' Dressmaker)*,[4] *L'Affaire Edouard (The Edward Affair)*, *Monsieur chasse! (Monsieur Has Gone Hunting!)*, *Champignol malgré lui (Champignol in Spite of Himself)*, *Le Système Ribadier (The Ribadier System)*, *Un Fil à la patte (Tied by a String)*,[5] *L'Hôtel du Libre-Echange (Hotel Paradiso,* [literally, *The Free-Exchange Hotel*]), *Le Dindon (The Sucker)*, *La Dame de chez Maxim (The Lady from Maxim's)*, *La Puce à l'oreille (A Flea in Her Ear)*, and *Occupe-toi d'Amélie (Keep and Eye on Amelie)*. These are not the only plays in which deception is used (in nearly all some form of deception plays a role), but because of the particularly large role it plays in these plays I shall refer to them as "deception formula plays."

The second major classification is the group of five "late one-act plays" which represent a major break in style and method from both his earlier one-acts and his full-length plays: *Feu la mère de Madame (Madam's Late Mother)*, *On Purge Bébé (Junior Gets a Laxative)*, *"Mais n'te promène donc pas toute nue!" ("Do Not Parade Around Stark Naked!")*, *Léonie est en avance (Léonie is Premature)*, and *Hortense a dit: "Je m'en fous!" (Hortense Said: "I Don't Give a Damn!")*. All of the plays in these two groups involve difficulties between husband and wife, or between lover and mistress. Feydeau also wrote a few plays based on another ancient theme: that of young people who want to marry in the face of parental objections. This group of "ingénue plays" contains only three examples: *La Lycéenne (The Schoolgirl)*, *Le Ruban (The Decoration)*, and *Le Mariage de Barillon (Barillon's Marriage)*. It is interesting because it illustrates Feydeau's treatment of one of the oldest themes in comedy and perhaps sheds some light on its relation to farce. These three groups contain all of the best known plays with the exception of *La Main passe! (Pass the Deal!)*, which is similar to the deception formula plays but is significantly different in structure and treatment.

In addition to these, Feydeau wrote two full-length plays early in his career which are based on mistaken identity. *Chat en poche (Pig in a Poke)* and *Les Fiancés de Loches (The Fiancés from Loches)* and ten early one-act plays (from *Par la fenêtre* [*Through the Window*] to *Dormez, je le Veux!*) which are largely built on individual situations involving deception or mistaken identity. Two of these one-acts, *Fiancés en herbe (Budding Fiancés)* and *Notre futur (Our Intended)* are not really farces, but share some characteristics of the other plays. In the later part of his career he began two full-length plays which show a marked departure from his earlier methods and were left unfinished; he collaborated on two plays to which his contribution seems to have been relatively small; and he wrote a farcical fantasy *L'Age d'or (The Golden Age)* and his most pretentious and serious comedy, *Le Bourgeon (The Sprout)*. Even this play, the least farcical of his full-length plays, contains elements of farce and is interesting because it deals seriously with themes which were treated quite differently in his farces.

Evolution of His Style

The plays cannot be neatly divided into precise chronological periods, but it is possible to detect gradual changes in his work over the thirty-six-year span of his career. It is difficult to know how much such changes were due to the evolution of the author's attitudes or to changes in society and theatrical tastes; they are probably a reflection of both. There are two major trends. The first is a movement toward greater verisimilitude in certain aspects of the plays, particularly in the initial premises, dialogue, and characters. Standard theatrical conventions which had been staples of the *vaudeville* form, such as the opening expository monologue, were gradually eliminated. The theatrical buffoons and improbable fools who inhabit the earlier plays were gradually replaced by characters much closer to reality. The language became more realistic, and comic advantage was taken of the idiosyncrasies of speech heard among the various inhabitants of Paris. Feydeau, always attentive to detail, even included lengthy footnotes admonishing his actors to use a more realistic style of acting.[6] The second trend was toward a more intense and almost savage comic vision. Both in treatment and in his choice of targets for laughter, the comedy of his later plays often borders on—but never crosses into—bitterness and cruelty. One of the last of the many monologues he wrote, *Un Monsieur qui est condamné à mort (A Gentleman Condemned to Death)*, ends, as the title suggests, with the innocent and completely bewildered narrator sent to the guillotine.[7] Suffering has always been a favorite subject of farce, but in his later plays Feydeau often goes well beyond the conventional cuckolds, pratfalls, and blows to focus on pains that are both more real and more extreme.[8]

These tendencies contributed to the value of his work, not by elevating it above the level of farce, but by intensifying its farcical quality. A sense of the reality of life as it is lived—or better, as it is felt—is a vital element of farce. This is particularly true of the more unpleasant realities. Feydeau's inclination toward the familiar is not irrelevant here. The reality of farce does not consist of discoveries or truths to which the audience must be educated; it is the reality of the familiar and the commonplace, of those things which are already known or believed to be true.

The Comedy of Misapprehension

Counterbalancing the unpleasant realities and the familiar pains is a sense of fantastic madness which is present in all of Feydeau's plays. In the majority of his plays he creates this madness by subjecting his characters to a world which had all the characteristics of a fun-house: well-oiled machinery propels its victims through a series of mirrored mazes, expected surprises, and absurdly frightening experiences. It ushers them past distorting mirrors and threatening apparitions, but it never abandons them and usually delivers them safely out on the other side.

To achieve this effect, Feydeau refined and developed techniques already characteristic of the nineteenth-century French *vaudeville*. This form, which has nothing in common with the American vaudeville, was a mixed genre which ranged from the sentimental to the savagely farcical. The term dates to the fifteenth century, when it referred to satirical songs that originated in the Vire valley of France *(val* or *vau de Vire)*. As the popularity of the songs spread, the term was corrupted to *vaudeville*. Toward the end of the seventeenth and into the eighteenth century, it became associated with the theatre as *vaudevilles* were incorporated into the plays of the fairs. These *"comédies à vaudevilles"* or *"comédies mêlées de chants"* eventually gave rise to two different forms: the *opéra-comique,* emphasizing original music and subordinating dialogue, and the *comédie-vaudeville,* with developed plots and songs adapted to known airs. By the beginning of the nineteenth century, the *comédie-vaudeville* was established on the Boulevard, where it was noted for extensive use of the *quiproquo,* broad physical humor, and a fondness for satirical and often risqué themes. Like the early farce, it combined a sense of everyday reality with extravagant buffoonery. This was the genre that Scribe "reformed" by creating the well-made play.[9]

Under the influence of Scribe and his successors, the songs diminished in importance and were often dropped altogether. In their place, Scribe gave the *vaudeville* greater verisimilitude and plots that were more logically constructed. This regularized *vaudeville* shared in broad outline many of the general methods and aims of the New Comedy of Plautus and Terence from which it was descended. Despite important differences between the two forms, they share a common method of comic dramaturgy: a technique of creating plots and comic action which is largely dependent on misapprehension or misunderstanding. Duckworth finds that the single feature all the plays of Terence and Plautus have in common is "mental error, or misapprehension." He concludes that "a general atmosphere of misapprehension seems by far the most essential factor in developing the action and producing the complications in comedy."[10] Misapprehension has two principal values to the creator of comic plays. It can provide a rich source of comic effects and can form the basis of a versatile yet simple method of creating comic plots. It is useful in the construction of plots because it offers a method of creating complications which, when the playwright chooses, can easily be dismantled and unraveled. In the simplest use of this technique, best exemplified by the formulas of New Comedy, the dénouement is provided in the standard final recognition scene. The dilemma in which the characters find themselves had often been resolved when the play opens. It is necessary only to inform them of the true situation in order to end the play. The audience is usually aware of the probable outcome shortly after the first scene. Only the characters remain ignorant until the dénouement.

In this kind of play the plot complications are more apparent than real because they result from mistakes or ignorance. Because the course of events is determined largely by misunderstandings or lack of knowledge, which in turn can be controlled by external circumstances, the most significant aspect of this form of dramaturgy is its manipulation by the playwright. In New Comedy, the prototypical comedy of misapprehension, the various schemes and counterschemes often have no real effect on the final outcome. The play ends when the playwright chooses to reveal the facts. If the sole aim of the author is to amuse his audience, this method has a certain harmony of form and content. Both the substance of the play—a series of amusing incidents—and the stucture of the plot are created out of mistakes and misunderstandings. Such plays may not fulfill the loftiest aspirations of the drama, but their means are consistent with their ends, and the recognition scene, which in New Comedy makes the whole play possible, has the virtue of being a simple and straightforward convention.

The convenience and adaptability of this method of dramaturgy may account for its continuing popularity among the many descendants of Roman Comedy. Shakespeare and Molière, among others, were able to use the methods and conventions of the comedy of misapprehension to create plays that go well beyond the simple popular entertainments which were their ultimate source. The comedy of misapprehension has also remained a staple of popular comic entertainment, not only because of the advantages which it offers the playwright, but because it ultimately avoids the logical outcome of the situations with which it appears to be dealing. The playwright, always in control, can avoid unpleasant consequences which the behavior of his characters might produce were they left to their own devices. It permits, if not a return to the status quo ante, at least an outcome which is acceptable and not disturbing to the audience—a conventional happy ending.

The same factors which account for the popularity of the form are also largely responsible for its most insidious effect on Western dramaturgy: an emphasis on manipulation by the dramatist rather than the "natural" development of the action through the characters. This emphasis became explicit, both in theory and practice, only in the nineteenth century, but it was inherent in comedies of intrigue which flourished from the Renaissance through the eighteenth century. The well-made plays of Scribe and his followers are direct descendants of Roman New Comedy, not simply because they use the same devices employed in the classical plays but because they share the dramaturgy of which those tricks are an integral part. However, what was a set of simple conventions for the Roman playwrights became for the well-made playwrights a complex game of skill. The simple recognition scene of New Comedy was unacceptable, not because it was false, but because it was too easy. Where Plautus simply lays his resolution baldly before the audience, the new rules demanded that the writer proceed by hints and suggestion. H.A. Smith wrote of Scribe that

> he hinges the most important developments on pure accident, but we have been so carefully prepared to expect this accident, or our eyes have been so persistently attracted to the spot

where something should occur, that, when it comes, it seems only a part of the natural train of life.[11]

Although the *vaudeville* benefited from the techniques of the well-made play by giving the *vaudevillistes* greater opportunities for juggling their characters into amusing situations, it always remained theatrical and frankly conventional. Unlike Scribe and the serious practitioners of well-made playwriting, most *vaudevillistes* practised their craft openly. They did not try to carefully conceal their tricks in order to give an illusion of reality. One of the reasons the serious bourgeois drama of the nineteenth century seems so wooden and cumbersome is the amount of time needed to make the plot manipulation seem "natural." Because their plots are so often based on secrets which must be kept from other characters but revealed to the audience, enormous amounts of time are spent in trivial dialogue, the sole purpose of which is to motivate exits or entrances and to provide exposition.[12] The unpretentious writers of *vaudevilles,* less concerned with such questions of apparent naturalness, were free to spend more time on the real substance of their plays, however trivial that substance might have been.

That is not the only advantage which the *vaudevillistes* had over their more serious colleagues. The well-made play evolved from the comedy of misapprehension, and the techniques which it developed continued to be more appropriate to the traditional comedy of intrigue and deception than to serious drama.[13] The plots based on secrets, the demand for an artificial order and "logic," the manipulation of events for the sake of theatrical effects, the emphasis on physical objects as determinants of human events—all these were ideally suited to the creation of farce based on misunderstanding. Even the subject matter of much of nineteenth-century drama would seem tailor-made for farce. The theme of sexual impropriety so dear to the nineteenth century had been a staple of farce since the Middle Ages. When Feydeau began writing he was able to build on a system of dramaturgy which was as perfectly suited to his style as if it had been designed for him specifically. The machine-like constructions of the well-made play were ideal containers for his natural sense of madness and fantasy. They imposed an almost abstract discipline of form which served both to contain and to heighten the lunacy.

The Logic of Vaudeville

Feydeau's first three one-act plays give little hint of the elaborate constructions which he was to create later. His first play, *Par la fenêtre* (1882), is a simple confrontation between two people. The comedy is based on their interaction, and the surprise twist of plot is simply a device to end the play. Both *Amour et Piano* (*Love and Piano,* 1883) and *Gibier de potence*

(*Gallows-Bird,* 1883) are relatively simple situations fabricated from cases of mistaken identity. *Amour et piano,* however, displays Feydeau's skill at cleverly prolonging a *quiproquo* and exploiting its full comic potential. The juggling of various misunderstandings was to become one of the principal features of his plays, and it plays a large role in his first full-length farce, *Tailleur pour dames* (1886). This was the first of the deception formula plays, and its warm reception may have been the reason he was so fond of the formula which was to provide him with many more successes. His plays were not always so well received, however. The five major plays which followed *Tailleur pour dames* were greeted with only a lukewarm response from both audiences and critics.[14] Interestingly, only one of these five utilized the deception pattern, while the string of successes which followed *Monsieur chasse!* (1892) until 1900 were (with one exception) all of the deception type. The principal objection to those five unsuccessful plays seems to have been that they were too wild and extravagant, that both characters and situations were improbable and illogical. Auguste Vitu of the *Figaro,* in appraising the original production of *La Lycéenne* (1887), suggested that the young author take the trouble to link his absurd situations together with some sort of logic, even if only apparent logic.[15] Edmond Stoullig complained of *Chat en poche* (1888) that "this young author was positively reckless with the audience, and they let him know that limits exist which may not be crossed." His reaction to *Les Fiancés de Loches* (1888, with Maurice Desvallières) was similar:

> Indeed, these two young fellows expected us to swallow anything, and they have leapt too easily into a region of inadmissible fancy... The *quiproquo*... produces the most improbable scenes and jokes of the most questionable taste. The authors have abused their license. They went too far.

Looking back on these plays from a distance of nearly a century, it is difficult to understand why the same audiences which so easily swallowed the absurdities of *Tailleur pour dames* objected to these other plays on the grounds of implausibility. To understand the kind of logic that was being demanded of Feydeau, one should look at some of the enormously successful plays he wrote later. Such a play was *L'Hôtel du Libre-Echange* (1894), built on essentially the same plan as *Tailleur pour dames* and several other plays in between. In writing of that play, Francisque Sarcey, one of the most influential and conservative critics of the time, provides insights into the nature of *vaudeville* logic:

> Previously, when he was beginning his career, M. Georges Feydeau just let his imagination run wild; he abandoned himself to his enthusiasm, lost sight of his objectives and strayed into fantastic situations which ultimately became tedious. He seemed not to be sure where he was going. But now that he has learned his craft,... he has today a sureness of touch and a control of his effects that is truly incredible.

> All of the fancies with which the play abounds, and which seem to spring spontaneously from a spark of imagination, are prepared and directed from afar. They surprise but never bewilder us, because we can predict them; we pratically expect them. They are determined by an infallible geometry,...
> There is not a detail in the play, no matter how unimportant it may seem, that does not have its justification and, at the right moment, does not contribute to the situation... Believe it: in a play by Feydeau, a character never enters and places his hat on a chair without my saying to myself: Aha! that hat was not put there for nothing!
> ... Without your realizing it, each of these details slips into your memory, is tucked away, and re-emerges only at the precise moment when the situation demands that you remember it.
> Now that is the genius of the *vaudeville*. Many a writer will repeat something three, four times to make it stick in your memory. You pay no attention. Feydeau suggests something with a stroke, quickly and without seeming to, and it is done. You will never forget it.[17]

He continues in the same vein throughout the entire review. The mathematical logic justifying every event, which Sarcy admires so, is essentially the "logic" of suggestion mentioned earlier in connection with Scribe, but here it has acquired the nature of a theatrical convention. It is an almost abstract game played by the author and audience, with precise rules understood by both. It is "chess problem logic" demanding economy in the use of all the pieces of the board.[18] The theatrical game is not so rigorous as that of chess, for the rules are rather simple. The first rule, as Sarcey suggests, is that everything which is introduced or mentioned must play a role in the action. In addition all such determinants of the action should be introduced as early as possible, preferably in the first act, so that they do not appear to have been invented for the occasion. They are among the original "givens" of the problem. Although Sarcey implies that this game demands tremendous skill from a playwright, in some ways it makes his job simpler. Because the audience expects everything to be used, all the author need do to justify an event is to introduce its "cause" earlier in the game. The improbable becomes probable solely by virtue of theatrical convention.

This game of chess problem logic is the fundamental means by which Feydeau manipulates his puppets both into and out of their many difficulties, particularly in the deception plays. He simply places his pieces in position in the first act, then propels them through a series of successive moves until the final curtain. As with the chess problem, economy in the use of the pieces is valued. In *L'Hôtel du Libre-Echange* many characters and objects have more than one function. Pinglet's sooty face prevents him from being recognized in the second act and helps to provide the dénouement in the third. And it does so because a towel which Pinglet uses to wipe his face is later used by Maxime, dirtying his face and causing him to be taken for Pinglet. Pinglet's illness at the hotel motivates a necessary exit, but it also gets rid of Marcelle's hat, forcing her to wear the veil which is vital to the outcome. Paillardin's dimissal of his servants provides a reason for Maxime and Victoire to be together at the hotel, and it also prevents Paillardin from learning of his wife's absence. This economy of means is part of the "logic" by which the plays operate. It provides an almost abstract and purely external means for drawing the various elements more closely together.

Tools of Manipulation: Objects and Appearances

The causal links between events are likely to be physical objects rather than human beings. For the playwright who juggles events, things are preferable to people as causal agents because they are much more easily manipulated. They can be lost or mislaid (like the keys in *Un Fil à la patte*); manufactured in identical copies (the trousers in *Monsieur chasse!*); or transferred from one person to another (like Marcelle's dress and the soot on Pinglet's face). Most versatile are the letters and other bits of paper which can be forged, misdirected, mislaid, and reproduced. If unaddressed, they can even find their way to more than one recipient, as in *Chat en poche*.[19] But even in farce objects have obvious limitations as agents of human events. The battle of people against things is properly the special province of farce, but the demand for logic and a degree of verisimilitude, however superficial, inhibited the fanciful tendency of farce to give objects special powers, to make them seem almost alive and capable of taking the offensive against their human adversaries. Yet there was one area in which, by social and theatrical convention, things were assumed to have extraordinary power over the lives of people: the business of deception and adultery.

Deception is standard fare in plays of intrigue and in the comedy or farce of misapprehension, but in the nineteenth century, deception in sexual matters was a major topic of serious as well as farcical plays.[20] By basing the majority of his plays on infidelity, Feydeau had chosen a subject which was not only distinctly appropriate for farce, but was regarded as acceptable in more serious (and presumably more logical) plays. Critics who objected to the implausibility of the unashamed fools in Feydeau's early plays apparently had no difficulty believing that anyone faced with the threat of scandal would be terrorized into behaving like a perfect madman. This became the principle by which Feydeau could convert his bourgeois characters into lunatics. The dread of scandal, rather than concern with moral values as such, is at the heart of even the serious plays written on this theme. Scandal, even more than adultery, is suited more to farce than to serious drama, not only because scandal is in itself a trivial concern, but because it hinges on appearances rather than realities. In a world dominated by a concern for bourgeois decorum, appearances become more important than facts. They are that world's most important reality. Appearances are easily manipulated and managed, however, and farce, ever fond of transforming and playing with reality, is totally at home in a world which has such an insubstantial notion of what is real.

Thus the fear of scandal not only provides Feydeau with a motive which transforms his characters into fools; it gives him a tool for turning their world into a madhouse. His characters are so preoccupied with appearances that they continually attempt to manipulate and control them. All that is necessary is to point them in the right direction and see to it that they always work at cross-purposes with each other. Once he has set them in motion, Feydeau simply provides them with a setting that both encourages their intrigues and increases the danger of being caught. Most of the ludicrous and embarrassing situations in which Feydeau's characters find themselves would not be possible without their own constant efforts at manipulating and deceiving.

Objects are able to acquire such incredible importance in Feydeau's world because they can constitute material evidence. Where appearances count for so much, objects which would otherwise be harmless become threatening simply because they have the power to incriminate. Feydeau never wrote an entire play around a single such material symbol of scandal as did Labiche in *Un Chapeau de paille d'Italie (An Italian Straw-Hat)* or Sardou in *Les Pattes de mouche (A Scrap of Paper);* however, most of the objects in his plays which seem so to dominate the characters derive their power from an ability to create or avoid scandal. Sometimes such things both threaten scandal and provide the means to avoid it, for example Marcelle's dress or the incriminating trousers in *Monsieur chasse!* Sometimes, like the torn clothing in *Le Système Ribadier,* they simply provide the dénouement, although incriminating objects—such as the *Figaro* of *Un Fil à la patte*—might appear at anytime to harass and bewilder their victims. Obviously, articles of clothing (or their lack) are especially important. There are few plays in which clothing does not play some role, either by its presence or absence. Clothing is a vital issue in a world which demands the appearance of respectability, and disputes over it can lead to desperate measures. In three of the plays *(Un Fil à la patte, La Main passe,* and *Occupe-toi d-Amélie)* questions of clothing drive Feydeau's normally non-violent heroes to the point of brandishing revolvers.

The characters are often harassed by objects which threaten to expose them. They can also be led astray by their preference for the evidence of physical objects over the testimony of their fellow creatures. Their lack of trust in each other is understandable in view of the tendency they all have to lie, but objects too can be unreliable witnesses. They can be misinterpreted in many different ways, forged, altered, destroyed, and planted on others. They are dumb and cannot correct the interpretations put on them nor can they stand for cross-examination.

Not all the objects which control the action do so through the threat of scandal. The concern with appearances creates an atmosphere in which things seem to be intrinsically more important than human beings. It is virtually a convention of the well-made form that objects have greater power than people to influence events. Camille's silver palate, without which he cannot be understood (in *La Puce à l'oreille*), is an example of the natural dependence of people on things. Its absence not only inhibits him as a person, but influences the action when he is unable to convey an important piece of information.[21] At times, however, Feydeau seems to prefer objects when human beings would do just as well. Homenidès' mistaken belief that his wife is unfaithful could easily be corrected by a simple explanation (as it ultimately is), yet Homenidès must first find physical evidence in the form of a letter which had been carefully prepared in the first act.[22] Anything written down is regarded as more reliable than human conversation. In *L'Hôtel du Libre-Echange*, Feydeau finds it necessary to use a telegram to prepare for Mme Pinglet's wild story about her nightlong adventure, yet the telegram arrives only minutes before Mme Pinglet herself.[23] When Ferraillon is told, in the second act of *La Puce à l'oreille*, that he might get life insurance at Chandebise's place, Ferraillon notes the address on his cuff, and the audience knows where to expect him in the next act. He does arrive, but his appearance has nothing to do with insurance or the address on his cuff. He is there only to return Camille's palate, which had also been inscribed with the address.[24]

The Inverted Pyramid

Such examples of wasted motion are infrequent, but they suggest how important the conventions of his "craft" are in Feydeau's work. As Sarcey said, he does not usually waste time giving elaborate hints to the audience about what is going to happen. He relied on the probabilities established by the convention itself. Because he worked within the conventions, the audience knew what to expect.[25] Unlike Scribe, who often spent the entire first act on elaborate exposition and ordered a complex array of facts and circumstances before setting them in motion, Feydeau starts his plays rather simply and creates the complications later. He once said of his method:

> If you compare the construction of a play to a pyramid, you must not start from the base in order to reach the apex, as has been the case until now, *I* invert the pyramid. I start from the point and then develop the complications![26]

The disadvantage of Scribe's method of building an enormous base to support a tiny pinnacle is that all the complications, which form the bulk of the play, are designed to make possible the *scène à faire*.[27] In Feydeau's method the complications exist for their own sake, or rather for the madness and frenzy they produce. He was able to accomplish this because, rather than directing all his efforts toward a predetermined conclusion, he merely returned to his place of departure, to the point of his inverted pyramid.[28] But a pyramid that can be made to stand on its head may not be weighty, and Feydeau's is constructed of little more than air. The problems in the deception plays are never very real, they are built on appearances. The planned adultery rarely takes place, and from a situation of apparent crisis and scandal his heroes are returned to an equally apparent situation of stability. The threat is easily removed because it was largely illusory in the first place.

The major obstacle Feydeau faced in using the deception formula was not in finding a logical way to get his characters out of their predicaments, but in preventing the apparent crisis from developing into a real one. For Feydeau's people, that means to avoid a situation that would precipitate an actual scandal. Their overriding concern with scandal makes the deception formula a particularly appropriate use of the comedy of misapprehension and the techniques of the well-made play. Despite the impression one may receive from watching or reading the plays, Feydeau's characters are largely the architects of their own destinies. The recognition scene of New Comedy provided an arbitrary dénouement which was imposed upon the characters, and the well-made play technique of preparing for the outcome with hints and suggestions did not make it any less arbitrary. But Feydeau's heroes are usually responsible for both complications and dénouement. They create the crisis when they are tempted into a scandalous situation, and produce the outcome by their successful flight from scandal. By manipulating them into a situation in which exposure seems inevitable, Feydeau only increases the probability of something that is always possible whenever one attempts deception. He uses the suggestive techniques of preparation primarily to bring the deceivers and the deceived together in an incriminating locale. Once he has them there, he merely guides their efforts as they do the work of manipulating for him.

Order and Chaos

The deception formula provided Feydeau with the means to create a fantasy of bizarre situations by starting with premises that his audience could accept as reasonably "realistic," that is, with characters motivated by fears like their own. This formula also satisfied the machinelike logic and materialistic aesthetics of Sarcey without letting these become an end in themselves, and provided the necessary discipline and order to counterbalance Feydeau's natural tendency to fantasy and lunacy. The chaos which is produced by the desperate flight from scandal is balanced by a sense of overall order and a feeling that the playwright always has control no matter how chaotic things may seem. Like the clown's pratfall, which combines apparent abandon with perfect control and precision timing, events which seem most abandoned often betray the skillful hand of the playwright. Apparently chance happenings always manage to fit into a overall and somehow logical pattern. When Pinglet and Marcelle are caught in a police raid at the Hôtel du Libre-Echange, they each give the other's name as their own in an attempt to pass as man and wife. This naturally results in their arrest, but it later has the effect of throwing the blame on to their innocent spouses. An equally fortuitous series of accidents shifts the responsibility to the maid and schoolboy, but the net result of all these accidents is the impression that the playwright could lift the guilt and place it with almost mathematical precision upon whosever shoulders he pleases.

The feeling of order in the midst of madness is increased as well by the nearly symmetrical arrangement of many of the plots. Starting from a situation of bourgeois stability and order, they move to a point of maximum disorder and impropriety in the second act and return to a situation of stability in the final act. Such symmetry is often reflected in the settings. In *L'Hôtel du Libre-Echange* and *La Puce à l'oreille* the setting of the third act is the same as that of the first, and the second act of both plays takes place in a disreputable hotel. The plays end as they began, with at least relative order restored to the household.

In some of Feydeau's earliest one-act plays there is less emphasis on this kind of order and symmetry, but in others, particularly those involving infidelity, it is even more striking than in the full-length deception plays. *C'est une femme du monde (She's a Respectable Woman)* and *Séance de nuit (Night Session)* both take place in a private dining room of a restaurant—a favorite setting for indiscretions—and in both plays the characters are brought together through a series of maneuvers and relationships which have the precision and economy of a mathematical formula. In *C'est une femme du monde* two men who are being unfaithful to their mistresses agree to share the same private dining room in order to show off to each other their latest conquests. Each of these conquests, posing as a respectable lady, turns out to be the other man's deceived mistress, and is also a former wife of the maître d'hôtel. Everyone in the cast has a relationship with at least one other person which is not discovered until the end. *Séance de nuit,* although even more complex, has the same sort of ingenuity and economy in its use of characters to serve more than one function. Even more than the full-length deception plays, these two short pieces illustrate the kinds of abstract patterns which can be developed from the use of plots based on misapprehension.

In nearly all of the plays Feydeau wrote before 1908, misapprehension, whether the result of deception or innocent mistakes, is both the basis of plot development and the source of most of the fun. Even in *Fiancés en herbe,* a simple vignette in which the usual plot complications are absent, the humor arises almost entirely from a special kind of ignorance: the naïveté of children discussing adult matters without understanding the implications of their words. The use of misapprehension is not always as appropriate to the action and the characters in these plays as it is in the deception plays, however. *Amour et piano* is more successful than many of Feydeau's early plays in this regard. The action, which develops from an innocent young girl being mistaken for a courtesan, ends with the implicit suggestion that the young man who makes the mistake would have been better off courting a proper young lady than attempting to get involved with an "actress"; in this way the mistake is given some significance. On the other hand, *Chat en poche* and *Les Fiancés de Loches,* two longer plays which are also based on mistaken identity, are sustained by a largely mechanical prolongation of the original error. The latter play, which seems primarily an exercise in developing the utmost madness from a single mistake, ends appropriately in a lunatic asylum.

Variations on the Theme

The deception formula was successful partly because the plot was so suited to the theme, but since this implies that both theme and presentation were essentially the same, it supports the charge that the deception plays are all simply variations on a single play. This is largely true, but not all of the deception plays follow precisely the pattern outlined for *L'Hôtel du Libre-Echange*. In *Champignol malgré lui,* for example, the action moves in the second act to a military base rather than a hotel or other trysting place, and in *Le Système Ribadier* the threat of scandal is brought right into Ribadier's home in the person of an enraged husband. Such differences are not entirely mechanical. They are usually accompanied by certain differences in tone and theme. In *Le Dindon* the principal threat of scandal is Vatlin's one-time mistress, Maggy. By not introducing her until late in the first act and not having her appear at all in the third, Feydeau is able to devote more time in the first and third acts to confrontations between people and less to the usual complications and misunderstandings. On the other hand, La Môme Crevette, a woman whose very presence threatens scandal, is onstage throughout most of *La Dame de chez Maxim* and dominates nearly all of the action by creating one disruption after another in Petypon's life. The former play stresses the frustrations of marriage and devotes much time to the conflict of husband and wife over questions of sexual morality, while the latter, presided over by the insouciant figure of La Môme, acquires something of a festival atmosphere from her carefree disregard of all normal conventions and restraints.

Un Fil à la patte and *Occupe-toi d'Amélie* differ significantly from the other deception plays because they have different starting points. Both begin in the salon of a *cocotte*, or courtesan, rather than a respectable bourgeois home, so that the usual procedure of introducing nominally respectable people into a scandalous situation and then returning them shaken but safe to the stability of their homes cannot apply. The *cocotte*, as a walking symbol of impropriety, has great power to disrupt the façade of respectability and create general panic when thrust into a bourgeois setting. She is more than immune to the scandal she produces; she thrives on it and uses it to her advantage. Thus the action of *Un Fil à la patte* reverses the usual pattern by moving the disreputable characters of the first act into a respectable home in the second. Bois d'Enghien is not a husband trying to escape his wife in order to enjoy an extramarital fling, but a lover who wants to leave his mistress in order to marry a wealthy young woman. Rather than running into his spouse at his trysting place, he meets his mistress at the signing of the wedding contract, where she outrages the future mother-in-law and causes the marriage to be cancelled. The action does not return the characters to their starting positions, however, because the young lady forces her mother to accept the marriage by herself causing another scandalous situation. Scandal is again the key to both complication and outcome, but instead of resulting from the flight of the main characters, here two characers—first the *cocotte* and then the ingénue—use the threat of scandal to obtain their own ends.[29]

Occupe-toi-d'Amélie moves even further from the standard formula because it revolves almost wholly about the world of the *cocotte*. The play has the usual second act bedroom scene which contains frantic attempts to prevent the discovery of infidelities, but instead of being the focal point of the play and the pinnacle of complications that must be unraveled in the final act, the second act here produces additional complications and a fourth tableau in which to straighten them out. As a result the play lacks the geometrical symmetry and economy of Feydeau's earlier deception plays. By the standards of the latter, it is loosely constructed, but it follows the logic of farce in carrying a situation to an unbearable extreme. Marcel's attempt to avoid marriage while reaping its benefits (the benefits of marriage being financial, not sexual) results in the most horrifying situation one of Feydeau's males could imagine—marriage to a *cocotte*.

New Directions

Occupe-toi d'Amélie is the last full-length play Feydeau finished without collaboration, and it is one of several attempts in the later part of his career to break away from the mathematical rigors of the deception formula. It is usually regarded as one of his finest plays, and its success may be due in part to the fact that it is less dependent on the formula than others.[30] After the success of *La Dame de chez Maxim* in 1899, he tried several times to move in new directions, but not always with happy results.

Some of these ventures departed radically from his usual practice. *Le Bourgeon* is a comedy which treats seriously many of the same themes on which his farces are based: sex and marriage, hypocrisy, and the role of the *cocotte* in (or out of) society. Because of the serious tone, it appears from our vantage point rather embarrassing in its commitment to an outdated code of sexual morality. *L'Age d'or* is a time-travel fantasy framed by a conventional plot of paternal objections to a daughter's marriage. Unlike *Le Bourgeon,* in which farce is largely relegated to a sub-plot, the general atmosphere in this fantasy is farcical, particularly in its treatment of sex and violence.

La Duchesse des Folies-Bergère (The Duchess from the Folies-Bergère, 1902) differs primarily in its development of the plot. This play weaves several threads of action together through five acts, and was understandably criticized as being "made up of several vaudevilles."[31] Although there is a kind of loose thematic unity which holds the various strands together, it lacks the economy and focus that were so highly regarded by Sarcey and others. Another play, *La Main passe!,* is interesting because it is superficially like the other plays that hang on the eternal question of adultery. Women often threaten adultery but are usually prevented from actually committing it. Even when husbands or wives are caught in compromising situations, they are the victims of mistakes and appearances. But in *La Main passe!* adultery is committed, and the guilty couple is discovered. Shaw once complained that "conventional farcical comedies are always finally tedious because the heart of them, the inevitable conjugal infidelity, is always evaded."[32] It is not evaded here, but the result is not especially fortunate. In spite of Shaw's objection, evasion is appropriate to a play such as *L'Hôtel du Libre-Echange* because it is consistent with the characters' attitudes. They ultimately avoid both adultery and its consequences because they fear scandal above all else. *La Main passe!* involves an actual breach of the moral code which Feydeau seems to have regarded seriously, for the lovers are duly punished.

The method of punishment is clever, amusing, and actually quite appropriate, but it is followed by a fourth act devoted to almost melancholy reflections on the consequences of adultery.[33] After these pious thoughts, when Francine runs off to find yet another lover, her behavior seems motivated by little more than the convenience of the plot. Since her sometime lover (now her husband) is allowed to rejoin his forgiving former wife, it seems clear that Francine is forced to pass from one man to the next because of the convention that an unchaste wife is forever "unclean," and not because of her arbitrarily "flighty" character. Having weighted down the main action of the play with the demands of conventional morality, Feydeau lightens the tone for two and one half acts with the antics of Hubertin, a broadly comic character whose actions, unfortunately, are only peripherally related to the main plot.

La Main passe! and *Le Bourgeon* suggest that Feydeau was searching for a way to deal with the real problems which arise between people because of the frustrations of sex and marriage rather than continue manufacturing artificial crises of misunderstanding and confusion, but both of these plays are marred by the necessity of warping the plot so as to demonstrate the validity of a code of sexual ethics. Only when he abandoned the question of extramarital sex was Feydeau able to find a satisfactory way of dealing with the conflicts of husband and wife without relying on intrigue and misapprehension. In his late one-act plays, beginning with *Feu la mère de Madame,* Feydeau abandoned the comedy of misapprehension and developed what was for him a new dramatic method. Misapprehension plays a role in these plays, as it is apt to in any farce, but it is no longer the principle on which they are organized. Instead these plays are based on a fundamental incompatibility between two persons which is steadily aggravated until it reaches a nearly explosive state. It was not an original method. Courteline had shown the farcical possibilities of putting two characters in conflict, each resolutely pursuing his own form of irrational logic.[34] Throughout his career, Feydeau had himself often used direct conflict between a husband and wife in individual scenes, but not through an entire play. The complications in the late plays are minimal, serving primarily to heighten the conflict and bring the differences between the two into the sharpest possible focus. The characters are more realistic than in his early short plays, but they seem scarcely less mad. In many ways quite ordinary and conventional, they exist in their own separate worlds, as firmly cut off from one another as if they were creatures from separate planets. Brought together by the unpredictable accident of marriage, they remain foreign and incomprehensible to each other. Incapable of communicating, they can only destroy one another.

This is a simpler, more direct, and perhaps more honest method of creating comic action, but it too proved limited in scope for Feydeau. He was only able to use it successfully in short plays where the steadily increasing tension is not broken by act divisions or obscured by complicating events. It is possible that if Feydeau had lived longer and retained his health, he might have written longer plays that were free of reliance on mistakes and misunderstandings, yet (unlike *Le Bourgeon*) wholly within his usually intensely farcical mode. As it is, two plays which seemed to be going in that direction were abandoned, while he went on to write several more short plays.

At the point at which each of these attempts breaks off, there are none of the misunderstandings or deceptions which sustain the plots of his earlier plays. *Cent millions qui tombent (One Hundred Million Windfall)* exists as the first two acts of a three-act play. There are a few scenes in the beginning of the first act involving the familiar business of hiding a lover, but this is soon passed over, and the characters quickly turn their attention to money, which is their preoccupation and the focus of the play. This is Feydeau's most savage portrayal of cupidity and one of the plays most dependent on the idiosyncrasies of character types for its comic effects. The plot is simple and straightforward. Paulette and her friends shamelessly try to flatter, pamper, or wheedle the formerly despised servant Isidore out of a share in the vast fortune he has apparently inherited. A reference to the brief duration of the Saturnalia suggests that Isidore's good fortune would have proved temporary in the third act, but there is little else to predict the outcome.[35]

In *On va faire la cocotte (Going to Play the Courtesan,* a two-act play, of which only one act exists), Feydeau returned to the theme of marital infidelity. The situation is similar to that of several other plays. A philandering husband is found out by his wife, who then plans revenge in kind. The state of affairs at the end of the act is parallel to that at the end of the first act of *Monsieur chasse!,* but in the earlier play the husband does not know that he has been discovered, and the wife does not intend for him to find out about her "revenge." This atmosphere of misapprehension becomes the basis for the frantic evasions and lies which make up the action of the remainder of the play. But when Emilienne learns, in *On va faire la cocotte,* of her husband's infidelity, she confronts him with the truth in a way that makes it impossible to deny. Both of them know exactly where they stand. Trévelin defies his wife and goes out with his mistress on his arm as Emilienne declares to his face, "Since you only go for sluts, that's fine! I'm going to act like a slut."[36]

We have little more than a cast of characters to tell us what Feydeau planned for the second act, but one can easily imagine an outcome consistent with the situation and the personalities of the characters involved: Trévelin forced to admit that he fears cuckoldry and scandal more than he desires the pleasures of sin, and Emilienne made to realize that the life of a "slut" is not precisely what she had romantically imagined. Yet Feydeau, the creator of such ingeniously complex puzzles, was unable to bring this relatively simple action to a conclusion, although he was still hoping to complete it six years after the first act was finished.[37]

Wisdom and Folly

The forms which Feydeau used were successful because even though they conformed to the social and theatrical prejudices of his culture, they were supremely suited to portraying the folly of those attitudes. This is not to say that Feydeau was criticizing or mocking the mores of his age. There can be little doubt that his attitudes were essentially conservative, and that he shared the prejudices of his contemporaries. If so, one might ask, how was he able to portray so accurately the folly of a scandal-obsessed society, if, as it seems, he did not really regard those obsessions as foolish?

In objecting to the evasions of bedroom farce, Shaw was asking that we critically examine our attitudes toward sex and scandal, but the play he offered as a "demonstration" of the proper role of farcical comedy actually demonstrates that people really need not be so foolish about these things, and so is not farcical at all.[38] Farce will not admit the possibility of an alternative to folly, for to concede the polarity of wisdom and folly implies the need for judgment, and farce abjures all judgment, whether rational or moral. It gives the only accurate picture of the region beyond good and evil, where the inhabitants are not supermen, but unashamed fools. Entering the spirit of farce is a declaration of irresponsibility, a temporary renunciation of the duties of wisdom and the right of judgment. It is an abdication which might justly be deplored if we could only be certain that our wisdom were real and our judgment sound. But we know that prejudice often takes the mask of wisdom and that judgment can be a cloak for hate or fear; so when farce insists that beliefs, prejudices, reason, and fear all shed their graver disguises to wear the cap and bells, its folly may be wiser than we know.

The irresponsibility of farce does not imply that it is simple. We are not easily seduced into discarding our serious attitudes toward ourselves and our feelings, and for every age and culture there exist limits which cannot be crossed. Feydeau's limitations were those of his age, and he accepted them even while—by exploiting their farcical possibilities—he portrayed them. If they prevented him from writing certain kinds of plays, they were the mainspring of others. The deception formula and the one-act plays of domestic conflict enabled him to probe the lives and feelings of his audience without straying from the path of folly. Both methods provided a distorting mirror in which they saw their lives reflected with a calculated degree of unreality. The nature of the reality shown in the mirror and the techniques by which it was distorted will be the subject of the next chapter.

3

The Inner Structure

> *The mechanism—although impeccable—does not explain everything. Others have been able to skillfully manage peripeteias and their works are no longer performed. They were nothing but good craftsmen. Feydeau's plays are made exceptional by their extravagance and especially by the streak of madness that runs throughout.*"[1]

Probabilities and Progressive Madness

Like Sarcey, many modern critics have commented on Feydeau's elaborate constructions and intricate machinery. But Feydeau himself had this interesting comment on the way he created his plays:

> I never write a scenario. I see a situation; I take it. Then I start out without knowing where, at random... Having come up against an obstacle, I jump over it, without evasion, without trickery or facile expedients. It's a principle of mine to pull myself out of everything.[2]

Feydeau implies that to have everything worked out in advance, to leave nothing to chance, would somehow be "cheating." He would not be playing the game honestly. The game of farce requires spontaneity, a feeling of improvisation. However much planning he actually did, he recognized that the vitality of his plays depended on a feeling of uncertainty and unpredictability that planning could not provide and might destroy. The wild air of improvisation which does so much to provide the buoyancy and gaiety of his plays could not be the product of a detailed blueprint. His repeated use of the same formula, with its "inverted pyramid," allowed him greater freedom to improvise than might at first appear, so that his plays create more the impression of an improbable and unpredictable juggling act than of a precise, well-oiled machine. This sense of unpredictable madness is at the heart of Feydeau, but even the madness is not without its rules and logic.

Elder Olson points out that even when comedy departs from normal or everyday probabilities it still follows understood patterns of rules, and he classifies the probabilities of farce as usually being what he calls "hyperbolical."³ The probabilities of exaggeration are generally the rule in Feydeau's farces as well, but they are complicated by additional rules. To some extent the probabilities are established by the conventions already discussed. The well-made play's demand for economy increases the "probability" that a character introduced in the first act will appear again in the second and third if he has the least excuse for doing so, although such an appearance may represent an extraordinary coincidence by normal standards. In the first act of *Un Fil à la patte* Bousin mentions that he is a notary's clerk. Thus, of all such clerks in Paris, it is he who fulfills that function in the next two acts.⁴ In *Champignol malgré lui* a maid who was fired in the first act just happens to find her next job in the home to which everyone is invited in the third.⁵ Characters may behave in ways which violate patterns of real life if there is a precedent in convention or tradition. Husbands blind to the attentions paid to their wives by other men were a firmly established tradition in *vaudeville*, and Feydeau carries such blindness to extremes. Vatelin, for example, is not the least suspicious when he finds a man nearly prostrate before his wife in *Le Dindon*, despite the fact that it is the third such occurrence.⁶ His indifference is the more striking since similar scenes in Feydeau are often the cause of general panic.

"Probabilities" of this kind are artificial and conventional, but they are an important part of the way Feydeau makes the improbable and bizarre seem logical and somehow acceptable within an atmosphere of accelerating madness. The acceleration is itself a part of the method. Feydeau once described his method of making a character seem more probable: "When I have a leading role who might seem improbable, I take care to provide him with a secondary character as a companion, one who...is even more improbable and, by contrast, makes the lead seem almost logical."⁷ The reverse is equally true: if a somewhat improbable character is made acceptable, he will prepare the way for the more fantastic one who follows him. Each step of the progressive lunacy in Feydeau's world builds on the previous one. However wild and improbable the action becomes, it usually begins in rather normal circumstances and everyday settings: "I always start out realistically. Something—the trick is to find it!—comes along to divert the natural progression of events from the course it should logically have taken."⁸ From this point the action becomes increasingly more complex and frantic until it finally seems that anything at all can happen. A simple mistake can snowball into disastrous consequences. The simple provincials of *Les Fiancés de Loches* mistake an employment agency for a marriage bureau and are led through a bewildering series of situations to confinement in an insane asylum. Lemercier's weakness for actresses eventually results in his being taken for a desperate murderer in *Gibier de potence*. The entire action of a play may be built on a mistake, such as Saint-Florimond's assumption of Champignol's identity, or even a minor character can be sent by an ill-timed move into a whirlpool of events beyond his control or comprehension.[9] Bousin's vain and foolish act of dropping his card into an anonymous bouquet leads ultimately to his arrest for indecent exposure in *Un Fil à la patte*. Like so many of Feydeau's victims, Bousin never quite comprehends what is happening to him and understandably concludes that he has fallen among a pack of lunatics.[10]

One of the reasons Feydeau can raise the level of acceptable madness so high is that the situation is nearly always more comprehensible and logical to the audience than it is to the characters involved. They cannot see the threads which weave events together; they are aware only that their stable world has been converted into a madhouse. They, even more than the audience, are ready to accept the proposition that "anything can happen," for they can make little sense of what has already occurred. When Tournel and Raymond see Camille appear from the revolving bed of *La Puce à l'oreille*, miraculously speaking with the help of his silver palate, they refuse to believe their eyes. After all, they had just seen the exact double of Chandebise appear magically from the same bed, and they assume this must be yet another magical twin.[11] In this world the improbable is expected and madness becomes the norm.

Once the playwright has lifted his audience and his characters to the highest possible level of madness, he must decide what to do with them—how to end his play. As with flying an airplane, coming down to earth may not be the most interesting part of the flight, but it is one of the most difficult. Lea wrote that the weakness in most farces is "at the end when the knots are cut and not untied."[12] She was referring specifically to the *Commedia*, but the same weakness can be seen in some of Feydeau's early plays. Plays like *Gibier de potence*, *Chat en poche*, and *Les Fiancés de Loches*, which are based on a central case of mistaken identity, end quite abruptly and with many questions left unresolved once the misunderstanding is cleared up. In farce we are not really interested in resolutions. We did not take off just to prove that we could come down again. Rather, we want to enjoy aerial acrobatics in the rarified atmosphere of fantasy and to defy the forces that would pull us back to reality. Yet it cannot be said that such abrupt endings are satisfactory, even for farce. Thrust suddenly back into reality, we become sharply aware that the fantastic world into which we had been gradually seduced was only an illusion. We had been secretly pleased at how much that mad world resembled our own, but the sudden ending makes us aware of the gulf between them.

Another of the advantages of the deception formula is that it restores order by means of the same logic which created the disorder. The resolution is a continuation rather than a denial of the previous action. Stability is restored, but it is just as insubstantial and often nearly as mad as the chaos that preceded it. Sometimes, as in *Le Dindon* and *La Puce à l'oreille*, the misunderstandings are cleared up and the characters are allowed to forgive one another and possibly to profit by their experience. In such cases the resolution brings us down from the level of farce and closer to conventional comedy, but just as often the madness continues to the end. Moulineaux, in *Tailleur pour dames,* persists in concocting new lies to the last line of the play, and stability returns in *L'Hôtel du Libre-Echange* only when Pinglet has driven the last incriminating witness from his home. In *Un Fil à la patte,* Bois-d'Enghien does finally get rid of his mistress and wins the young bride he wanted, but only because his fiancée finds the sinful past he was trying to discard irresistibly glamorous.[13] Such characters may find the "happy" endings which they have been seeking, but their newly found paradise is as appropriate to their foolishness as was their recently endured hell.

Happy endings are not required, but endings which are consistent with the original premises are. The late one-act plays have their own form of accelerating madness, but there are no tricks to elevate us into a world of fantasy. There is only an increasing tension between two people which usually ends when the distracted husband leaves the field of combat in an impotent rage. There is no resolution of the crisis or return to stability because there is no need for one. There are no intrigues or misunderstandings to be resolved and the conflicts, although essentially trivial, are as real at the height of the madness as they are at the beginning. The crises in the deception plays are like a magician's tricks. They are the product of mirrors and sleight of hand. The transition back to reality is necessary to complete the illusion. In the late one-act plays the same level of reality—the same degree of "hyperbolical" probability—is maintained throughout, and the conflict is carried through to the inevitable explosion.[11]

Exaggeration and Truth

The exaggeration of reality in Feydeau's plays varies both in kind and degree. Exaggeration is not always comical. As Eastman says; "It is the *too* much—always and absolutely—not the much, that is funny." In order to be comic, exaggeration must go "beyond some humanly reasonable bounds."[15] This does not mean that the greater an effect or a character is exaggerated, the funnier it is likely to be, or that it need be gross to be effective. At times such "reasonable bounds" lie remarkably close to actuality. Domestic strife, such as that portrayed in Feydeau's late work, is a favorite theme of comic writers because such situations find even the best of us approaching our limits of petty and selfish stupidity. Feydeau goes just beyond these limits in making his married combatants—especially the wives—totally blind to all but their own interests and points of view. Comic exaggeration is usually most effective when it most successfully welds together reality and unreality, when the traits it draws manage somehow to appear at once strikingly true to life and absurdly impossible. The couples in Feydeau's late plays are extreme without departing far from reality. One of them at least may have re-created events that actually took place in the Feydeau household. His son Jacques claimed that he was the original hero of *On purge Bébé!* and that "things happened pretty much as they did in the play."[16]

In Feydeau's earliest plays the exaggeration is much more heightened and lifts us immediately into a fantastic world which derives its comic power from its blissful unconcern with the standards of our own. The opening line of *Gibier de potence* tells us the sort of world we are entering. Plumard is just finishing writing a letter which he signs, *"an anonymous citizen... who won't give his name."* Plumard, who lives appropriately at 7, rue aux Anes (Street of the Asses), later explains how he came to marry an actress:

> I was a herbalist, Monsieur, with respectable morals. One day Mademoiselle Lamballe sent for me because she was feeling ill. She was having dizzy spells, but thanks to my care... she felt great the next day, and two weeks later, I married her. Five months after that, I became a proud father! My wife gave me a fat, healthy baby... That's a very rare thing, you know. I wanted, in the interest of science, to send off a report to the Academy of Medicine, but my wife was against it.[17]

Plumard is more an exaggeration of an ancient theatrical type character, the happy cuckold, than he is of observed reality. Thus twice removed from reality (like the other characters in the play), he seems less an exaggeration than an inhabitant of some land of happy fools whose only relation to real life is their obvious freedom from its restrictions.

Extreme forms of exaggeration are not always of this kind. Bentley suggests that the exaggerations of farce, although apparently excessive, still maintain contact with reality because although "the external facts are distorted," farce is always faithful "to the inner experience."[18] As he sees it, farce shows not what we do, but what we would like to do. It expresses, usually by direct physical action, what we feel but usually keep to ourselves. Like Freud, Bentley stresses the expression of feelings of aggression and sexual desire. While these are present in Feydeau's farces, they are not the only aspects of the "inner experience" that are exaggerated. The most common and most often exaggerated mental state for a Feydeau character is fear of exposure. Discovered in a compromising situation, as they always are, they run like frightened rabbits. Their fear is instantly translated into flight—into direct physical action. The reaction is automatic and unthinking. Confronted with exposure, they can think of nothing else. When his wife surprises Plantarede with his mistress in *Je ne trompe pas mon mari (I Don't Cheat on My Husband),* his terrified impulse to flee is so great that it never occurs to him until later that his wife had made her startling appearance from under the covers of another man's bed![19] Feydeau's heroes will do anything to escape scandal. If the door is not free, they may go out the window. If that is not possible, they will look for someplace, however ridiculous and improbable, to hide. When finally cornered, they will manufacture desperate and absurd lies.

The exaggeration of fear is complemented by the exaggeration of joyful relief when the fear is removed. Terrified at the thought of Jambart's return, Barillon's household is suddenly comforted with the reminder that Jambart must be dead. He was devoured, they assure themselves, by a man-eating fish. Dancing and singing for joy, they shout, "He was eaten up! He was eaten up!" *(Le Mariage de Barillon)*.[20] After Yvonne learns that the messenger who had brought news of her mother's death *(Feu la mère de Madame)* had actually come to the wrong door, she jumps for joy as she hears the fateful bell ringing at the door of the adjacent apartment: "It's our neighbors who lost their mother!"[21] As Bentley suggests, such reactions are likely to be physical. Many a guest whose appearance is inopportune finds himself shoved unceremoniously into the next room, and Barillon picks up an insulting telegraph boy and has him carried bodily off stage.[22] If they are prevented by the situation from reacting physically, they are apt to betray their anxiety by becoming so distracted that they appear mad. In *Le Dindon,* Pontagnac is so upset when he learns that the husband of the woman he has been pursuing is an old friend that he gives her money to keep quiet, apparently thinking for the moment that she is a servant.[23] Later in the same play, Vatelin is surprised in his hotel room by Soldignac, an Englishman (despite his name) who is trying to obtain evidence of his wife's adultery. Knowing that the unsuspecting wife is in the bathroom, Vatelin becomes nearly incoherent:

> *Vatelin.* ...She's not here! She's not here!
> *Soldignac.* Who, my wife? Don't I know it! The commissioner must be about to trap her right now.
> *Vatelin.* Right, yes, yes, yes.
> *Soldignac.* To be absolutely certain, he has had her followed since six this morning. Aren't you interested in what I have to say?
> *Vatelin.* Oh, yes! Yes, yes! You said: "Sick...She's sick!"
> *Soldignac.* Oh no, not now.
> *Vatelin.* Oh dear! She died! Well, that's the way it goes.
> *Soldignac.* No, no, I said "My wife—"
> *Vatelin.* Oh, right! Your wife—who's right there...
> *Soldignac.* Huh?
> *Vatelin.* Who's right there—on rue Roquépine![24]

If the characters' reactions are exaggerated, so often are the stimuli which produce them. As the play progresses, their troubles grow beyond all reasonable bounds. They are haunted by the things they dread most, and their most secret fears materialize before their eyes, like the newspaper in *Un Fil à la patte* which reappears with the magical certainty of a hydra's head. Feydeau's often quoted "rule" of always bringing together people who should on no account meet applies to things as well as people.[25] The demons who haunt these people usually have been created as a result of the characters' own attempts at deception, but they need not be. Barillon's troubles only partly stem from a deception, yet he seems to be caught up in a nightmare in which his worst imaginings are realized. It is not enough that he is married to the woman who was to be his mother-in-law (and whom he finds physically repulsive), or that her husband's return from the dead makes him first a party to bigamy and then a cuckold; the world seems to have conspired in nightmare fashion to remind him of his shame and humiliation. He himself has barely learned of the mistake that has made Mme Jambart his wife at a time when all Paris seems to have heard of the man who married his own mother-in-law. When the "family" flees to the country to escape the growing scandal, they are followed by children singing mocking and obscene songs, and a theatre manager gives them free passes in order to boost sales with a sign reading "The bigamist of Bois-Colombes will be present at this performance."[26]

Fatalism and Farce

Bentley suggests that the structure of coincidences in farce becomes the equivalent of fate, a force outside ourselves to which we (or the characters in the play) must submit.[27] Such a concept of fate seems particularly appropriate for Feydeau, because his characters are often governed by a destiny which has its own inexorable logic quite beyond the conventional "logic" of manipulated events which was discussed earlier. The nature of this irrational logic is suggested in remarks made by Jean-Louis Barrault. Calling attention to the dream-like quality one sometimes finds in Feydeau, he said that one of the characteristics of his work "is to make concrete the association of ideas. Several ideas develop together—and immediately the thing exists."[28] The association of ideas transformed into concrete images sounds more like the experiments of the surrealists than nineteenth-century farce, yet there is a certain similarity between the surrealists' attempts to make manifest the life of the unconscious and the tendency of farce to express the "inner experience" in physical terms. It is not simply that the characters openly and often violently express normally repressed emotions; the world in which they live seems to reflect those thought processes, much as the dream world is created by the mind of the dreamer. In Feydeau, the pattern of coincidences which controls the fate of the characters is not random, nor as arbitrary as it might seem. It is so closely related to the desires and fears of the characters that it seems at times to be produced by them.

Sometimes, particularly in the opening scenes, fate seems to be working in their favor. Pinglet, in *L'Hôtel du Libre-Echange,* barely mentions his lust for his neighbor's wife and chance conveniently arranges to throw her into his arms. He searches for an appropriate *maison de rendez-vous* and several circulars of such an establishment appear almost magically—in his wife's hands.[29] That perhaps should have given him a hint as to what was in store for him, but like the other would-be lovers in Feydeau who find themselves suddenly fortunate, he learns only later that the gods were tempting him to a comic hell. If it seemed for a short while that fate was responding like a genie to his every wish, the illusion was temporary. But fate is not indifferent to him, nor is he without influence on his destiny. On the contrary, like most of Feydeau's characters, he seems to have a knack for calling disaster down upon his own head.

Fools as well as tragic heroes seem to have a special relationship with fate. Welsford argues that the privileged place of the court-fool to say what he pleased and the prominence of fools and folly in certain religious and folk festivals both had their origins in the ancient practice of deliberately inviting vituperation in order to bring good luck. It is, she says, "a form of that universal human instinct, the dread of... the sin of 'hubris' or presumption."[30] It can be seen even in educated people who insist on touching wood whenever they happen to mention their own good fortune.

> The malign power of the Evil Eye... exists in a vague, undefined way suffused throughout the universe... To praise oneself or be praised by others is a sure way of attracting this queer, cosmic jealousy, and conversely the surest way to evade its unwelcome attraction is to depreciate oneself or be mocked by other people.[31]

The role of the fool was to draw this "cosmic jealousy" onto his own shoulders, and possibly, because fools were often regarded as immune to the Evil Eye, to transfer some of his own good luck onto those he mocked. Feydeau's fools serve also to draw the jealousy of fate onto themselves, and they too are immune from its worst effects.[32] They tempt fate as surely as Agamemnon treading on the red carpet, but being fools, they escape the catastrophe reserved for kings, and are ultimately allowed to return to their folly.

With this strange power watching over Feydeau's world, to boast of one's prowess invites certain impotence, and to declare with confidence that something is impossible is to guarantee that it will occur. We need only hear Chanal, in *La Main passe!*, dismiss as totally absurd the idea that his wife might have a lover, to know that he is, or soon will be, a cuckold.[33] When Pinglet assures Marcelle that the seedy hotel *(L'Hôtel du Libre-Echange)* to which he has brought her is the perfect place for their rendezvous because "it would be bad luck indeed if we met someone we know here," her husband sneezes in the next room, and Pinglet jovially answers the hidden voice with "God bless you!"[34] The same malicious Providence insures that Follavoine's "unbreakable" chamber pots will be smashed into pieces *(On purge Bébé)*, and that Brigot's boast of his sexual exploits will cause his nephew to be threatened with a cuckold's horns *(Le Mariage de Barillon).*[35]

A closely related superstition holds that if one speaks of the devil he is sure to appear, so if one wishes to doubly defy fate, one need only declare that his appearance is impossible. There is nothing more certain in Feydeau's world than the imminent arrival of anyone whose presence is declared unlikely, especially if that person's entrance will destroy an alibi. In play after play, all that is needed to bring a character on stage is another character's insistence that the absent person is hopelessly ill, never leaves his remote country home, or is confined to a wheelchair by crippling rheumatism. The audience knows this and expects the new arrival, but the characters never seem to learn what disastrous effect their words have. Duchotel is caught twice in *Monsieur chasse!* He has been visiting his mistress under the pretext of going hunting with a friend in the country; a friend, Duchotel tells his wife, who never comes to Paris. The minute he leaves, the friend walks in the door. The wife soon learns that the two have not seen each other in months, and that Duchotel's hunting companion has never been hunting in his life. Later, when his wife confronts him with his lie, he continues to bluff, thinking his reluctant alibi has returned safely to the country:

> Ah, well, for heaven's sake! Just because Cassagne told you—so then you thought—? But don't you know about Cassagne? That's his sunstroke. Then you didn't know that he got sunstroke in Africa, and ever since he's had these lapses of memory? Well, you see? You ask him if he goes hunting—he says "no," of course! And he's sincere! He doesn't remember! Not a hunter—him? Oh, sure!—I wish he were here, really! To say that in front of me. I just wish he were here![36]

One scarcely need say that the next line belongs to the servant, announcing the arrival of M. Cassagne.

This vein of comic fatalism and the note of bitterness some have detected in his plays have caused certain critics to see an almost tragic undercurrent in Feydeau. As early as 1913 Nozière wrote that his plays had the

> mathematical rigor of a tragedy. A kind of fatality controls the action and constrains the hero to submit to every consequence of a fault or a peril. Certainly Feydeau loves lunacy... But beyond that, he is subjected to a superior law, as Wotan obeyed the Nornes. The god of *vaudeville,* he too, is the slave of a supreme and reasonable force.[37]

There is a danger that this sort of observation may lead one to discover more profundity than exists in these farces, so it is well to seek the meaning of this sense of "fatality" in Feydeau's work. Welsford does not speculate on the origin of the "universal instinct" she describes, but it is not unreasonable to conclude that, like so many superstitions, it represents an attempt to impose order on an uncertain universe, an attempt that creates a picture of the cosmos which more accurately reflects our own mental processes than the unpredictable workings of the external world. We create an avenging destiny by projecting our jealousy and outrage at the lies and presumptions of others onto an indifferent universe. But the idea of destiny confirms our fears as well as our sense of justice. We cannot mention our good fortune without fearing to lose it, and the more we fear, the more apt we are to see the cause of our fear in some unseen force waiting to take away what is precious to us. What we fear most is uncertainty, so we perversely convert chance into a positive force which is increasingly tempted to rob us the more we have to lose, and we create from our imaginations a cosmic tendency to produce order through the operation of chance. In Feydeau, this transformation of chance into certainty has almost mathematical precision.[38]

There is nothing mystical about this comic sense of fate. It stems from a theatrical convention that is used by many comic writers to create a sense of expectancy in the audience. But this is not a purely arbitrary convention. It has a basis in human psychology that makes it particularly appropriate for farce. When the convention is used by a playwright such as Scribe to make a coincidence seem somehow more "natural," or simply to create a dramatic *coup de théâtre,* it may rightly be criticized as artificial or false.[39] In Feydeau's hands, the improbability of the device is flaunted, not hidden. It becomes part of the method by which the disorderly world of dream fears is made both concrete and precisely predictable, and by which the improbable is made certain.

Conflicts, Contradictions, and Transformations

The actualization of submerged mental states through the association of ideas is a major part of the dream-like quality which critics like Barrault find in Feydeau's plays, but it is not the only one.[40] The irrational logic of farce, like that of dreams, depicts the world (including the world of our imaginations) in a changed aspect. The Freudians maintain that the true content of dreams is disguised to escape the psychic censor. In much the same way, Feydeau presents brutality, catastrophe, and humiliation transformed by absurdity. Many of the situations in Feydeau's plays, if encountered in life, could be as painful as those of tragedy. Our suffering is always lessened if we are allowed to suffer nobly and grandly. What we truly cannot bear is humiliation, being exposed to the world as the petty, weak, and pitiful creatures we fear we really are. It is this sort of nightmare world to which Feydeau's creatures are subjected. Like a nightmare, it becomes increasingly absurd and impossible as it becomes more terrifying. What would be painfully embarrassing is transformed into laughter and fantasy, because, although we may recognize our nightmares, they have been stretched beyond the limits of the possible.[41] The distortion takes many forms, but one of the most common is the inappropriateness of a character's response to a situation. When threatened with exposure, his or her reaction is usually an exaggerated, headlong flight. Yet when actually caught in an embarrassing situation, the character often tries to act as if nothing at all were out of the ordinary. When Lucette, in *Un Fil à la patte,* discovers Bois-d'Enghien hiding in a closet, he calmly explains, "You know, there are times in life when one needs to be alone—And how've you been since I saw you last?" Later he is trapped in his underwear on the landing of his apartment just as a wedding party descends from the floor above. With nowhere to run or hide, he gallantly bows and offers his best wishes to the scandalized bride.[42]

Both the frantic flight and the affectation of nonchalance which follows are reactions to the same typical nightmare fear: the threat of exposure. Both reactions emphasize this fear while placing it in a slightly unreal context. When exposure is merely threatened, the reaction is extreme and physical, drawing attention to the fear itself in a way which appears out of proportion to the threatened cause. Quite often (as in the scene in which Bois'd'Enghien frantically hides newspapers that everyone else regards as innocuous) the threat appears in the guise of a perfectly ordinary object or event, and is not seen as threatening by most of the characters on stage. But when the threat is realized in all its enormity, the reaction is to ignore it completely. Either cause or reaction is given a complete, physical expression, and the other is proportionately diminished. Each situation is an example of what Bentley calls the farcical dialectic: the bringing together of "wild fantasies and... everyday and drab realities."[43] The fantastic improbabilities of a nightmare come into direct conflict with the bland surface of everyday life in an explosive collision of the ordinary and the extraordinary.

The *quiproquo* provides an excellent means of exploiting such conflicts by presenting two versions of the same event, one bizarre or shocking and the other bland and ordinary. It may simply be a question of a character acting in ignorance of the true situation. Moricet, in *Monsieur chasse!,* unknowingly duplicates the scene with Bois-d'Enghien on the stairway. Alone in his apartment with another man's wife when he hears the voice of the law demanding entrance, he dresses hurriedly—including gloves and hat—in order to have an irreproachable appearance when he opens the door. Unfortunately, he forgets in his panic to put on his trousers, so that from the waist up he is dressed to go out, and from the waist down he is undressed for bed.[44] This is another instance of farce's tendency to express its themes and situations in strongly physical terms. Moricet's appearance is a striking visual metaphor for the situation in which he finds himself: in spite of his attempts to "cover up," he is literally "caught with his pants down."

Moricet's neglect of his trousers is a simple mistake by comparison with many of the elaborate *quiproquos* for which Feydeau is famous, but it shares the characteristics which make mistakes and misunderstandings such fertile devices for the writers of farce. In the first place, mistakes provide a bridge between the ordinary and the bizarre by permitting ordinary characters to behave through ignorance in an extraordinary or fantastic manner. Whether or not the mistake itself was foolish (they are often quite natural and reasonable under the circumstances) they cause their victims to look and behave like fools. Just as misapprehension gives the writer of the second, or "mechanical," type of farce a means of controlling events and shaping the plot, it also allows him to control his characters' foolishness. A simple mistake can induce an otherwise ordinary character to behave with the apparent abandon of the most irresponsible and improbable *zanni* while always maintaining the necessary link with reality. There is no shortage of fools in Feydeau, but most of the outrageous and foolish behavior with which his plays abound is the result of characters' operating on false assumptions. Occasionally such ludicrous behavior is the result of deliberate trickery on the part of other characters. Such is the case in *La Dame de chez Maxim* when Môme Crevette convinces the credulous Gabrielle to rush to La Place de la Concorde to receive the "word" through which she will conceive the future savior of France.[45] The best known example of such trickery is the famous wedding scene in *Occupe-toi d'Amélie* in which Marcel finds himself married to a notorious *cocotte* in spite of his plans to avoid marriage altogether.

Such cases of a character deliberately and successfully making a fool of another are comparatively rare. More often the mistakes and misunderstandings seem to arise from apparently random accidents in an atmosphere of general confusion. Often a character is caught in a ludicrous situation because his own attempts at deception have backfired. Moricet's overlooked trousers and Marcel's wedding are examples. Another occurs when Duchotel tries to convince his wife that he has really been hunting. He habitually returns from his escapades with "game" he has picked up at the local butcher, but this time the slightly deaf merchant supplied him with several pâtés which Duchotel unwittingly presents to his wife as proof of his honesty.[46] Duchotel's lies are typical in that they rarely have the effect intended. If they don't result in making the perpetrator himself look foolish, as in this case, they are apt to cause entirely unforeseen misunderstandings and confusions. Another inveterate liar, Moulineaux, produces nearly all of the multiple misunderstandings in *Tailleur pour dames* by his constant and often desperate fabrications. His intention is merely to deceive his wife, but in the process he inadvertently makes fools of everyone in the cast, himself included. Characters seem to be led into the greatest absurdities, however, through the operation of blind chance and innocent mistakes. It is chance that leads Tournel and Raymonde to get on their knees to an alcoholic hotel porter in *La Puce à l'oreille*, kissing him and begging his forgiveness.[47] Their confusion is the result of the age-old device of exact physical resemblance, but a much more complex series of accidents causes Duc Pitchenieff *(La Duchesse des Folies-Bergère)* to unwittingly act as a procurer for his own wife.[48] The unfortunate duke is in much the same position as the lawyer Charançon in *L'Affaire Edouard,* although the consequences for the latter are not as severe. He merely defends an unknown woman (who happens to be his wife) from charges stemming from an illicit encounter, and unknowingly directs several insults at himself in the course of his eloquent plea.[49] These and many more are fools by circumstance more than by nature. They are ordinary people thrust by the playwright into extraordinary situations.

The ability to turn ordinary people into fools is not the only advantage of the *quiproquo.* It has other transformational possibilities as well. Part of the persistent popularity of the *quiproquo* and its verbal equivalents—the double meaning, the pun, and the play on words—lies in the illusion they create that things and ideas can be made so malleable. They create the intriguing and fantastic impression that meanings, ideas, and even things need not be constant, that they can be altered, twisted and transformed at will. They weld together normally incompatible images into strange new shapes and invite our imaginations along unexplored paths. Even a simple mistake, like that of Moricet, provides the opportunity to bring together two jarringly incompatible images to create a kind of sartorial chimera: part impeccable and elegant, and part humiliating and ridiculous.

Many of the mistakes in Feydeau, particularly the extended misunderstandings in the early plays, are even more bizarre. The prolonged *quiproquos* of *Chat en poche* and *Les Fiancés de Loches* and the multiple misunderstandings woven through the plot of *Tailleur pour dames* have little meaning other than to raise the level of madness to a point at which the normal laws of probability seem to have been suspended. We sense that we have entered a kind of wonderland, a world of imagination. It is not the kind of fantasy world presented in Lewis Carroll's famous story, where events can be understood only as part of a dream or fantasy. But imagination clearly precedes reality because it is the characters' false concepts of the situation which are the primary determinants of the action. We are encouraged to view the world through the eyes of the character while at the same time being constantly reminded of how far that view is from reality. Pure fantasy allows us to enter a world in which the normal laws of existence have been suspended, but in this case we are introduced into a world of imagination which operates in direct defiance of those laws, which skips lightly across the face of reality like a flat stone across the surface of a pond. Like the stone, its repeated collisions with the surface allow it to gain new elevation and continue its precarious flight through the air, rather than causing it to sink abruptly beneath the surface, as we had feared. This world of imagination, created through misunderstanding, is even more versatile than the skipping stone, for it can unexpectedly change its shape or direction. It does not achieve the heights of pure fantasy, which soars free of reality. It is restricted, however loosely, by the laws of natural probability, and thus acquires the air of a game of skill in which the playwright must increase the atmosphere of fantasy while constrained by the laws of reality.

Such manipulation and perpetuation of misunderstandings were among Feydeau's special skills. Especially in the early plays, there are a number of misunderstandings at once, sometimes within the same scene, which will combine to create new misunderstandings even as some of the first ones are being cleared up. A complex web of mistakes is spun in which each individual's misinterpretation of the situation indirectly influences the others in a logically evolving pattern of confusion. In the majority of the plays the mistakes result largely because of attempts at deception, but in a few cases the entire plot is a tissue of misunderstandings created from innocent mistakes. In *Chat en poche* there is one central misunderstanding which becomes the foundation for all the subsequent mistakes and complications. The central error is Pacarel's belief that Dufausset is a famous young tenor from the country whom Pacarel hopes to exploit. The confusion is sustained through the three acts by a series of additional mistakes which help to bolster the original error just as it seems inevitable that the truth must come out. At one point Dufausset mentions having heard the choir of the Sistine Chapel. Because of the phrasing of Dufausset's remarks, the others think that he became a member of the choir and are shocked at the thought of the surgery required for such membership. Everything Dufausset says seems to confirm their conclusion, including his explanation that he visited the Chapel because he was feeling depressed as the result of an unhappy love affair.

> *Dufausset.* I can tell you that I had one of the greatest jolts of my life there.
> *Landernau.* I believe it.
> *Dufausset.* I had no sooner gone in, Monsieur, than I felt myself seized by all those singers with their celestial voices—floored, bowled over—I was no longer a man, Monsieur. I was—Ah, I don't know what I was—
> *Pacarel.* Don't try. [Aside] Poor fellow!
> *Dufausset.* Anyhow, believe me when I tell you that I wept, yes sir—like a calf, when that happened.
> *Pacarel.* Ah! I didn't realize that when that happens calves—
> *Landernau.* No doubt it's the thought of the stew-pot.
> *Dufausset.* It was ecstasy, that's what—to the point that I didn't even pay attention to what was happening to me.[50]

As both Pacarel and Landernau had thought that Dufausset was trying to seduce the other's wife, this new misunderstanding adds an additional complication, one which is compounded when Dufausset later asks to marry Pacarel's daughter.

Throughout the play an atmosphere of fantasy is maintained by a perpetual discrepancy between fact and interpretation. Our imaginations are invited to play with meaning and see how long we are able to dance lightly above the face of reality. The mistaken interpretations need not always be bizarre or extraordinary, but they are made to seem so because of the marked contrast with the true state of affairs and sometimes with other, equally mistaken interpretations. Because the fantastic atmosphere so often depends on this tension between reality and appearance, the playwright is often at pains to keep the contrast before the audience. The principal function of the aside in Feydeau's work is to heighten these contasts. He uses it to call attention to the difference between a character's true thoughts and feelings and those he expresses to others, and also to make clear to the audience his misinterpretation of events when it would not be plain from what he says aloud.[51]

Although it is typical at the height of the confusion for every character on stage to be acting under one or more delusions, Feydeau is usually careful to ensure that the audience be able to keep the various misunderstandings separate. Even when the audience is momentarily kept ignorant of the facts, the effect is to heighten the sense of the fantastic and the feeling that anything can happen. A good example of this technique is the scene between Amélie and Adonis in the opening of *Occupe-toi d'Amélie*.[52] The audience is as surprised as the guests when she takes her attractive servant onto her knee and kisses him, and they are surprised again at the dramatic announcement that Amélie and her servant are brother and sister. The temporary illusion that Amélie may be sleeping with her young servant was acceptable because it did not far exceed the limits of what the audience would deem possible under the circumstances. The world of the *cocotte* was, by bourgeois standards, a fantastic place where normal standards and values were flouted or ignored, and Amélie's shocking behavior just seems to flirt with the limits of the audience's expectations. Here, as elsewhere, Feydeau builds his mad world on a foundation of realism, stretching to its limits his audience's perceptions of what is possible by displaying reality in its most fantastic light.

The Playwright as Magician

The paradox of these elaborate misunderstandings is that they combine an atmosphere of extravagance and abandon with an awareness of the skill and precise manipulation required to keep the confusion from collapsing. Quite often mistakes depend on exact phrasing which seems natural and spontaneous enough in the situation, but which is capable of more than one interpretation. Feydeau calls attention to this need for precision in a footnote to a speech in *La Dame de chez Maxim* which warns the actress playing

Gabrielle against inserting a single word which would make the speech unequivocal and end the confusion.[53] Feydeau's purpose is not simply to manipulate people and events for the purpose of shaping the plot—the conventional aim of the well-made playwright—his real purpose is the transformation of reality through the distortion of images and meanings. The farce playwright is not merely a juggler, but something of a magician. He is an alchemist who transmutes base reality into the bizarre.

The writer of well-made farces differs from the stage magician in that he is not trying to create illusions by means of secret tricks. He is playing with images, showing how one thing can be made to *appear* like another, rather than pretending that he can actually bend the laws of nature. Yet some of his appeal is drawn from the same sources as those of the magician. Using different kinds of "sleight of hand," each attempts to delight us with surprises, make us expect the unexpected, and create the charming sensation that facts can be manipulated and changed. The image of the magician is particularly apt for Feydeau. While most of his tricks and transformations, like those of other *vaudevillistes,* are based on various forms of misapprehension, his plays are filled with devices which are much like those of a professional conjurer. In *L'Age d'or,* one of the principal characters *is* a magician who uses his art to extract the Follentin family from numerous difficulties. Although Gabriel is the only real magician among Feydeau's characters, there are many others who have plans for making people vanish. The best known of these tricks is the revolving bed thoughtfully provided to its customers by the management of the Hôtel du Minet Galant. Designed to transform an amorous couple into a sick old man in the event of unwelcome visitors, it serves to produce a number of surprising appearances and disappearances throughout the second act of *La Puce à l'oreille.* A similar device is the trick cabinet and moaning horn of *La Duchesse des Folies-Bergère* which permits the Duchess to be in two places at once.[54] Other devices, designed to trap rather than conceal lovers, also produce surprising results. A secret chamber in an old castle turns out to have been provided by its builder with a system of mirrors which permit those outside to view the hidden room without being seen in *Le Circuit (The Road Race),* and the ingenious plan in *Le Dindon* to trap a pair of guilty lovers with electric bells also produces unexpected excitement in the lives of an elderly couple.[55]

His fondness for tricks and gadgets was not the only way in which Feydeau demonstrated his liking for magical effects. He also made use of the magical qualities inherent in two apparently contradictory trends of his time: the rising popularity of mysticism and the supernatural on the one hand, and that of science and technology on the other. However opposed they might be philosophically, science and mysticism each have a similar hold on the public imagination: the fascination with the wondrous and extraordinary. The scientific fantasies of Jules Verne had exploited and propagated the image of the scientist as a creator of miracles, an image helped even more by the stream of discoveries and inventions which brought science and its wonders into the daily life of nineteenth-century Europeans. Feydeau explored the comic side of scientific fantasy in the third act of *L'Age d'or*, but he was also fond of the startling effects which could be produced by more commonplace wonders of science, such as the phonograph in *La Main passe!* and the previously mentioned electric bells of *Le Dindon*.

Feydeau also exploited the surge of interest in the occult and the supernatural which swept Paris in the last decade of the nineteenth century.[56] Like most Parisians, Feydeau undoubtedly had more faith in the miracles of science than in the power of the occult, but he was more than willing to use public awareness of the supernatural by creating comic apparitions of his own in *L'Hôtel du Libre-Echange, La Dame de chez Maxim,* and *Occupe-toi d'Amélie*. In these cases Feydeau seems to be mocking the belief in otherworldly powers, but there was another area of mysterious power which generated intense interest and which Feydeau—whether because he believed in it or because it suited his purposes—accepted at face value. The intensively debated and dimly understood practice of hypnotism became the core of two Feydeau plays: *Dormez, je le veux!* and *Le Système Ribadier*. In some ways hypnotism was an area in which science and the occult overlapped. It was seriously studied by reputable doctors, yet its strange powers over people did not quite fit the largely physical and materialistic image of nineteenth-century science. The wonders of hypnotism and the marvels of physical science were useful to Feydeau separately, so it is not surprising that in *La Dame de chez Maxim* he combined them to create the *"fauteuil extatique,"* a machine which induces an hypnotic trance at the touch of a button. As usual with Feydeau, fantasy was based on reality, and even this extraordinary machine was not entirely the product of his imagination. It was based on the invention of a Dr. Moutier, a specialist in electrotherapy. As if to authenticate the imaginary invention, Feydeau credited the real doctor with its creation in the original version of the play, although the name was later changed at Dr. Moutier's insistence.[57]

The touches of stage magic, the scientific gadgets, and the toying with the supernatural are all a part of a larger tendency toward the surprising and the bizarre. Feydeau's plays produce one surprise after another in the manner of a magician's act. His settings, with their many doors (nearly all are interiors), resemble those boxes used by illusionists to produce rabbits and make goldfish and people vanish. However, in Feydeau's plays it is the characters, not the audience, who are bewildered by the transformation the playwright makes in their circumstances. As Claude Berton has pointed out, even Feydeau's language has some of the quality of a magician's performance:

> It is abrupt, jolting, slangy, elliptical, crammed with ridiculous and bewildering juxtapositions of ideas, like the tuxedo of a prestidigitator which from sleeves, pockets or collar brings forth fishes, flowers, an omelette, soap bubbles or a cannon ball.[58]

The Familiar and the Exotic

In addition to using theatrical tricks to transform reality into strange new shapes, Feydeau chooses wherever he can subjects which themselves combine the qualities of the real and the strange. Hypnotism, spiritualism, and wonderful new inventions were all a part of the world that was familiar to Feydeau's audience, yet they also seemed exotic and strange. The same combination of the familiar and the exotic can be found in many of Feydeau's characters. This is particularly true of the many foreigners, who are among the most extravagant personages in Feydeau's assortment of fools. Foreign visitors were a common sight in Paris, especially during and after the 1889 Exposition, and Feydeau probably expressed the feelings of many Parisians when he wrote to a journalist, *"Where am I? For a week abroad—in Paris! But not for long, because I'm afraid I'll forget how to speak French."*[59] Like many comic writers, Feydeau allows himself considerable latitude in portraying the strange behavior and bizarre manners of foreigners, treating them all as more or less mad. Still, he was exaggerating less than might first appear in depicting some of these characters, for the reputation Paris had acquired as a center of pleasure and licentiousness drew a large number of well-publicized eccentrics and adventurers. At least one of Feydeau's most extraordinary foreigners was inspired by a real person.[60]

Another of Feydeau's sources of real yet extraordinary characters was the *demi-monde*. No other aspect of life under the Third Republic was as inherently theatrical and fantastic. The *grandes cocottes,* who were the heart and soul of this illicit world, were creatures who lived on notoriety and publicity. Theirs was a theatrical world, not just because many were actresses and singers, but because success depended less on beauty than on the aura of glamour and excitement they generated through extravagance and scandal. Like certain modern film stars, they lived on legends of their own creation and traded in fantasy as well as sex. They created a world well suited to Feydeau's purposes because it strove for outrageousness and deliberately defied the normal restraints of respectable society. It cultivated, in short, much the same kind of freedom from civilization's rules that fools have always enjoyed, and turned itself into the kind of topsy-turvy world on which farce thrives.

These examples illustrate the tendency of farce to establish its excursions into the fantastic firmly in contemporary reality. With one exception, all of Feydeau's plays take place at the time they were written and deal with familiar characters and themes.[61] The exception, *L'Age d'or,* actually begins in a contemporary setting, then moves into the past and future in a series of dream sequences. Yet even here the familiar and the exotic are combined in a way that is characteristic of farce. When farce goes beyond the realm of everyday living and treats exotic or historical subjects, it is apt to do so on a level which is thoroughly familiar to its audience. Rather than using history or foreign lands as a background, it is inclined to give farcical treatment to well-known characters and incidents from novels, films, or legends, and so slips easily into parody or burlesque. Here the usual movement from the commonplace to the unusual is reversed. Starting with material that is more exotic than familiar (although it contains elements of both), it often draws further into the realm of the commonplace through the easy expedient of anachronisms.[62] In *L'Age d'or* both the familiar story and the anachronisms are a logical consequence of the use of dream sequences. Follentin falls asleep while reading Dumas's popular novel *La Reine Margot* and his dream loosely resembles incidents from the novel. In the second act Follentin is transported into the reign of Louis XV, but again the major characters are those made familiar through popular fiction. The anachronisms are limited to those that would naturally result from traveling backward in time. As usual with Feydeau these absurdities follow a logical development. The technique of combining the exotic and the everyday, however, is the same as that of modern "spoofs" and parodies.

The Two Sides of Sexual Fantasy

If Feydeau's treatment of familiar reality is part of a system of conflicting extremes, so too is his treatment of the "inner experience" of which Bentley speaks. In Bentley's Freudian view, farce depends on tendentious joking, on the desire to attack and expose; sex and violence are mainstays of farce and, in farce, they both assume the form of aggression. Certainly sex and violence are an important part of Feydeau's plays, but the treatment is more complex than that suggested by Bentley. Of the two, sex is by far the more important to Feydeau, as illicit sex is the basis of most of his plots. Bentley may have had Feydeau in mind when he wrote that farce

> offers a special opportunity: shielded by delicious darkness and seated in warm security, we enjoy the privilege of being totally passive while on stage our most treasured unmentionable wishes are fulfilled before our eyes... In that application of the formula which is bedroom farce, we savor the adventure of adultery... without taking the responsibility or suffering the guilt.[63]

Yet this description gives an incomplete idea of what actually takes place in a Feydeau farce. It is true, as Bentley suggests, that Feydeau's plays and other bedroom farces can be seen as elaborate jokes on the frustrations and trials of marriage. But having forbidden desires *expressed* on stage is not the same as having them *fulfilled*. Farce thrives on evoking strong emotions and converting them into laughter, not on vicariously satisfying illicit desires. And repressed sexuality represents not just one emotion, but a conflict of opposing emotions. Sexuality is repressed where it is desired but feared, and Feydeau gives full physical expression to both sides. In his plays sex is both a temptation and a terrifying threat. In Freudian terms, the super-ego is given equal time with the libido.

This dual attitude toward sex is inherent in plots in which attempts to fulfill illicit desires are met with frustration, exposure, and humiliation. Feydeau does not attempt to moralize or to demonstrate that humiliation is the inevitable outcome of violations of the moral code, but he does dramatize the conflict of desire and fear, carrying both to extremes to produce the most effective collision between them.[64] As in a dream, the conflicting emotions have a way of materializing through a process of association, assuming grotesque and exaggerated shapes, but unlike a dream, where nothing is certain or predictable, here everything is controlled and justified through the well-made logic of material causation.

In the deception plays, this conflict is apt to culminate in an establishment such as the Hôtel du Libre-Echange, a place where a woman might casually request a pack of cards from a bellboy, unconcerned with the fact that she is stark naked.[65] Such suggestions of licentiousness soon dissolve into images of fear and humiliation, and erotic freedom becomes scandalous anarchy. Sexual fantasies materialize only to be transformed into nightmares which drive the frightened bourgeois back to the safety of their homes. The formula of the deception plays permits a retreat from the world of dreams and nightmares, but the action of farce does not always offer such a logical means of escape.

Le Mariage de Barillon illustrates even more clearly than the deception plays how the action of farce can make manifest inner frustrations and secret terrors and give them nightmare proportions. Barillon is a middle-aged man who plans to take an eighteen-year-old bride, and is opposed by a young rival whom the girl greatly prefers. The contrast of Feydeau's play with Molière's *L'Ecole des femmes*, perhaps the most famous expression of this ancient theme, helps show the difference between the logic of farce and that of comedy. Molière's play is grounded in reality throughout. Given the natural psychology of the characters involved, it logically demonstrates the folly of Arnolphe's plan to marry a young girl yet avoid the dangers of cuckoldry. But the action of Feydeau's play, while it begins with a similar premise and reaches much the same conclusion, takes a course in which the logic of reality is left far behind. Although Barillon looks forward to his marriage with the lovely young Virginie, he cannot stand his future mother-in-law. It is not that she is hostile to him; on the contrary, she is much too affectionate. She is forever kissing him, forcing him to hide the fact that he finds her repulsive. Then, through a ridiculous but apparently unalterable mistake, he finds himself married to the mother rather than the daughter. As absurd as this situation is, he is constantly reminded that it is in some ways quite appropriate, for the mother is close to his own age. The girl even begins to call him "mon petit papa."[66] But Barillon fails to see any justice in this development and complains loudly of his predicament: "On the one hand, to love a woman I can't marry, and on the other, to have married a woman I can't love! Oh, no, it's too much!"[67]

Barillon's plight is an absurd caricature of the situation in which many middle-aged men find themselves. They resent the fact that the women they married many years earlier are no longer youthful and attractive, and they yearn wistfully after lovely young women who are beyond their reach. Barillon's strange predicament is in one way quite normal. But his troubles do not end there. At the beginning of the play, he is threatened with cuckoldry by his youthful rival. Even after he is married to the mother, he is in danger of wearing horns, but the threat has undergone a bizarre transformation appropriate to this nightmare world. Jambart, his new wife's rightful husband, materializes from the dead, and now either husband will become a cuckold should the other exercise his conjugal rights.

When an annulment is granted at the end of the play, Barillon resolves to remain a bachelor, just as Arnolphe is advised to stay single at the close of Molière's play. But in Arnolphe's case the advice is a logical conclusion drawn from the action of the play, which in turn was a direct consequence of Arnolphe's own foolish plan. In *L'Ecole des femmes* the initial situation contains the premises of a logical argument which is developed through the plot. The situation which begins Feydeau's play gives rise to a host of associations that materialize into grotesque and changing shapes. The oppressive mother-in-law fuses with the unattractive wife, the reluctant bride becomes a rebellious daughter, and the rival in love re-emerges as a suitor for the daughter's hand. Assuming the role of wronged husband, Barillon is twice threatened with cuckoldry, but in both cases it is he who emerges as the usurper when at the end of the play mother and daughter both claim their "rightful" husbands. Barillon's rivalry with Jambart becomes a grotesque parody of his claim to Virginie because the young man's right to Virginie is as "natural" as Jambart's right to be Mme Jambart's husband.

Sexual fantasies in Feydeau's plays, whether of adultery or a lovely but inappropriately young bride, always have a dark side that evokes associations of fear, frustration, or scandal. While the plots dramatize this conflict of desire and fear, there is one character who, more than any other, personifies it. She is the *cocotte,* the glamorous symbol of sensuality and license, a personification of erotic fantasies. She is also a destructive threat to society and respectability, a wrecker of marriages and fortunes. Like Astarte, she represents both sensuous pleasure and forces of terrible destructiveness. This dual role is seen clearly in *La Dame de chez Maxim*. La Môme Crevette is charming, attractive, clever, and vivacious, yet her mere presence is enough to turn Petypon's life into a nightmare. His association with her is made as suggestive as possible. First she is discovered in his bed, and then he finds himself inadvertently "married" to her. But Petypon is permitted no pleasure from the relationship. While she is in his bed, he spends the night under an overturned sofa, and, when he remembers nothing from the evening before, she assures him that nothing took place between them.[68] The pretence that La Môme is his wife helps to bring out the ambivalence in attitude toward the *cocotte*. When he objects to her posing as his wife, she mocks him with "you don't mind it a bit!"[69] If that were not enough, his uncle, who is unaware of the deception, keeps reminding him of the contrast between La Môme and his real wife by calling the latter "an old bag."[70]

Ambivalence toward sex shows up in more subtle ways, as when Armandine is made to think that the love-sick bell boy is afflicted with a serious illness—a disease called puberty.[71] The joke acknowledges the fact that the awakening of sexual desire in a young man is sometimes a mixed blessing. Sexuality in young women could not be treated so directly because of the convention that young women were innocent of such desires, or at least of any real knowledge of sex. Yet in Feydeau's plays there is at least a hint of ambivalence toward this common assumption. For one thing, his young heroines are often more forward and knowledgeable than was acceptable. One of them goes so far as to insinuate to an undesirable suitor that he will become a cuckold if he insists on marrying her.[72] In plays where the young women are conventionally innocent, their innocence is often the source of sexual jokes based on their naïveté regarding the real nature of marriage.[73] The plot of *Amour et piano* is a joke of this kind, although it is not based on naïveté, but on the fact that the young lady is mistaken for a *cocotte*. These jokes do not go so far as to suggest that young innocence is a sham, but they do call attention to the fact that in spite of their purity young women do have a sexual nature, if only as the object of sexual desire.

If the innocence of young unmarried women is highly charged with sexual meaning, it may also have produced mixed feelings toward sex on the part of married women. In *La Main passe!* Francine argues that a bride should have no hint as to what awaits her on her wedding night. She concedes that "Maybe Caroline will have a bit of a shock. Maybe she'll say: Oh, my! What's this? But at least that has the virtue of surprise and the effect won't be spoiled."[74] Francine seems to think that the best the young bride can expect is a disagreeable surprise.

But despite (or perhaps because of) this abrupt introduction to the pleasures of the marriage bed, married women in Feydeau are not immune to the temptations of adultery. Francine herself has already taken a lover when she gives Chanal this illogical advice. Their motives are usually less frankly sexual than those of their male counterparts, however, and, because they are more sensitive to the dangers of exposure, they are quicker to back out of an amorous adventure. Francine is the most forthright adulteress among Feydeau's heroines. She is the only one to admit that her original reluctance and protestations of virtue were a sham. She concedes that if her lover had not been so persistent she would have been forced to play the part of the aggressor herself.[75] Others, such as Angèle in *Champignol malgré lui*, are much less candid. She is prevented from having an affair with Saint-Florimond (she had gone so far as to give him her house key) only by an unfortunate chance which threatens their discovery, yet she insists on calling her terrified retreat from infidelity the "triumph of my virtue."[76] With Angèle, as with most of Feydeau's characters, fear of discovery or of reprisal takes the place of genuine moral commitment. But in the case of married women, reprisal can be a motivation as well as a deterrent to adultery. Most of Feydeau's husbands fear cuckoldry far more than they do exposure of their own infidelities. As a result, the wives are apt to see adultery as the ultimate weapon in the battle with their husbands, and they are more easily tempted by rage against their spouses than by the ardor of a would-be lover. Pinglet, who is otherwise not much of a lover, takes advantage of this in *L'Hôtel du Libre-Echange* by inflaming Marcelle's anger at the insulting remarks made by her husband. She promptly acknowledges the wisdom of his strategy when she tells him, "Oh, Pinglet, you are ugly!—But you know how to speak to a woman's heart!" At any other time, she admits, "I would have pushed you away in disgust."[77] Marcelle is merely annoyed by her husband's neglect, but most women resort to this drastic weapon only to retaliate for their husband's infidelities. Once they have determined to go through with it, however, they give no more thought than Marcelle to the attractiveness of their chosen avenger. "And don't you think I'm going to be choosy!" says Mme Pontagnac in *Le Dindon*. "I believe that would only prevent me from savoring my vengeance! No sir, no matter who, the first idiot I come across!"[78]

Mme Pontagnac's attitude fairly represents the role played by the adultery of wives in Feydeau. While it is clear that many of these women are less than candid in their protestations of virtue, the principal target is not the exposure of feminine hypocrisy. Feydeau uses their attempts at infidelity primarily for the threat they pose to their husbands' well-being. It is a masculine point of view. The stress is on the danger of cuckoldry rather than the psychology of the women involved. Yet, while the danger is always present, the threat rarely materializes. Feydeau was curiously circumspect in treating the infidelities of women. Nowhere does a *ménage à trois* have the central role it occupies in Labiche's *Le Plux heureux des trois (The Happiest of the Three)* and in numerous medieval farces. Most of his contemporaries viewed the adulterous wife as an extremely serious subject, and Feydeau either shared their view or deferred to their sensibilities. When adultery occurs its effect is carefully diminished by the manner of presentation. The unwritten law of the Boulevard was that although a man might be forgiven for unfaithfulness (and often was), an adulteress must not go unpunished.[79] Only in his last play does the principal female character commit adultery and escape both detection and punishment.[80] Duchotel's mistress in *Monsieur chasse!* is never seen, and the only woman to be forgiven for adultery also never appears on stage.[81] We never meet Irène's cuckolded husband in *Occupe-toi d'Amélie*, and Maggy does not appear after the second act of *Le Dindon*, allowing the audience to forget the probable consequences of her infidelity.

It is interesting that Feydeau, who has a largely deserved reputation for being able to treat any subject in a comic vein, should appear hesitant in dealing with the situation often assumed to lie at the heart of this kind of farce: the scheming wife, her lover, and the cuckolded husband. Until late in his career, when he virtually abandoned the subject of adultery, his plays end with the restoration of respectability and order. This requires that nothing irrevocable happen in the meantime, and to Feydeau's audience a wife's infidelity was an absolute bar to the return of respectability. To forgive her would be shocking and therefore unacceptable, but to punish her while her male accomplice is forgiven could be just as bad, for it would call attention to the injustice of the double standard. The latter situation actually occurs in three of his plays *(Monsieur chasse!, Le Dindon,* and *La Main passe!),* but Feydeau is careful to hide the irony of the situation from the audience. In the first two plays the mistress's fate (divorce in both cases) is de-emphasized so that it is lost from view during the final reconciliation scene. In the third, the woman is made to seem incorrigible, doomed to continue making the same mistake in an endless series of divorces and re-marriages.

Despite this lack of honesty in dealing with the subject, it is still the central feature of many of his plays. It represents the ultimate threat, the supreme disaster, the worst thing that can happen to a bourgeois *ménage*. Feydeau uses the threat, like all other forms of disaster that menace his characters, to drive the action of his plays forward. The powerhouse which keeps the plot moving and the characters scrambling frantically just out of the reach of catastrophe is fueled principally by sex. In this sense the main role of sex is negative rather than positive. The characters are much less motivated by sexual desire than they are by their fear of its consequences. Even as they are giving in to temptation, foreshadowing clearly draws our attention to the difficulties that their little escapades will cause them. Illicit sex is always fraught with danger and usually ends in frustration. Legitimate unions are plagued with fears of inadequacy and unattractive, unresponsive mates, as well as the perpetual fear of deception. Women are seen as sex objects, but in that role they do more to thwart than to satisfy male desires. The typical married woman manages to frustrate her would-be lover even while threatening her husband with a cuckold's horns. When sex is discussed, as it often is, it is expressed in terms that are often grotesque or pathetic. When the frustrated Pinglet complains in *L'Hôtel du Libre-Echange* of his unfulfilled desires, he declares: "I've got lava in me! Bubbling lava!—I just don't have a volcano!"[82] Pontagnac, the profligate in *Le Dindon,* has already claimed that his wife is crippled by rheumatism. When he explains his numerous infidelities by describing his spouse as "a novel I've often leafed through," Lucienne remarks, "Yes, without mentioning that it's perhaps no longer easy to turn the pages."[83]

The Role of Violence

Feydeau's characters may dream of sexual fulfillment, but their fantasies are born of frustration and inadequacy and somehow always reflect their origin. But if sex is viewed at least with ambivalence, the other principal motive force of farce, violence, is shown in an even more negative light. Feydeau's heroes are almost invariably the targets rather than the perpetrators of violence. Feydeau is reported to have said that

> in my plays there are two kinds of characters: those who deliver the kicks in the rear—and those who receive them. The latter have the best roles, because they get the laughs....[84]

For the most part such "kicks in the rear" are metaphorical rather than actual. Real blows are infrequent, although threats abound. Violence is itself subsidiary to sex in that it is usually brought on by the general disorder of which sex is the cause. Physical threats are a logical result of the rule that disorder is carried to its extreme, and because the disorder is usually sexual in origin the threat is often posed by jealous husbands or lovers, for example, in the form of a challenge to a duel. Such displays of aggression rarely come from Feydeau's timid bourgeois heroes. Most of the violence, whether actual or threatened, is produced by energetic and unpredictable foreigners, particularly the hot-blooded and jealous Latins. Aggressiveness is a trait common to nearly all of Feydeau's foreigners, regardless of their origin. When they want something they are direct and single-minded in its pursuit, with little concern for the turmoil they produce in the process. General Irrigua of *Un Fil à la patte* is one of the most violent and extreme, but he expresses the attitude of most foreigners when he explains to the terrified and bewildered Bouzin why he plans to kill him: "Becoze I no like when something he ees in my way. And when ees an obstacle, I no jump over eet! I get rid of eet!"[85]

The violence they produce may take rather bizarre forms (such as the duel proposed in *La Puce à l'oreille*), but to them it all seems perfectly normal.[86] When Duc Pitchenieff becomes angry with his butler (as usual in these cases, the fault lies entirely with the master), only the fact that he is not in his own country prevents him from applying the knout to the unfortunate servant *(La Duchesse des Folies-Bergère).*[87] The women are less physical. Dotty, the American heiress in *Je ne trompe pas mon mari,* is well endowed with aggressive determination but is not at all violent. Maggy, the unfaithful English wife in *Le Dindon,* is more capable of extreme measures. She is not only willing to use the feminine ploy of threatening suicide, but, as an expert boxer, she can effortlessly knock her lover to the floor when he tries to oppose her.[88] The only truly violent character who is not a foreigner is Hubertin, in *La Main passe!* Even he could be said to be under foreign influence, because he is violent only when drunk, and he blames his drinking on his American wife. Consequently, he feels, "you can't say that I get smashed. No, I—I become Americanized!"[89]

The fact that foreigners are the most aggressive characters on the scene does not mean that Feydeau's heroes are incapable of violence, particularly with servants and others who are not in a position to retaliate. Most of the violence that actually occurs results from the characters' frantic efforts to flee disaster and is thus less a consequence of aggression than of desperation. On rare occasions desperation may drive them as far as it does Pinglet, who is emboldened to punch his friend Paillardin in the eye, but they usually limit themselves to roughly shoving people whose presence is embarrassing into the nearest hiding place.[90] They do all they can to avoid violence, but it seems to haunt them wherever they go. They may feel obligated by social pressures to fight duels, but they will try anything possible, even devious or dishonorable, to get out of them. Barillon has what he thinks is a foolproof method of avoiding such unpleasant encounters. Whenever he has a quarrel with a stranger, he hands his adversary the card of a famous fencing master rather than his own.[91] Savinet, in *Le Système Ribadier,* is no less anxious to avoid combat, but he is not so devious. As a wine merchant, he approaches the question with the directness and rationality of a businessman. Although he has caught his wife in adultery, he demands only that her lover keep silent about the affair: "After all, for whom do we have duels? For the sake of society. Well, so long as society is not informed..." Only if the affair becomes known will he engage in a duel. And in that case his businessman's logic refuses to accept the possibility that he will be the one to be killed: "Those are the prerogatives that belong to us, the offended husbands. We certainly ought to have some! The lover has the duty to let himself be killed."[92] Later he retracts even this limited threat, for business considerations come first. Feydeau's bourgeois simply do not have the temperament for dueling. The ancient aristocratic concept that ties honor to combat is foreign to the souls of these business and professional men. Petypon is a physician, and when his military uncle and others are determined to force him into a duel despite his adamant and repeated refusals, he turns on them: "So you insist that I fight? All right, fine!—I've got the choice of arms? I take the lancet!"[93]

One might ask whether Feydeau is mocking the cowardice of these reluctant combatants or is attacking the outdated institution of dueling in these scenes. On the evidence, it seems likely that his sympathies were close to those of the servant who bursts out laughing when she hears that her master is engaged in a duel, and explains: "That always makes me laugh when I hear someone say: 'He's going to have a duel.' I think that's so stupid."[94] But Feydeau was no more conducting a campaign to eradicate the custom of dueling than he was consciously promoting chauvinism in his portrayals of foreigners. Duels and foreigners, and mocking, unsympathetic servants as well, are all manifestations of an uncertain and threatening world which is perpetually menacing one's well-being and dignity.

Dignity and decorum are the major casualties of Feydeau's violence. Major threats are avoided, but minor assaults, which leave the body unscarred yet rip away the fabric of self-esteem, are fairly common. In *La Puce à l'oreille,* Chandebise escapes a bullet in the chest at the hand of Homenidès, but cannot seem to avoid kicks in the rear delivered by the sadistic Ferraillon. Petypon manages to get out of the duel his uncle would force on him, but is made to endure the humiliation of numerous slaps in the face. Physical violence exists not for itself, but as a part of the more intangible violence inflicted upon the stability of respectable life, symbolized by the fragile equilibrium of the *ménage bourgeois.* This sort of violence, directed at order and respectability, is at the dramatic core of nearly all of Feydeau's plays. When his treatment of this central conflict changed, so did the nature of the physical violence in the plays. In the last plays, in which the action ends with domestic catastrophe rather than a resolution of the crisis, the slaps and kicks disappear, but the duels remain. At the end of two of the latter plays, the hero is faced not only with destruction of his domestic peace, but with an armed confrontation of which the outcome is by no means certain.[95]

The Integration of Conflicts in Farce

Feydeau's plays, like so many other farces, thrive on the exploitation of pain: not just physical pain, but humiliation, deformities, embarrassments, and all of the gross and grotesque realities of life. They also allow for the expression of hostility and aggression—and these different aspects of farce are not unrelated. Penelope Gilliatt, discussing farce in film, makes the paradoxical observation that "brutality can be funny if it is directed at someone whom we all really agree we must protect, such as children and animals."[96] One need not be a committed Freudian to concede that this sort of brutality in farce acknowledges the feelings everyone has had toward certain exasperating but helpless creatures, or that it can be a healthy antidote for excessive sentimentality. But since farce commonly derives laughter and joy from what is painful and unpleasant, it is reasonable to conclude that farce can employ *this particular form* of aggression precisely because we would usually find it shocking and unpleasant. Our laughter is not merely a disguise for hidden brutality. It is an acknowledgment of opposing forces within our souls, of both the forbidden hostility and the horrified reaction to seeing it acted upon. At this fundamental level of emotional response, farce differs radically from melodrama, its sibling in the family of popular drama, because where farce integrates, melodrama polarizes. Melodrama encourages us to project all that is evil and ugly onto others, and in so doing discourages us from acknowledging traits which, after all, seem to be the exclusive property of villains and scoundrels. It also *justifies* our aggression and cruelty by portraying their targets as unworthy of sympathy. The amoral atmosphere so often noted in farce does not justify or excuse. It is not a license to act as we please, but an amnesty under which we can admit our faults without fear of guilt. To the extent that the amorality of farce serves to mitigate evil, it does so not by portraying it as virtue, but as folly. Melodrama insists that the evil lies without; in farce we can confront the conflicts within our own souls.

The central conflict in Feydeau's plays is the classically Freudian one of civilization versus the libidinous forces of anarchy, narrowly conceived as the conflict of bourgeois respectability and unrestrained sexuality. The latter is given full and—when confined to the limited world of the *cocotte*—even favorable expression. However, the basic point of view is that of the bourgeois who, however tempted, ultimately views license with alarm and chooses domestic stability, providing he can find it, in spite of all its restrictions. This theme is inherent in nearly all of the plays, but is made explicit in *L'Age d'or*. Follentin, beset with troubles and frustrations, yearns for an earlier and more violent age in which he could be free to vent his anger with the sword. When he gets his wish in a dream, he quickly becomes the victim rather than the perpetrator of violent attacks. Barely escaping with his life from the mayhem of the St. Bartholomew's Day Massacre, he is transported to the age of Louis XV and is delighted with the sexual license of the court until he realizes that the same moral standards apply to his wife and daughter. He fares no better in the decadent twenty-first century, discovering too late that the orgy he has eagerly attended has assembled to experience the ultimate sensation—in the act of self-destruction. When he awakes to find that his frustrations in the present have vanished, he piously proclaims: "The Golden Age—it's right in our hands."[97]

Because it is seen from this fundamentally conservative point of view, the conflict tends to resolve itself along the lines of the basic farce dynamic: the clash of reality and fantasy. As we move from the world of bourgeois stability and frustration into the realms of freedom and anarchy, the world becomes progressively more fantastic. The clear-cut division between dream-world and reality which is evident in *L'Age d'or* is exceptional. The change is usually gradual, accomplished partly by means of the action, but particularly by the nature of the characters themselves. Representing the poles of the conflict between anarchy and civilization are the gay abandon of La Môme Crevette and the timid respectability of *le docteur* Petypon, but all of the other characters participate in it. The next chapter will examine how the nature of the characters is determined by the role they play in the conflict.

4

Character: Disrupters and Victims

The Community of Fools

One of the most distinctive aspects of the plays of Feydeau is the scarcity of "normative" characters—characters who stand on the side of wisdom and good sense. One of the few examples is the Marquis in *Le Bourgeon*, Feydeau's only serious comedy. Other than the Marquis and a few of the other characters in the same play, Feydeau's people are all committed, albeit in different ways, to the pursuit of folly. No group or type of character is given favored treatment. Major as well as minor characters, young and old, ingénues and *cocottes*, young lovers and tired businessmen, masters and servants—they are first of all fools who rarely learn from the difficulties their folly produces. Occasionally the resolution brings a small increase in wisdom to some of the characters, but they are usually slow in accepting the lesson and give little assurance that its effect will be long lasting.[1]

The atmosphere of forgiving festivity which concludes many comedies, in which foolish characters admit their folly and join in with the general merrymaking, is uncharacteristic of Feydeau. Even when, as in *Monsieur chasse!*, the play ends with an admission of guilt and forgiveness, both the confession and the pardon are apt to be the result of coercion rather than the expression of genuine contrition and amnesty. Like Molière, Feydeau did not believe in the possibility of educating fools. *Le Ruban* offers a good illustration of Feydeau's inclination to see only folly in all of his characters and to sustain that folly to the end. One of the two strands of action in that play parallels that of Labiche's *Le Voyage de Monsieur Perichon*. In both plays two young men are competing for the hand of a young lady. The one, calculating and cynical, attempts to win approval by appealing to the vanity of the father or guardian. The other, preferred by the girl, is straightforward and ingenuous. The heroine of Labiche's play is conventionally but not excessively demure, and the young man she loves, although naïve, is brave and admirable. But in Feydeau's play, the girl is wild and aggressive; her intended, bumbling and weak. She initiates a number of plans which he merely attempts, unsuccessfully, to carry out. He does not avoid playing on the uncle's vanity because he is above such tricks; he is just not clever enough. For her part, the girl has no qualms about manipulating her guardian's weakness. In Labiche's play the resolution comes about when the father finds out that he was being used, and he appears to learn a lesson about his own vanity. In *Le Ruban* Dardillon gets the girl only when an accident suddenly makes him valuable to the uncle.

Rarely in Feydeau is a character what he or she should be according to the conventional standards of behavior or morality. If, as some maintain, comic action typically revolves about the *alazon*, or imposter, who pretends to be more than he is, and the *eiron* who claims to be less than he is, one would have to categorize the majority of Feydeau's characters as "imposters."[2] But one would have to distinguish between them and the kind of Plautine imposter or braggart whose claims to self-importance are ridiculously excessive or even impossible. Paginet, the uncle whose pretensions to the Legion of Honor are manipulated by the young people in *Le Ruban,* is one of the few characters dominated by this sort of comic hybris. He hopes to receive the coveted honor on the basis of his refutation of Pasteur, a paper in which he "proved" that microbes do not exist. The pretensions of most of the characters are considerably more modest. They claim merely to be normal, yet they never quite make the mark. The comic contrast results not from a discrepancy between claim and performance, but from a simple inability to meet the basic standards of behavior for someone of their position in society. They may easily be tempted into displaying excessive vanity, but it is not a dominant character trait, merely one of many petty weaknesses. Tartuffe and other outstanding imposters of comic literature, however ridiculous they may be, are still awesome in their audacity. None of Feydeau's characters is nearly so grand. Not one of his bourgeois heroes would have the effrontery to pass himself off as a nobleman, but when an enterprising maître d'hôtel improves his business in *Séance de nuit* by giving titles to all of his customers, they smilingly accept their new rank without protest.[3] Tournel is greatly pleased, in *La Puce à l'oreille,* to be described as a ladies' man, but he feels he must demur.

> *Tournel.* Oh, no! I've got charm, that's all.
> *Chandebise.* There! He's got charm! Come on, Killer! I didn't make you say that! And anyway, there are women who have committed suicide for you! True? Yes or No?
> *Tournel.* [*modestly*] Well—one!
> *Chandebise.* Aha!
> *Tournel.* But now, she's doing quite well.[4]

Despite his vanity, he cannot help but reveal the truth.

Vanity is one of the most common failings of Feydeau's people, but it is never their single defining characteristic. There are no "humors" in Feydeau, no grand comic obsessions. There are also few "comic professionals," characters whose role in the play is dominated by their calling and whose comic failings are associated with a profession. Except for police commissioners and a few others, we seldom meet Feydeau's characters in their professional capacities. Their professional failings are not ignored. They are included with all of their many other idiosyncrasies. The doctor Landernau complicates a simple question of cuisine by describing the killing of a bird as an involved surgical operation, but the fact that he is a doctor has little else to do with the action of *Chat en poche* or his character development.[5] There are a few genuine comic professionals, such as a self-important midwife who browbeats the expectant father with technical terms, and the police commissioner who is openly delighted at a family's tragedy because so few exciting crimes occur in his district.[6] But these are relatively minor roles, and we see them only in their professional functions. We might surmise that they do not carry their professional "tics" into their personal life from the comments of another police commissioner. Bridois, in *Monsieur chasse!*, makes a careful distinction between his official attitude toward adultery and his attitude "as a gallant gentleman."[7] There are a few whose personalities are strongly flavored by professional preoccupations, such as the actor Snobinet, whose wardrobe and conversation both come from the theatre.[8] The only one whose life is dominated by professional obsessions is the wine merchant Savinet of *Le Système Ribadier*, who even sells a cask of cognac to his adversary in the midst of discussing a duel.[9]

Feydeau uses professions primarily as marks of identification which can be manipulated in a confusion of persons and roles (e.g., the doctor taken for a dressmaker in *Tailleur pour dames* and the salesman passed off as a lawyer in *L'Affaire Edouard*), but they may also be given symbolic or thematic significance. In *L'Hôtel du Libre-Echange* the contrast between the personalities of Paillardin and Pinglet parallels the difference in their occupations. Pinglet, the builder, complains that his friend and associate, like all architects, is impractical. He drafts beautiful plans which ignore the physical requirements of buildings.[10] Paillardin also has a beautiful wife whose physical attractions he ignores, and Pinglet regards this neglect as a shameful waste. The same thematic contrast is seen in the scene between Maxime, the philosophy student who studies love in the pages of Descartes, and a soubrette whose knowledge of the subject is considerably more down to earth.[11] In *La Puce à l'oreille*, Chandebise's occupation, *assurance* (insurance), is significant in that all of his difficulties stem from problems of *assurance* (self-assurance, confidence).[12] Professional concerns are often important in the late one-act plays because they point up the husband's role as breadwinner in the battle of the sexes. Because Follbraguet *(Hortense a dit: "Je m'en fous!")* is a dentist, we see vivid evidence of the effect his losing battle has on his vocation. The suffering of his patients increases visibly as his wife's tyranny becomes progressively more insupportable. There may be thematic significance as well. In *"Mais n'te promène donc pas toute nue!"* Ventroux is a politician whose concern with favorable public exposure is undermined by his wife's fondness for self-exposure of a very different sort. And Follavoine, in *On purge Bébé!* is thwarted in his attempt to sell chamberpots by Julie's obsession with her son's constipation.

   The names Feydeau gave his characters often suggest their clownish roles and set the tone of the play. Many of his names, particularly in the early plays, are comic without being symbolic or meaningful. Some, like Pinglet, simply have a comic sound. One of Feydeau's favorite devices was to use names derived from, or sounding like, common nouns, identifying his characters with animals or objects. The hero of *Champignol malgré lui,* whose name suggests *champignon,* or mushroom, is the most famous of these unfortunate characters, but there are many others. Lanoix de Vaux (walnut, calf), the reluctant young suitor in *Chat en poche;* Charançon (weevil), Gratin (crust), Baloche (village fair), and Pinçon (bruise) in *L'Affaire Edouard;* and Poche (pocket) in *La Puce à l'oreille* are only a few. Some names have comic associations with a character's occupation. Bousin, in *Un Fil à la patte,* writes the kind of vulgar songs that are sung in the cheap taverns his name suggests. Saboulot, whose name sounds like *sabouler* (to scold), is the schoolmaster in *La Lycéenne,* and the midwife in *Léonie est en avance* is Mme Virtuel. Hochepaix (pronounced Hoche-pet, "shake-fart") and Ventroux (dry wind), the two politicians in *Mais n'te promène donc pas toute nue!",* have appropriately "windy" names. A few names are ironic. Paillardin *(L'Hôtel du Libre-Echange)* is a sexless homebody, not the libertine his name implies. Angélique, in the same play, and Angèle, in *Le Système Ribadier,* are among the most shrewish of Feydeau's wives. Others have names more appropriate to their personalities. Two of Feydeau's most ironic characters have names derived from the word *fine* (sharp, sly, cunning): the sharply sarcastic Finette in *La Lycéenne,* and Finache *(fine hache,* "sharp hatchet"), the sardonic doctor in *La Puce à l'oreille.* True to his name, Rigolin is looking for a good time *(rigoler)* on the town in *Séance de nuit,* and his friend Fauconnet brags of his ability to hunt down female prey. The list could go on, from the false tenor Dufausset in *Chat en poche* to the effervescent Mme Giclefort (spout-strong) of *Je ne trompe pas mon mari.* Toward the end of Feydeau's career, as his lunacy became less playful and increasingly fierce, names suggesting madness began to appear: Follavoine in *On purge Bébé,* and Follbraguet and Mme Dingue (screwy, nuts) in *Hortense a dit: "Je m'en fous!"* These names reflect the greater intensity of Feydeau's later farces, but like so many of the earlier names, they also accent the weaknesses, inadequacies, and victimization of the majority of Feydeau's characters.

The Disabled in Body and Soul

The name of Toudoux (all-soft), the meek husband in *Léonie est en avance,* would be suitable for many Feydeau characters. Along with other names, like Charançon (an insect) and Champignol (suggesting a mushroom), it stresses the characteristic of Feydeau's personages that has made some critics feel he was uninterested in character psychology: their insignificance and weakness.[13] It is not simply that his characters are dwarfed by the avalanche of events; they are small from the start. Feydeau's people are little people. Except for the foreigners and *cocottes* (who will be discussed at length later), there are no grand comic personalities drawn in broad, bold strokes, who can dominate the stage and the action and leave an indelible impression on the memory. They are victims not only of circumstances, but of their own many inadequacies. Elizabeth Nusbaum Smith, using many examples from Feydeau, has described the milieu of farce as the "society of the incomplete."[14] Even when Feydeau's characters are broadly and implausibly painted, as they are in the early plays, they are outstanding only in their inability to meet the most minimal standards for sane, rational human beings. They are fools masquerading as normally functioning members of society. These mental incompetents may have their own sort of logic which they follow with great confidence. Brigot, in *Le Mariage de Barillon,* describes himself as "punctuality itself" because he arrives an hour early for every appointment. And if the person he was to meet does not arrive within thirty minutes, he promptly leaves.[15] Plumard thinks he is rather clever, although his wife's most flagrant behavior did not arouse his suspicions until he had read *Othello* ("A drama by an Englishman—who writes rather good French for a foreigner.") Then he immediately thinks of suffocation, but finds that a bit too English for him.[16] In the later plays such gross mental defects disappear, at least in the major characters, and are replaced by a multitude of more plausible failings.

The most prevalent of these shortcomings are moral in nature, but they are not limited to ethical myopia. Feydeau's characters are not simply amoral; they are defectives—morally, mentally, and physically. Feydeau does not single out moral faults for special comic treatment. One of the reasons for the consistently farcical tone of the plays is that all of these different types of defects are treated with a similarly detached comic objectivity.[17] Feydeau achieves this objectivity partly through another kind of defect in the characters, for there is another way in which the term "incomplete" is particularly appropriate for these creatures. While their primary defects may be quite common and human, they are accompanied by another which is not altogether natural. It is as if something had been surgically removed from their personalities. Penelope Gilliatt describes this crucial omission while reviewing a production in English of *La Puce à l'oreille:*

> The houseboy [Poche] is incessantly victimized and bawled at, but nothing shakes him. Like all figures in farce his self-esteem is impregnable. In the stylizing process his capacity for pain has been cut away. Another character achieves the unlikely task of making a cleft palate hysterically funny for exactly the same reason; unlike many afflicted men, he luckily has no idea of the way other people see him. To his own loving mind he is a perfect enunciator and it is other people's ears that need cleaning out.[18]

The quality that sets all of these characters apart is their fortunate oblivion with regard to their defects. Their imperfections may be very like our own, but their blindness is superhuman. They are literally "shameless." The oblivion need not be total in the way an outright fool is oblivious to the standards which govern normal people, but within its limits it is absolute.[19] It is the only aspect of their personalities that could properly be called "perfect." Distinctions must be drawn, for these characters *are* capable of humiliation. But the source of their humiliation is invariably external, usually the result of a preposterous mistake. It is shame, the awareness of their own failings, of which they are incapable.

Fools like Poche who are impervious to any form of humiliation are not uncommon, though they are usually relegated to the minor roles. The primary imperfections of the major characters are usually quite common. Bassinet *(Tailleur pour dames)* is simply a crushing boor. At one point in the play, he enters a room and everyone flees. His wife is furious at the insult, but he cheerfully replies, "Oh, no. That happens to me all the time."[20] The violence which Irrigua, in *Un Fil à la patte,* inflicts on the French language is greater than that with which he threatens his enemies, but this might be expected of a foreigner. Then he reveals that he once taught the language. When this announcement is greeted with surprise, he explains that "een my country, I have spoke eet good. Here, I do not know why, I spoke eet bad."[21] Understandably numerous are those faults, such as lust and selfishness, which are quite common, but which morality demands be suppressed for the sake of society's preservation. Thommereux *(Le Système Ribadier)* defends himself when his attempt to seduce his host's wife is rebuked as "sordid" *(infame)*: "It is sordid! Yes! But it's human!"[22]

The amorality of farce characters is a function of the same sort of blindness which allows Poche to be impervious to every assault on his dignity. It allows them to treat every sort of defect, moral or otherwise, as if they did not exist. Moral and mental defects often go hand in hand when rationalizations and twisted logic are used to excuse blatant violations of the moral code. Clarisse, the heroine of *"Mais n'te promène donc pas toute nue!",* can see nothing wrong in undressing in front of her son. That, she claims, is more appropriate than that her husband should see her unattired:

> When I married you, ... I didn't know you; and, bang, overnight, because of a fat gentleman in a tricolor sash to whom we said "I do," it was alright! You saw me stark naked. Well,

that—that's indecent!... As for my son, though? He's my flesh! He's my blood! Well, then, if the flesh of my flesh sees my flesh, there's nothing improper about that![23]

Clarisse's argument at least sounds logical, but often such reasoning is supported by nothing but selfish emotion. When Cassagne's inopportune arrival destroys Duchotel's alibi in *Monsieur chasse!,* Duchotel puts all the blame on Cassagne, as if common sense dictated that he check such things before a visit.[24] Duchotel's selfishness becomes even more blatant a little later when he refuses to exonerate a friend who was arrested by the police for a violation committed by Duchotel. When his feeble excuses for not helping fail to satisfy the friend, he declares flatly, "I only know one thing—I was not caught, I am not caught! I'm not budging from that."[25]

Selfishness may even be masked as morality. Ferraillon, who runs a hotel that is lovingly designed to encourage adultery, condemns the local bistros as an offense to public morals because his employees have a disposition to get drunk.[26] It is typical of Feydeau that the persons most likely to be frank about their selfishness are those in professions which are ideally obligated to serve the public. Most of Feydeau's professional humor comes from the cavalier unconcern of those in service occupations for the people in their charge. Doctors, not surprisingly, head the list. Their attitude toward their patients is neatly summed up in *La Dame de chez Maxim* by the surgeon Mongicourt. Although an operation he performed could not have saved his patient from death, he objects to having it called useless. An operation, he calmly argues, is never useless; if it does not profit the patient, it always profits the surgeon.[27] Other characters take this attitude in doctors for granted. In *Tailleur pour dames,* Bassinet hopes that his physician friend will recommend his vacant apartments to the doctor's patients. The apartments, he assures the good doctor, are very unhealthy and should help boost his practice.[28] Politicians are also excellent targets for this sort of humor. When his wife observes that the country is always more peaceful when the legislature is not in session, the Deputy Ventroux, exasperated at the female inability to understand practical matters, declares, "But my darling wife, we're not there in the assembly so that the country will be peaceful!"[29] But professional callousness is not limited to the loftier occupations, as Séraphin proves by the brutal disregard with which he treats the clients of his domestic employment agency in *Les Fiancés de Loches.*[30]

Blindness to one's defects is often itself the result of human selfishness and vanity. When Raymonde worries, in *La Puce à l'oreille,* that the fake love letter she is composing might be exaggerated, Lucienne touches on a basic principle of Feydeau's characterization by replying that such things always seem exaggerated to others, but never to oneself.[31] Another reason why these people fail to live up to the highest moral ideals is that they are following other standards, unacknowledged publicly, but much closer to those practiced in society at large. When Pontagnac arranges, in *Le Dindon,* to reveal a friend's infidelity in order to take advantage of the wife's "revenge," he admits what he is doing is a rather low trick. But, he concludes, "I have an excuse—it's to have his wife."[32] This is not just pointless cynicism. It acknowledges the code that secretly admires the philanderer who successfully seduces a married woman, but condemns absolutely the traitor who betrays that philanderer to his wife. Theoretically, adultery is condemned in both men and women, but the practice is quite different. A sympathetic friend tries to explain to Massenay his wife's unforgiving attitude toward his adultery in *La Main passe!* Young girls, he consoles him, receive a lot of false ideas: "they hear a lot about marital fidelity—so, they imagine that it's meant for the husband."[33] A character in *C'est une femme du monde* turns infidelity into a principle of behavior. He feels that he should have the same respect for his mistress as he would for a wife; therefore he cheats on her.[34]

Money and Appearances: The Basic Values

The standards of sexual morality followed by men are quite different from those demanded of women, but there are other standards which apply equally to all inhabitants of this world. The twin values of money and appearances dictate the rules by which all the characters really live. Scandal is a major preoccupation, but the concern with appearances goes well beyond the fear of scandal. The reason Angèle gives for not being unfaithful to her husband in *Champignol malgré lui* is that he is one of the foremost painters of his time.[35] She does not value him personally; she does not even care for his paintings; it is his name that matters. But even this is a pretext; the real reason she insists on remaining faithful is her fear of being caught. Guilt is purely a matter of being found out, as Suzanne acknowledges in *Tailleur pour dames:* "It's just that if someone should see us!—I would be guilty indeed!"[36] Moricet *(Monsieur chasse!)* expresses the same thought more cynically in his attempt to seduce a less willing wife, and Madame Latour, who has learned by experience the rules of the world, says later in the same play: "Society will pardon bad behavior; it won't pardon a scandal."[37]

Appearances can replace earthy as well as idealistic values. Raymonde is a stylish, chic young woman in *La Puce à l'oreille* who thinks it would be exciting and romantic to have a lover, but she is not interested in going to bed with him.[38] The sixteen-year-old Catulle yearns for a liaison with a *cocotte* in *Un Bain de ménage (Household Bath,* with a pun on *pain de ménage,* "household bread"), but his primary motivation is not sex. He is anxious to show off to his schoolmates, particularly to one who has already acquired that most sought after badge of prestige.[39] There are those who are quite cynical about their pretenses and wear their hypocrisy easily. Hochepaix, a politician who has publicly called his opponent the worst names he could think of, hastens to assure him (now that he has use for him), "Believe me, that doesn't reduce in the least my esteem for you."[40] The main concern of Feydeau's characters, however, is with the face that they show to the world. Vatelin, in *Le Dindon*, admits that he is not bothered by a lecher who follows his wife in the streets. He would be upset if it made him look foolish, but as long as it is the other fellow who looks silly, he does not mind.[41]

The face they show to the world is greatly dependent on money, and finances are never very far from their thoughts. Money is not usually the principal concern of the plot, but when it is, as in *Cent millions qui tombent*, the characters display their greed in its brightest colors. In that play the characters range from Serge, the ruined aristocrat whose cavalier attitude toward money represents a love of ostentatious spending rather than indifference, to Mittwoch, the Jewish entrepreneur whose ability to make money earns him epithets like "crapule" and "fripouille" as well as grudging admiration. Serge is willing to throw his money away at the roulette wheel, but holds people like Mittwoch, who own the tables, in contempt. Mittwoch thinks Serge rather foolish, but since people insist on gambling, he wishes they would do it at his casino rather than at Monte Carlo.[42] Although the others look down on Mittwoch and the "filthy" business of making money, they soon demonstrate that there are few limits to their own willingness to debase themselves for the sake of money.

The scale of values that sees extravagance as a sign of nobility has some curious results. When Serge's mistress finds out that he has lost all of his money, she is delighted. She loves him all the more now, not in spite of the fact that he is penniless, but because of it. What excites her is the thought that he ruined himself for *her*. But it goes without saying that she will now have to find someone who can pay.[43] Serge, however, is an exception; ordinarily the esteem due to a person is in direct proportion to the amount of cash he has. When Isidore is transformed from a despised servant into a revered millionaire, he is treated like nobility by all the other characters in the play. Isidore is taken in by their flattery, as well he might be, for they are as sincere as they are capable of being. They have no other values, and for them a man with millions *is* a great man. A title would be advantageous, they feel, for it is important to have the marks of greatness as well as its substance; but titles are not difficult to acquire. Isidore might acquire a title through the Pope; after all, Mittwoch asks, if Moïse Guttelbach and Samuel Hofmeyer can do it, why not he?[44] Isidore is not used to money, and he takes a while to learn its true value. He is surprised when Snobinet makes him a standing offer of free tickets to the theatre, so Snobinet has to explain: "If people like you had to pay at the theatre, to whom would they give the free passes?"[45] Isidore must learn that money is not just something with which to buy things; it has absolute value, is respected and esteemed in its own right.

The characters of *Cent millions qui tombent* have unparalleled opportunities to display their greed, but they are not exceptional. The constant preoccupation with money shows up in many ways, although it is seldom the principal concern of the plot. Most of the plays dwell on questions of love and marriage (or more accurately, *lust* and marriage), but the two seldom coincide. Marriage is generally a financial affair, and love an activity that takes place beyond its boundaries. Saint-Florimond *(Champignol malgré lui)* reveals that he is planning to get married even as he is hotly pursuing another man's wife. When asked if his prospective bride is pretty, he exclaims: "Is she *pretty?* An income of sixty thousand francs!"[46] Saint-Florimond fails to get either bride or mistress, but others are more fortunate. Bois-d'Enghien is forced to give up his mistress in *Un Fil à la patte,* although he does so in order to acquire a large dowry. Marcel is unusual in that he manages, in *Occupe-toi d'Amélie,* to use a false marriage so as to obtain his patrimony and keep his mistress.

Even in pursuit of what they feel is the only true (i.e., illegitimate) love, their minds are not far from the cashbox.[47] Moricet tries in *Monsieur chasse!* to convince the object of his desire that the expression "I love you," which had at one time escaped her lips, is like an instrument of exchange, a kind of non-negotiable bond redeemable upon demand.[48] Even the moral question of marital fidelity is expressed in financial terms. There is a lengthy argument in *Le Dindon* in which love is metaphorically represented as money. Lucienne and Pontagnac debate whether a husband could be rich enough, or have the right, to make "a few foreign investments."[49] These people do not do everything for the sake of money, but they do nothing without first considering the cost. Taking this attitude for granted, Lucienne thinks she can rid herself of a man who is following her by entering an expensive jewelry store. Unfortunately, the cad is experienced and waits on the sidewalk outside.[50] Bois-d'Enghien *(Un Fil à la patte)* can afford to be generous with the flowers he sends his fiancée, for, as he is quick to point out, he has a flat rate with the florist.[51] He expects a rich return on his investment in any case; one does not send flowers for nothing. Earlier in the same play, Bouzin is shocked to learn that a beautiful bouquet in Lucette's salon has been sent to her anonymously. Hating waste, he slips in his own card, "so that someone will profit by it."[52]

The Role of the Physically Impaired

Given the pervasiveness of moral deficiencies among Feydeau's characters, the physical defects seem unimportant by comparison. The actual number of such disabilities is fairly small, but they are among the features of the plays that leave the most lasting impression. Although relegated to minor roles, they do much to establish the atmosphere that distinguishes Feydeau's plays, a feeling of entering a side show in which the freaks are both very like ourselves and impossibly unreal. They began to appear shortly after the extravagant fools of the early plays had disappeared, and it is possible that Feydeau had them in mind when he spoke of using an absurd minor character as a kind of counter-foil to make a more important character seem more acceptable.[53] The absurd minor figures also serve another important function. They set the tone of the play and establish the light in which the more realistically conceived characters will be seen. They help to guarantee that no note of seriousness will creep in as we observe the more common faults, defects, and sins of the major characters.

The disabilities that spark the gaiety include such standard items as false teeth, bad breath, and deafness, but the most common problems are those afflicting the use of speech. Ever since Pierre Pathelin's bleating shepherd, farce has been fond of debasing that most human of traits, the lack of which does so much to rob us of our distinctiveness and reduce us to the status of animals. In this foreigners are very like those with speech defects, for they are comic primarily because of their inability to use language properly, or their tendency to speak in gibberish which to the native might as well be the bleating of a sheep.[54] Speech problems are of a different order; stuttering and cleft palate are real disabilities that are usually regarded seriously. But when Feydeau portrays speech problems they are made to seem almost illusory and unreal. Not only are the afflicted unperturbed by their problems, but at times the defects disappear. Mathieu's stammer *(L'Hôtel du Libre-Echange)* is quite severe, but only when the weather is bad; at other times he is fluent and voluble.[55] Lapige *(Le Main passe!)* is a jovial mason who is a good deal more eloquent than might be expected of a laborer, until he becomes excited and involuntarily barks like a dog.[56] A character in the same play stumbles and stammers when around the woman he loves, but is the most poised and confident of men at all other times.[57] These characters are not just extreme, they alternate between opposing extremes without ever touching the middle ground. It is as if their disabilities could be turned on or off with the flick of a switch.

Camille's cleft palate in *La Puce à l'oreille* provides the most striking example. Although his speech is incomprehensible to most people, he makes no allowance for others' inability to understand him. He behaves no differently than when, with the aid of a prosthesis, he is able to speak with normal clarity. The contrast is all the more pointed because of the reaction of others. No one listens patiently, slowly trying to make out what he is saying while trying to hide the inevitable embarrassment which accompanies such scenes in life. Either, like the members of the household, they understand him perfectly, or they are bewildered by everything he tries to say. Even his personality accents the contrast. Although at home he cultivates an image of seriousness, he is actually something of a playboy, and his defect has apparently no effect on his amorous adventures.

The more unusual defects receive extravagant treatment, but they set off the more common human afflictions. The most common of all are those associated with one's age. Feydeau does not idealize youth by contrast with age. His young men are often bumbling, rash, or slow, and they are nearly all rather simple or naïve. But the emphasis is on the problems of those no longer young. There are no portraits of extreme old age; these are just middle-aged men and women who yearn for the lost energy and good looks of youth.[58] The men may, like Pinglet in *L'Hôtel du Libre-Echange*, try to prove their youth by having an extramarital fling, or they might seek youth in the form of a young and lovely wife. They find it impossible to understand why the pleasures of youth should be denied to them. Saboulot *(La Lycéenne)*, although thirty years older than his seventeen-year-old fiancée, persists in his determination to marry her in spite of the abundant proof she gives him of her ability to make his life miserable.[59] If a middle-aged man does manage to obtain a young wife, fate conspires to remind him of his age. Ribadier's humiliation is compounded when both his wife and her would-be lover are mistaken for his children in *Le Système Ribadier*.[60] More often they see their own age reflected in the no longer attractive faces of their wives, a constant reminder that youth has left them. Women are not exempt from the folly of forgetting their ages. They never lose faith in their ability to attract men. On the numerous occasions when they are misled into thinking someone is making advances, they are only too anxious to be fooled.[61]

Orbits around the Bourgeois Household

Feydeau's protagonists are endowed with a kind of negative universality; their faults, failings, and sins form a lowest common denominator of humanity which their audience could not fail to recognize. They are unexceptional also with respect to the roles they play in society. At the heart of Feydeau's world is the *ménage bourgeois,* and his protagonist is apt to be at the center of the household, occupying the role of breadwinner and husband. Most of the other characters are defined by the roles they play in relation to the central *ménage:* servants, wives, would-be lovers, in-laws, and friends of the family. The farther one moves from this household, the more fantastic is the action and the more extraordinary are the characters, while at its center stands the timid bourgeois, frightened and harassed, desperately trying to preserve his values of respectability and tranquility from the forces he perceives as menacing his fragile domain. Outside the circle that marks the limits of the bourgeois *monde* exist two major groups that are the most extraordinary and threatening of all: the foreigners and the *cocottes*.

There are some figures who are not technically excluded from the circle of bourgeois respectability, but at times assume a role like that of the menacing outsiders. The military men are similar to the foreigners in their propensity for violence, but are considerably different in temperament. They are not hot-blooded or unpredictable. Encountered in a civilian setting they might appear quite amiable, but once they assume their military role, either in the barracks or when considering a duel, they become methodically violent and brutal.[62]

But one large class of persons at the heart of the respectable household often shares important aspects of the *cocotte's* role in the plays. Any member of the female sex, except older or unattractive wives and spinsters, might at times function as a violator of sexual decorum and an instigator of scandal. Even respectable women take advantage of the fact that for this society respectability depends primarily on female, rather than male, behavior. *Cocottes,* married women, and even ingénues find it easy to create scandal and use it as a weapon against their lovers, husbands, and families.

It was mentioned earlier that most of Feydeau's characters could be classified as "imposters" in that they are less than they should be by normal standards. Where the complementary role of *eiron* is to be found in Feydeau, it is likely to be fulfilled by a woman. The classic *eiron,* Plautus's tricky slave, is not actually self-deprecatory. He is one who, through cleverness and cunning, is able to exceed his assigned role in life and prevail over his superiors, an achievement virtually impossible off the stage. He is not more than he pretends to be, but more than he would ever be allowed to be in real life.[63] Although the difference between their assigned role in society and the role they are permitted on stage is not as extreme as it is for Plautus's slaves, Feydeau's women often behave in a similar fashion. As a rule his women are more aggressive, self-confident, and clever than his men. Where trickery is successful, it is likely to have been initiated by a woman. The reversal of the sexes is one of the oldest themes in farce, but Feydeau's women are not just the usual nagging and domineering shrews. Often they are genuinely superior and more sympathetically portrayed than the men with whom they are contrasted. But whether they are sympathetic tricksters or insupportable shrews, the trait they are most likely to share is the willingness to blatantly disregard conventional proprieties.

The extremes represented by the bourgeois husband and the *cocotte* can be seen more generally throughout the plays of Feydeau in the opposition of male and female, and the way in which it is manifested depends considerably on the social roles of the combatants, whether they be husbands and wives, lovers and mistresses, or fathers and daughters. The last mentioned of these, the young lady whose future marriage is in question, is the most neglected of Feydeau's heroines. This is not surprising, for ingénues do not usually play a large role in his plays, and the few plays in which they are featured are not among those which were most successful originally or those most often revived.

The Ingénue as Trickster, Clown, and Fool

The reason his ingénues were not well received is not difficult to find. Feydeau's young ladies are the least conventional of all his characters. Considering his normally close adherence to social and theatrical conventions, his unusual treatment of marriageable young women might seem at first surprising, particularly because no other stock figure of popular comedy has varied as little throughout the ages as has the ingénue. But Feydeau breaks with tradition only in that his young women are drawn in a manner consistent with that of his other characters. From the *Commedia* to the Marx Brothers, where farce has included conventional plots of love and marriage, the young lovers are usually set apart from the other characters; they are non-fools only temporarily involved in the world of fools. The alternative is often to omit the young lovers entirely and concentrate on the problems that follow marriage rather than those that precede it, as in many medieval farces and in the majority of Feydeau's plays.[64] Where Feydeau uses young lovers, they too are portrayed as fools and clowns.

Most of the ingénues in Feydeau's theatre are minor roles, but there are a few notable exceptions. The ingénues who occupy minor roles are apt to be comically simple, naïve, and helpless.[65] When the ingénue is important to the play, she is aggressive, determined, and quite as willing to shock her guardians as to defy them. Finette, the heroine of *La Lycéenne,* was the first and most audacious of his unconventional ingénues. *La Lycéenne* is the only one of his plays solely devoted to lovers who wish to get married against parental opposition. In the typical farce on this theme, the young lovers enlist the aid of clever clowns who, with a combination of foolishness and cunning, help to bring about the happy ending. But Feydeau's *innamorati* have no need of *zanni,* for they take those roles for themselves. They are the most irresponsible and irrepressible clowns in the play. Their names indicate the relative nature of their clownish roles. Finette is the clever and aggressive one, taking all the initiatives and making all the plans. Apollon Bouvard, the handsome young ox, makes no plans of his own, but has a talent for making the best of a situation by improvising with wild abandon, even though he may not fully understand what is happening to him. He succeeds in making his opponents look foolish because he is indifferent to looking foolish himself, while Finette, the disrupter, victoriously rides the tidal wave of anarchy and establishes herself as undisputed queen of topsy-turvy land.

Part of her claim to that rank is suggested by the play's title. The law which had provided for the establishment of *lycées* and colleges for women was only seven years old at the time the play was produced and was still the subject of considerable controversy.[66] The picture of a *lycée de jeunes filles* painted in the second act of Feydeau's play is a realization of the worst nightmares of the opponents of female education. The girls lack any trace of feminine decorum and behave like unruly schoolboys, playing cards, throwing spitballs, and fighting. Finette proves her right to reign over this world in an encounter with the school bully ("Sophie l'intombable") whom she knocks to the floor in an impromptu fight. She takes advantage of the girls' military training by leading an armed rebellion before she flees with Bouvard. As in other Feydeau plays, the second act is set in a place where normal bourgeois pieties are systematically violated, but here the den of iniquity is an institution of higher learning.

Feminine decorum is not the only quality overturned; feminine virtue is also at stake. Shapiro points out that one of the greatest fears of the opponents of female education was the possibility of sexual encounters between teachers and students, so the *pion* who both rewards and punishes his charges with kisses had strong overtones for the audience.[67] This concern with the corruption of female innocence is also reflected in Finette's personality, for she delights in violating the taboos designed to preserve virgin ignorance. Even before she is sent to the *lycée* she indirectly threatens Saboulot with adultery if he insists on marrying her, and reveals that she was expelled from boarding school because she was carrying on an amorous correspondence with a young man.[68] When she hears herself described as "barely nubile" she mischievously tries to elicit an explanation of the word by feigning ignorance.[69] Both the first and third acts are climaxed with the kind of vulgarly risqué songs that are routinely described as "not fit for young ladies' ears."[70] Finette is instrumental in causing the first to be sung and sings the second herself in a public performance. In the third act it is Bouvard, not she, who becomes more sober and begins to worry about proprieties.

Finette is one of the few truly ironic persons in Feydeau's theatre. Particularly during the first act she uses her presumed girlish innocence as a cloak for improper remarks and sarcastic attacks on her would-be husband. Although she employs her irony to expose the folly of an "imposter," she does so by exceeding the limits of civilized behavior and so proves herself to be a different sort of fool. The play is a fantasy of overturned values, and the fantasy is accented by the fact that the attack is led by the figure who should normally be the symbol of those values in their purest form. The final song, which requests the indulgence of the audience and asks them to forgive the *lycéenne* her streak of madness, suggests the festival spirit in which the play was meant to be received, but the words were wasted on the critics. Vitu, after complaining of a total lack of verisimilitude, attacked the heroine as "a badly brought up, impertinent minx of the most unbearable sort;" he did not comprehend that the lack of realism was directly related to Finette's freedom from normal social restraints.[71]

Henceforth Feydeau's ingénues were more subdued, even when they shared aspects of Finette's personality. Viviane, in *Un Fil à la patte,* has an unromantic concept of love which, despite her sheltered existence, seems to be based on a surprisingly close observation of the world. Her opening lines show that she is not quite as innocent as decorum demands she pretend to be, and her observations on love and marriage are cynicism in the guise of naïveté.[72] She is unconcerned that her future husband is handsome, because she has noticed that whenever there are two men in a household, the husband is always the less attractive. She wants a husband who has had plenty of mistresses because the value of a man is determined by supply and demand; the more others want the thing, the more valuable it becomes. A husband is like the Legion of Honor, coveted "firstly, for the esteem in which one is held, and secondly—because it makes others mad with envy!"[73] She is quite willing to act on her beliefs, and in the end she borrows Finette's trick of getting what she wants by creating a scandal.[74]

Simone, in *Le Ruban,* does not have Viviane's notion of love based on vanity, but she is matter-of-fact about using the vanity of others. She is willing to accept the world on its own corrupt terms and is never shocked that it is not what it should be. When her uncle tells her that he is giving her in marriage as a quid pro quo for the decoration he seeks, she does not murmur a word in protest. She merely acts accordingly, quickly tricking him into postponing the ceremony by appealing to his vanity and selfishness.[75] She always appears in command of the situation, meeting each new unfavorable development with equanimity and a change in strategy. Only when a combination of circumstances and the bungling of her young man brings her trickery to an end does she openly defy her guardian, and then she is fiercely adamant.[76]

The last of Feydeau's ingénues is not a farce character, but she has much in common with those just described. Huguette is not a trickster, but in many ways she opposes the conventional ideal of femininity. She is strong, athletic, resourceful, and unconcerned when others find her behavior shocking. This lack of concern, along with an open and generous spirit, she has in common with Etiennette, the *cocotte* with whom she shares the plot of *Le Bourgeon.* Symbolically, the ingénue and the *cocotte* represent opposite extremes on the bourgeois scale of respectability. Feydeau often explored the comic possibilities of turning that scale upside down. In plays like *La Lycéenne* and *Le Ruban,* he assigns the ingénue a role much like that of the *cocotte.* In others, he used misunderstanding to combine the two roles. In *Amour et piano,* an innocent young lady is mistaken for a *cocotte,* and in *Occupe-toi d'Amélie,* a courtesan poses as a virginal bride-to-be. Even when he treats them seriously, however, as he does in *Le Bourgeon,* there is a remarkable similarity in Feydeau's portrayal of ingénues and *cocottes.*

Husbands, Wives, and the Sanctity of the Hearth

Feydeau shows strong and determined young maidens in a favorable light, but the picture darkens considerably after they marry. Marriage is a battleground, and the husband, being the weaker of the pair, is always at a disadvantage. In the opening monologue of his first play, *Par la fenêtre,* Feydeau provides a preview of the husbands that would follow. Hector fits the classic pattern for hen-pecked husbands, having traded a dominating mother for a shrewish wife. It was his mother, in fact, who chose both his wife and his career, and he unhesitatingly accepted both decisions.[77] Hector is cheerful about his situation, but the attitude of the weak husband later changes considerably, as when this character reemerges for the last time as Follbraguet, in *Hortense à dit: "Je m'en fous!"* The hero of Feydeau's last play is the most pathetic of husbands. Like Hector, he is caught in the middle of a dispute between his wife and his maid and loses to both sides. He is easily as pathetic in the ease with which he is manipulated by a few kind words from the maid as he is when being intimidated by his relentlessly shrewish wife. Husbands are not always as thoroughly dominated by their wives as in Feydeau's first and last plays. The battle between the two can take many forms, but the best a husband can usually expect in any encounter is a hasty and undignified retreat. Even his nominally superior position in the eyes of law and custom does not always work to the husband's advantage. Clarisse is quite willing to use her husband's presumably greater intelligence as a weapon against him in *"Mais n'te promène donc pas toute nue!",* and Follbraguet's weakness is all the more apparent (and dangerous) because as the nominal head of the household the responsibility for his wife's irresponsible actions falls on him, despite his powerlessness to prevent them.[78]

When the issue is adultery, Feydeau's husbands fall generally into two categories: the habitual philanderers, and the more timid types who are not really suited for such adventures, but who are capable of being tempted if conditions are right. The philanderers, less numerous and more likely to play a secondary role, are more enterprising than the other husbands, but they ultimately prove no match for their wives. With the exception of Ribadier, who prides himself on originality, they are neither very clever nor original in their methods of deception.[79] Their principal talent is an ability to lie no matter how damning the evidence against them, but their fabrications are more notable for the imagination they reveal than their plausibility. It is only in the inventiveness and sheer audacity of their excuses and lies that Feydeau's bourgeois husbands ever exceed their usual mediocrity.

In accordance with the simple, commonsense justice that prevails at the end of Feydeau's plays, the libertines are usually exposed and humiliated. The only exception is Moulineaux, in *Tailleur pour dames,* although the escapade he attempts during the play is a total failure. He is also exceptional in having a simple and weak wife who requires the services of her mother to do battle with her husband. Feydeau's mothers-in-law are conventionally unbearable, but they are not numerous because most of the wives are more than capable of standing up for themselves. The wives of libertines are usually more clever than their husbands, but clever or not, they have one advantage over their husbands; even the most shameless of philanderers is like his more timid brethren in his fear of scandal, and especially of the humiliation of cuckoldry. After *Tailleur pour dames* the threat of horns is always part of the punishment which profligate husbands must incur. The methods by which the punishment is inflicted vary. Léontine, in *Monsieur chasse!*, soon regrets her first angry impulse to pay her husband back in kind and resorts instead to irony and sarcasm. She finally forces him into involuntary confession by making him believe that his *mistress* has been unfaithful.[80] Angèle, in *Le Système Ribadier,* has ample opportunity to be unfaithful, but chooses to make the punishment fit the crime in another way. Since her husband committed his infidelities while she was in a hypnotic sleep, she pretends that some unknown man, or possibly several, took advantage of her helpless state.[81] Massenay receives his punishment in *La Main passe!* when his mistress becomes his wife. Because she was unfaithful to her first husband, he is tormented by the fear that she will be unfaithful to him.[82]

At the heart of the sexual battle between husband and wife is a concept of the nature of marriage and the sexuality of women that makes adultery, if not inevitable, at least a constant threat. In most of Feydeau's plays the causes of the dispute are obscured in the farcical emphasis on its catastrophic effects, but when he re-examined the question late in his career he looked more closely at the psychology and motivations of the combatants. The characters of *On va faire la cocotte* are more realistic than those of the earlier plays, and the comedy results directly from differences between the two spouses in attitude and point of view, rather than the exaggerated portrayal of feared consequences. Watching Trévelin gives us a better understanding of why so many Feydeau husbands find adultery irresistible even when they have young and attractive wives. His wife Emilienne is affectionate and vivacious, but Trévelin still finds it necessary to seek sexual excitement beyond the confines of marriage. In the opening scene she tries to show her affection, telling him that she is unconcerned with the appearance of the room because she wants only to look at him. She is annoyed when he shrugs off this show of affection as if it were only to be expected:

Emilienne. That's beautiful! Why, you vain thing. You think it's only natural that I look at you? That's your due?
Trevelin. After all, my dear, we're married! The law says—

Emilienne. Oh, sure, the *law!* Well, when it comes to times like this—if there were only the law to make me look at you, well let me tell you, honey...
Trevelin. Go on—you little anarchist![83]

Shaw's famous aphorism on the popularity of marriage is invalid in Feydeau's world; sex in marriage is not a temptation but an obligation.[84] The excitement exists only outside of the legal bond. Trévelin's calling his wife an anarchist is more than a playful or joking rebuke; it reflects his entire attitude toward marriage. Marriage represents the law, and its formal obligations discourage spontaneity. Trévelin's attitude is much like that of a husband in *Je ne trompe pas mon mari* (written at about the same time), who explains why his attractive wife has a chilling effect on him: "Just at the right psychological moment, all that family upbringing comes up before my eyes: the father, the mother, the governess. That takes the wind out of my sails!"[85] His wife is not frigid or prudish, but the aura of sanctity society has built up around the chastity of respectable women produces the same effect.

Trévelin is not simply deaf to the tender and seductive appeals of his wife; he finds them vaguely threatening and shocking. Qualities that would be attractive and exciting in a mistress are disturbing in a wife. Trévelin is trapped by his notion of what a proper wife should be; although he finds that image unexciting, he is unable to tolerate any deviation from it in his own wife. Emilienne would be content to find excitement within the bounds of marriage, but she is understandably envious of the attentions men lavish upon *cocottes* while neglecting their own wives. Yet while Trévelin is quick to point out that his wife's ideas about the glamorous life of a courtesan are unrealistic, he is unconscious of the irony that his own behavior justifies his wife's complaints. Between them they present a picture of marriage as an institution which seems almost expressly designed to produce sexual dissatisfaction even in the most compatible of couples.

While both men and women have their reasons for being attracted to illicit relationships, they have even stronger reasons to fear them. Both male and female see sexual license as the supreme threat to the sanctity of marriage, but they have dissimilar views on the nature of that threat. For men, the chastity of their wives has primarily a symbolic function, but in this world where appearances count for everything, the symbolic value of chastity is supreme. Its violation constitutes the ultimate attack on a husband's authority, respectability, and dignity. No action of his own, however foolish, could make him feel as despised and ridiculous as being publicly known as a cuckold. As their wives are less sex objects than symbols of chastity and respectability, the male characters tend to put the pleasures of sex and the institution of marriage into separate and mutually exclusive categories.

The reaction of wives to the adventures of their husbands is simpler and less artificial. They are motivated by pure jealousy and possessiveness. They simply do not want to share their husbands with anyone else. To maintain their exclusive rights they are willing to violate society's most sacred taboo and create the most feared kind of scandal. Feydeau's men are usually intrinsically weaker than their women, but their greatest weakness lies in the fact that their worst fears are at the mercy of their wives. Thus even in the plays dominated by lecherous husbands, the principal threat to bourgeois morality and fear of scandal comes from women rather than men. Feydeau's women are not content to be seen as mere symbols to be fought over and guarded by fearful males. They are quite capable of using their chastity for ransom to get what they want.

As if acknowledging that they are faced with superior forces on the domestic battleground, Feydeau's husbands became more timid and less adventurous in the later plays. Even Trévelin, although he is deceiving his wife, uses the tricks of a weakling to get what he wants, pouting and sulkily trying to make her feel guilty for making demands on him.[86] If, like Petypon in *La Dame de chez Maxim* and Pinglet in *L'Hôtel du Libre-Echange,* they are middle-aged men with unattractive middle-aged wives, husbands can take little comfort from the fact that they are no longer faced with the possibility of cuckoldry. Wives unable to threaten desecration of the household gods set themselves up, *faute de mieux,* as High Priestesses of marital piety, intimidating their husbands with an excess of prudery. But if the wives have lost the most effective weapon in their arsenal, their husbands are no longer fit for the battle. Free from his wife on a rare spree, Pinglet revels in the wines, liquors, and cigars which his wife normally forbids him, but a few minutes later he feels ill and wishes his helpmate were present to nurse him.[87] Other husbands would be glad to forgo extramarital pleasures for the sake of domestic peace. Vatelin, in *Le Dindon,* would like to be able to forget the momentary lapse from fidelity he suffered while away from his wife, but the past comes back to torment him, and his wife extracts her full measure of revenge.[88] Chandebise *(La Puce à l'oreille)* has no thought of adultery. His only fault is in giving his wife some slight reason to suspect him, but that is enough to bring upon him humiliation, degrading physical abuse, and the threat of sudden death.

The conflict of spouses becomes more direct and intense in the late one-act plays, but the values of bourgeois respectability are still at the heart of the dispute, although the issue is no longer adultery. The initial quarrel in *Feu la mère de Madame* is similar to that in many of the earlier plays, but in a different key. Again a husband seeks excitement outside the home and is countered by a wife who threatens to bring the same kind of "excitement" into his own home. Lucien is a clerk with artistic pretensions. Not ambitious enough for adultery, he is content with voyeurism, seeking "artistic inspiration" by staring at the breasts of a nude model. His wife is furious at this slight to her own bosom, which she threatens to exhibit for evaluation at their next dinner party.[89] Accused of not sufficiently appreciating his wife's torso, Lucien is first menaced with having to share it with the world, and then suffers the ignominy of having his wife's breasts pawed by a male servant.[90]

The situations in *On purge Bébé!* and *"Mais n'te promène donc pas toute nue!"* are similar. Husbands whose professional concerns make them acutely aware of appearances and the importance of what they deem proper behavior are pitted against wives who are unconcerned with the basic principles of bourgeois decorum. In each case the foolishness of the husband has its exact counterpoint in his wife's madness. Follavoine, singleminded in his role as businessman and breadwinner, fails to see anything absurd or undignified about his dream of selling unbreakable chamber pots to the army; and his wife, who in her role as housewife has a disorderly passion for order, cannot understand why, as a mother, she should not put her son's constipation above all other concerns. Clarisse and her husband have somewhat loftier ideas of themselves. He sees himself as a glamorous politician, courting public acclaim, although he cynically makes deals with those who have publicly insulted him. She declares herself above the petty opinions and prejudices of society, but her fine words are only an excuse for exhibitionism.

In the final two short plays, the wife no longer need rely on scandalous or shocking behavior to destroy her husband's fragile peace of mind; her domination is now virtually complete. In these portraits of domestic incompatibility we can see how far the evolution of Feydeau's characters has come. These are not the oblivious fools of the early plays, unconscious of their gross defects and amoral in their total lack of a sense of guilt. In the late plays his characters are much more complex and realistic than those simple fools, but they are still unaware of their faults and usually incapable of guilt or shame. In the last two one-acts, however, (as in *On va faire la cocotte*) guilt and shame are weapons used by one spouse against the other. In *Léonie est en avance,* Toudoux is alternately blamed for being the cause of his wife's pregnancy and consequent suffering and browbeaten with constant reminders of his uselessness and insignificance in the great drama of childbearing. When his wife's condition turns out to be hysterical, he is berated for not having been able to produce an heir. *Hortense a dit: "Je m'en fous!"* presents the husband as a comic Lear, stripped of all but his title, who must discover that rank without power is a dangerous thing. Even as his wife bullies and orders him about, she castigates him for his inability to fulfill his role as protector and head of the household.[91] In each new scene—with his wife, the servants, and his patients—Follbraguet demonstrates a different aspect of his impotence, finally renouncing his title as he is thrown out of his own apartment, the lease to which is in his wife's name.

Puppets and Pawns

The later plays focus so intensely on the conflict of husband and wife that the other characters fade into insignificance, but in the earlier plays others have roles of varying importance within the orbit of the *ménage bourgeois*. The first of these is the wife's would-be lover, a figure who, following timeless tradition, is always the best friend of the unsuspecting husband. For the most part the would-be lovers are rather inept and never as brash or enterprising as the philandering husbands. As lovers they have little to recommend them besides persistence, but that they have in abundance. They may have once received some small encouragement from the object of their affections, and that is enough to sustain them, no matter how cold she may subsequently become. Despite their persistence, they are sometimes quite timid. Coustouillu, the eloquent statesman of *La Main passe!* is reduced to a stammering fool in the presence of the lady he loves, and Thommereux *(Le Système Ribadier)* even leaves the country out of fear of deceiving his best friend. Yet, each manages to pursue his beloved through two successive marriages. They have few individual traits or characteristics, for their principal function is to create embarrassment for either husband or wife.

The would-be lovers rarely get anything but humiliation and abuse for their efforts, but in this they are like most of the minor characters who exist principally to serve the plot. Often the most victimized of Feydeau's characters have only a small role in the mechanics of the plot but are caught up in the machinery and left bewildered and frightened, not understanding what has happened to them. Some, like the confused and frustrated bridegroom in *L'Affaire Edouard,* have no plot function at all.[92] Like innocent pedestrians in the path of a runaway automobile, they merely get in the way as the crazy machine begins to accelerate. Perhaps the saddest of all is Belgence in *La Main passe!,* a friend of the family whose earnest efforts to be helpful are fruitless. Later, he accidentally brings about a reconciliation of husband and wife. Then, having served his purpose, he is immediately discarded by his ungrateful friends. Feydeau even stresses his role as puppet and victim by referring to him in the cast of characters as "a minor character...who has no importance."[93]

Servants and Masters

Among the few purely functional characters, there are understandably many servants. Nevertheless, there is no other single class of Feydeau's characters that is as varied in treatment and personality as the servant. Some, like most of the servants in *La Main passe!,* are simple yet earnest and dutiful. There are also a number of conventionally self-important butlers who see themselves as the real masters of the household; however, there is variety even in these. Samuel, the self-assured butler of *L'Affaire Edouard,* is quick to point out to everyone he meets that Samuel is not really his name:

> "Lot's of folks think I'm Jewish because I'm called Samuel. But that's not my real name. I only took it because it helps in business."[94]

His pretension is all the more striking because servants often had to change their names to suit the whims of their employers. Bastien, in *La Duchesse des Folies-Bergère,* had to become an Arnold because his masters already had a dog named Bastien.[95] Another servant has loftier aspirations. Tiburce, the domestic in *Chat en poche* imagines himself in love with his fat and homely mistress, and complains that "it's acceptable for a lover to love his mistress, and not acceptable for a servant to love his mistress—what's the difference?"[96] Firmin *(La Lycéenne)* has no pretensions, but seems overqualified for his position as servant. Formerly a prizewinning student at the *lycée,* he is hired by his pompous bourgeois master to give a literary tone to the household, while his classmate, who envied his ability to win all the honors, is now a schoolmaster.[97] Although often briefly sketched, servants may be more individualized than their masters. Rédillon, for example, the conventionally irresponsible *fils de famille* in *Le Dindon,* is watched over by a valet whose regard for his employer can only be described as maternal.[98] While the portrait of the valet is not developed, it is more vivid than that of the master.

Even as his plays became more realistic, Feydeau betrayed his fondness for portraying servants as extravagant and irrepressible clowns. Although most of the servants are victims of events as well as scapegoats for their masters' frustrations, Feydeau occasionally allows them a brief Saturnalian triumph over their betters. The only play which employs the Plautine theme of a servant who bests his master through his own initiative is *Dormez, je le veux!* Unlike the tricky slave of Plautus, Justin is not engaged in a constant battle of wits with his master; the secret of hypnotism gives him effortless control over his employer. He wields his power with great relish and abandon, not only making his master do all the work, but forcing him to make a fool of himself in the presence of his fiancée. On the few other occasions when Feydeau's servants play the destructive clown, they are unconscious of their disruptiveness. Charlotte, a sweet provincial naïf, is unaware of the alarming complications she creates for Angèle and Saint-Florimond in *Champignol malgré lui* by her cheerful eagerness to please, but in their eyes she is an appalling nemesis whose every appearance brings a new embarrassment. Bretel, the servant-clown who dominates the action of *Les Pavés de l'ours (The Bear's Embrace),* is another naïf. He is considerably more aggressive than Charlotte, but no less cheerful and well-intentioned. And he is just as bewildered when he is angrily thrown out after having demolished his master's wedding plans.

Dormez, je le veux! and *Les Pavés de l'ours* were produced about midway in Feydeau's career, following a number of successes which, relying on the mechanics of the deception formula, had employed realistic but bland major characters. In these two short plays Feydeau again freely exploited broadly drawn clowns like those of his earliest plays, but instead of giving all of the characters the same clownish proportions, he reserved the clown's role for the servant, who was allowed to disrupt the more "serious" world in a temporary reign of folly. This ancient theme, in which the rule of disorder is produced or accompanied by a reversal of social roles, was used by Feydeau in two longer plays. The Saturnalia is specifically mentioned in *Cent millions qui tombent*, where the action involves a servant who is treated like a king and is waited upon by a Prince.[99] In this case the servant is not an active or disruptive clown. Rather, his role in the action is passive, but his sudden fortune gives others an opportunity to debase themselves. The overturn of the social hierarchy is the single theme which runs through the several strands of action in *La Duchesse de Folies-Bergère*. La Môme Crevette has become a Duchess; a butler whose good fortune permits him a holiday normally beyond his means is first taken for a count and then for a high-ranking diplomat; a young king goes on a spree like a common schoolboy and is physically abused for not paying a bill; and a drunken *pion* is mistaken for the king and accorded a royal reception. One of the acts is set in Maxim's, a place where both a king and a butler could go on holiday from their respective roles, and the festival atmosphere of Maxim's pervades the whole play.

But the overturn of accepted values and the disruption of order is not normally a question of reversals within the social hierarchy. The opposition of servant and master is as exceptional in the plays of Feydeau as it is common in those of Plautus and Molière. Although the patriarchal society of nineteenth-century Europe bears some resemblance to that of Republican Rome, the threat to social stability in Feydeau arises more from sexual scandal than violations of barriers within the social hierarchy. When such violations occur, they are usually produced by wives and daughters, rather than servants; the most important forces of disruption, however, come from a world technically excluded from the accepted hierarchy. Women—the *cocottes*—naturally dominate this topsy-turvy world, but they have active assistance in their attack on bourgeois values from the other group of disruptive outsiders: Feydeau's energetic foreigners.

The characters considered so far have been primarily citizens of the bourgeois world. It is they who are measured by their petty inadequacies, and they who are victimized and threatened when the plot's infernal machinery picks them up and carries them helplessly through the maze of sexual intrigue.

In Feydeau's own phrase, they are those who receive the "kicks in the rear."[100] The foreigners and *cocottes*, who deliver the kicks and ride the whirlwind unscathed, are created according to different principles. The members of the bourgeois world are negatively comic—weak, hypocritical, fearfully ridiculous—while the outsiders are positive, strong, aggressive, and self-confident. The outsiders are not without standards of behavior. The standards of the *cocotte* are those of the respectable world turned upside down and inside out. And the foreigners, unlike the French bourgeois, have no difficulty living up to their own code of conduct, but that code is always bizarre and usually violent.

Foreigners and the Assault on Civilization

One of the characters in *Le Dindon*, having nearly been bowled over by Soldignac, refers to him as an "energumen."[101] It is an appropriate description for most of Feydeau's foreigners. Not only do they seem possessed by some frightful and superhuman force, but at times they are like agents of the darker world, evoked to materialize and scourge the earth whenever humans are tempted to sin. These demons are the shock troops in the assault on civilization that is presided over with queenly grace by the *cocotte*. They are most often found within her orbit, but they are apt to appear whenever one enters the world of illicit love. Whenever one risks the creation of some kind of scandal, these nightmare apparitions are likely to materialize as if they were physical manifestations of unconscious fears. This is true even of the English, despite their reputation for phlegmatic impassivity. Soldignac and his wife Maggy are like ghosts from a forbidden past who come back to haunt Vatelin in *Le Dindon*. Soldignac, the businessman from London, is coldly indifferent to the scandal he might create in his businesslike approach to divorce; and Maggy, formidable as a wife and terrifying as a mistress, affectionately calls Vatelin "ma fille" before she knocks him to the ground.[102] Another Englishman, in *La Puce à l'oreille*, is like a sex-starved animal waiting by the entrance to his lair in the Hôtel du Minet Galant for any unsuspecting female who might wander close enough to be pounced upon and dragged into his den.[103] One need not go to a disreputable hotel to be plagued by the foreign menace. Once Hubertin has become sufficiently "Americanized" (i.e., drunk), it seems natural that he should appear in the bedroom of an adulterous couple, terrorizing them with a pistol and throwing their clothes out the window.[104] The most ferocious of all are the Spanish-speaking gentlemen, figures who bear strong resemblance to the Capitain of the *Commedia dell'arte*, and for whom murder is one of the most likely consequences of love.

Physical violence is not the only threat foreigners pose for civilization. Their abuse of language is only the most obvious example of their disregard for the forms and conventions that are the hallmarks of civilized society. More important is their blatant lack of concern with scandal. Nothing marks them as savages as clearly as their shamelessness in questions involving sex. Whether they are pursuing someone who has caught their fancy or are seeking revenge on a cheating mate, they are never furtive, but show an energetic disregard for propriety. The two foreign women, Maggy and Dotty, ignore the restraints society has placed on their sex. They go after the men they want with an aggressiveness that few of Feydeau's men could muster. This disregard of propriety is not just a matter of their easy usurpation of the male role in courtship. Dotty, the American millionairess of *Je ne trompe pas mon mari*, has no concept of those important distinctions between classes upon which civilized society is based. Recognizing her lack of experience in matters of love, she has no qualms about soliciting professional advice on the subject from a notorious courtesan. Far from recoiling in horror from the presence of such a woman (the civilized response), she treats Bichon's profession as blandly as she might a dentist's. For her part, Bichon discovers a common bond with the American girl when she learns that her father made his millions selling pigs:

> Bichon. Made his fortune with pigs? Oh! How many must it take?
> Dotty. Lots.
> Bichon. You're telling me![105]

Foreigners and *cocottes* are both outsiders, if for different reasons. But the American and the *cocotte* have something more in common. They are both parvenus, having found success in defiance of class distinctions and in professions others find distasteful.

The association of foreigners with illicit sex is more than just chauvinism or the convenience of the playwright. The reputation which Paris had acquired as the most sinful city in Europe drew many pleasure-seeking tourists, so that while Paris was seen abroad as the pleasure capital, foreigners could well be viewed by the Parisians as more than usually prone to the temptations of the flesh.[106] Some, like Soldignac, were businessmen who took advantage of their trips to Paris to sample the city's most important tourist attraction. Soldignac, in his methodical way, has left a standing order with a Paris *cocotte* for one night of pleasure each time he is in town.[107] Many of these foreign pleasure-seekers were well publicized, particularly if they were rich or titled. Lorcey says that General Irrigua, the South American adventurer in *Un Fil à la patte,* was based in part on a real person, the president of a South American country who came to Paris for the purchase of arms but spent the money from his country's treasury in self-indulgence. General Irrigua admits that he is under sentence of death, but the fate of his real-life antecedent was even worse. He was lynched by a mob when he tried to return to his country.[108]

There were many stories of visiting royalty who sought out the favors of the queens of sensuality—the renowned *grandes horizontales*—and Feydeau makes use of the royal patronage of *cocottes*. Bichon even claims to have been assigned to the shah of Persia by the French government.[109] Her story is not implausible; it was said that the president of the Senate kept a list of those *cocottes* most worthy of presentation to royalty, and was consequently one of the first dignitaries called upon by visiting princes.[110] Foreign aristocrats do not have quite the same function in Feydeau's plays as ordinary visitors, and are shown in a different light. They are not the scourge of straying bourgeois like so many of the other foreigners, although they know how to make life difficult for their inferiors. Instead, they are found only within the orbit of the *cocotte* and are the final adornment to her fantastic presence. They complement and legitimize her role as the monarch of her special world. Technically a pariah, she is sought after and virtually worshipped by princes who are only too happy to debase themselves by entering her topsy-turvy world. For while they legitimize her lofty claims, they cast doubt on their own legitimacy and claims to seriousness. Their role in Feydeau's world is that of kings doing homage to the queen of fools.

As a result they are not savages who threaten civilized values, but the holders of genuine claims to a place at the pinnacle of civilization who have chosen to debase themselves. They maintain the marks of their rank and authority even in absurd circumstances and thus remind us of the extent to which they abuse their real and symbolic position. Their language is evidence of their position. Feydeau's foreign royalty and the members of their entourages speak consistently better French than his other foreigners and are most apt to be comic in their use of language when they attempt colloquialisms or slang. Prince Nicolas of Palestrie, in *Occupe-toi d'Amélie,* is fond of telling everyone that he dislikes formality even while insisting on the respect that is his royal privilege. He is, as he says, a *farceur,* and he debases his authority in the pursuit of his "farces," showing no concern that the victim of one of his practical jokes has died as a consequence.[111] The conflict between his fondness for playing the clown and the nature of his position is further emphasized when he encourages intimacy with the maid, whom he nevertheless regards as little better than a slave.[112] Another royal *farceur* is Serge, in *La Duchesse des Folies-Bergère,* whose schoolboy pranks are little in keeping with his recently acquired title of king. He might well play the clown, for his royal establishment has already been invaded and undermined by the presence of La Môme Crevette, who is presently married to a duke and will soon become the king's mistress. Even if they did not marry into the aristocracy, many *cocottes,* both in the plays and in real life, gave themselves aristocratic names. Considering the willingness of many nobles to ruin themselves for a *cocotte,* she might almost appear to have the right. In one instance at least, a *cocotte* was given what amounts to a royal license. In 1901 King Leopold II of Belgium wrote to Emilienne d'Alençon, who had risen from poverty to riches as a courtesan, inviting her to join him on a hunting party and suggesting that she call herself "la comptesse de Songeon" (Countess of Dreamland).[113]

The Cocotte, Queen of Fools

The king of Belgium was acknowledging an established fact, that the *cocotte* was an institution, a recognized symbol of fantasy and outrageousness. As such, she was ideally suited to the use that Feydeau makes of her. She could play the role of Mother Folly, presiding over a festival of overturned values and ranks, because that was much the role that she played in life. When Feydeau assigned the same role to the ingénue in *La Lycéenne,* he was greeted with commercial failure because he was violating convention. Although the reversal of social roles was perfectly in keeping with the spirit of farce, his audience could not accept that sort of treatment of its most sacred symbol of passive purity. Feydeau's use of the *cocotte* presented no such problem.

This is not to say that Feydeau adopted the *cocotte* with reluctance. He was clearly fond of her and included her in about half of his plays in both major and minor roles. Even when her role is small, she manages to be among the most colorful of Feydeau's characters. He rarely included characters who were not essential to the action, but when he did, they were apt to be *cocottes.* Targinette, the dancer in *Le Ruban,* has nothing to do with the plot, yet is given a lengthy scene with the protagonist.[114] The nameless *cocottes* in *La Lycéenne,* who are part of the background against which Finette scandalizes her parents and fiancé, merely provide atmosphere. There is Olympe, the aging former *cocotte* in *La Puce à l'orielle,* who was known in her youth as "Culotte de peau" (leather britches) and once had herself served up nude on a silver platter.[115] Even when she does not appear on stage, the *cocotte* might serve as an evocative image of license, as in *Amour et piano* and *Un Bain de ménage.* The image of the *cocotte* is also used in *Hortense a dit: "Je m'en fous!"* Follbraquet, the dentist who is oppressed in so many ways, is denied even a glimpse of the famous Caroline Otéro when she is treated by an associate.[116] The forlorn hero of Feydeau's last play can only yearn hopelessly for the extravagance, freedom, and fantasy that the *cocotte* represents.

The *cocotte* is not always gay and fun-loving. At times she can be an avenging fury, particularly when she is being deserted by a "protector" who wants to get married. She might even be a bad-tempered vixen like Paulette in *Cent millions qui tombent,* whose nasty disposition, always under control when there is a question of profit, is nakedly displayed in her treatment of the servants. But generally the *cocotte* is a *"brave fille,"* spirited, charming, and blithely content with her role, although she is never sentimental when it comes to business. The most striking thing about the *cocottes* is that they alone among Feydeau's undeviatingly selfish characters are capable of altruism. Unselfishness is not common even among them; what is unusual is that it should be found at all. The specific form it often takes would also be surprising except for the fact that it follows a well-established theatrical convention. In several of the plays the *cocotte*, who personifies the antithesis of bourgeois values and is seen as one of the most serious threats to bourgeois stability, actively and unselfishly helps to restore the façade of respectability. In *Le Bourgeon*, she goes so far as to make a melodramatic sacrifice for the preservation of society's sense of decorum. Writing of that play, Robert de Flers noted ironically that "in the theatre, *demi-mondaines* are the greatest defenders of the family and the social order," and suggested that the French bourgeoisie should show its gratitude by erecting a monument to Marguerite Gautier.[117] Unfortunately, Feydeau expects us to take the heroine of *Le Bourgeon* seriously and to accept at face value her resignation to her fate: "We are here on earth to give pleasure, to give love. It is not our place to provide a hearth. Let us be content with our role."[118]

That role is acceptable in his farces because we are not asked to become sentimental over the exclusion of the tainted woman from respectable society. She is an irresponsible clown with no desire to join the world that excludes her. If she acquiesces, or even actively helps, in the restoration of respectability, she does so in a way consistent with her role as clown. Miranda can easily afford to volunteer as a scapegoat at the end of *L'Affaire Edouard*. Like the fool who is thought to be immune to bad luck, she is impervious to a scandal that would ruin the respectable woman she is protecting.[119] Although nothing we have learned of her character prepares for her spontaneous gesture, it is essentially that of the fool who cheerfully resigns her throne after her temporary reign of folly and allows the return of order.[120] Even La Môme Crevette is willing to help save Petypon from scandal, although her behavior is more believable and consistent. She goes along with the scheme in which she plays the role of wife because she thinks it a lark, and is as irresponsible in acting her part as she is when she abandons it. The transformation undergone by Bichon in *Je ne trompe pas mon mari* is more inconsistent than that of Miranda. Lighthearted but caustic through most of the play, she suddenly puts her ingenuity and persuasion to work to prevent the rupture of a marriage, even though her action leaves her without a protector.[121]

The sudden altruism of Bichon follows the convention noted by Flers that has pariahs supporting the very society that excludes them. Inconsistency of a similar sort was actually part of the legend that surrounded the *cocotte*. Caroline "La Belle" Otéro was one of the most famous and cynical *grandes cocottes* of the Belle Epoque. Men killed themselves for her and she remained indifferent. She could have had a number of men who were young and handsome as well as rich, but she chose one who was ugly and old, but *extremely* rich, and she treated him with disdain while taking his money. Yet she was reputed to have helped less fortunate friends, and, much like Paulette in *Cent millions qui tombent,* remained faithful to one lover for some time after she had ruined him. Manson describes her as "stingy and generous, compassionate and cruel."[122]

The variety of her legend enabled Feydeau to make the *cocotte* and those surrounding her into some of the most interesting of his characters. *Occupe-toi d'Amélie* is praised by Lorcey as being the most accurately observed of Feydeau's plays because of its picture of the characters in Amélie's orbit, but in describing these people as both "improbable and real" Lorcey suggests why they were so appropriate for farce.[123] Improbable yet real, they were ideal for Feydeau's mixture of fact and fantasy. The "reality" on which he had drawn was both fact and legend, and the legend had been created both in the theatre and outside of it. The year 1852 had seen both the premiere of *La Dame aux Camélias* and the establishment of the Second Empire, which gave rise to the famous courtesans who were responsible for the reality behind the legend. For the second half of the nineteenth century the sinful woman, adulteress or courtesan, was to be a common image in theatre and literature.

Whatever a sociologist might say about the nineteenth-century obsession with fallen women, its effects on the drama were mostly unfortunate. It matters little whether the guilty woman was wept over as a sentimental heroine or painted as an unrepentant villain and cast out, the result was to trivialize the drama. It is not true that the nineteenth-century drama of adultery seems trivial merely because our standards of sexual morality have changed. We need not share Sophocles' concept of religious duty, Euripides' view of incest, or Shakespeare's belief in the nature of kingship to be moved by Antigone, Phaedra, or Lear. Rather than engaging in a moral struggle whose proportions we can appreciate even if we do not accept its precepts, these unfortunate women were mere scapegoats, the passive receptacles of collective guilt and fear. Confined to a submissive role or made outcasts by convention, they could be effective neither as tragic heroines nor as villains, for they were not permitted the moral dimension or responsibility required by either of those roles. Feydeau lacked the originality to create a Nora or Hedda who could defy the restrictions of her sex, but he had an advantage over most of his contemporaries in his instinctive understanding that their conventionally subordinate place in society allowed women to be effective only in the role of clown. The most consequential of his female clowns were the *cocottes,* because as outcasts they enjoyed the fool's traditional freedom from responsibility. The most ironic comment to be made on the folly of the society depicted by Feydeau is that the extravagant clowns on which his portraits were based did not require the license of a king or the religious sanction of a Saturnalian festival to assert their dominance. In some ways they did dominate society, commanding the center of attention and dictating its fashions.

The real position of these theoretical outcasts is reflected in the ease with which Feydeau's courtesans rule over their world. His most famous *cocottes*, La Môme Crevette and Amélie d'Avranches, fill their roles effortlessly and with supreme self-confidence. Although Amélie dominates the action of *Occupe-toi d'Amélie*, she does so with detachment. She rarely initiates any action, but is content to observe the folly of others and to use it to her profit, cheerfully trimming her sails to whichever wind might blow. She need not work or scheme like the intrepid Plautine slave in order to make fools of others; the fools and schemers alike come to her, and she presides serenely over them all. Confident that she can profit from whatever chance throws her way, she is even tempted by marriage when it is thrust upon her. She soon rejects it, not like Etiennette in *Le Bourgeon*, with a deep sigh of regret, but with the realization that marriage can only mean trouble. As an outcast Amélie can never be more than Queen of the Fools, but in a world in which fear of scandal makes fools of all those who claim respectability, that may be the grandest title of all.

5

Conclusion: Thoughts on the Significance of Feydeau and the Value of Farce

Me dis tu que dame Folie
Est morte? ma foy, tu as menty;
Jamais si grande ne la vy,
Ne si puissante comme elle est.
—***Les Sotz nouveaulx,***
farcez, couvez

Limitations of Serious Criticism

The differences in the critical assessments of Feydeau have sometimes been extreme. According to Voltz, for example, Feydeau's characters are empty shells who have only the negative virtue of allowing talented performers free rein to create as they please, whereas Jean Morgan has declared that Feydeau excelled other *vaudevillistes* purely because of his characters.[1] Few of his contemporaries regarded his plays as even worthy of serious comment. In 1901 Brander Matthews was able to write a book about French playwrights of the preceding century without once mentioning Feydeau's name.[2] Even his admirers saw nothing beyond the laughs and the mechanics of the plots. Sarcey, while praising one of Feydeau's plays, conceded that "you could throw it into Schopenhauer's crucible, and it is certain that you would not draw off a drop of philosophy."[3] Modern defenders, on the other hand, claim to have discovered more than a drop of philosophy beneath the gaiety. Feydeau has been hailed by Paul Morand as "the only heir of Greek tragedy" because "he poses the great problem of fatality, on which time has no effect." Others have found an affinity in his plays with Jarry or with Shaw, or have seen him as the precursor of Dada, Surrealism, Pirandello, or Ionesco.[4] Roger

Steiner finds that "Feydeau's plays do not grow old because they have nothing to do with particular intellectual trends of the age, particular social attitudes or problems," while others see in him a hidden satirist (Shapiro) or an astute observer of manners and morals (Lorcey).[5]

If the variety of interpretations proves anything, it is that Feydeau's art is much more complex than was suspected by his contemporaries, despite its real limitations. But there is a danger in these attempts to elevate Feydeau to respectability and admit him into the circle of durable artists. The *Times Literary Supplement*, reviewing Shapiro's translations of Feydeau's plays, wondered at the apparent need felt by intellectuals to canonize past writers and performers of farce.

> If we are honest, it may be doubted whether the intellectual ever enjoys farce as much as he pretends. He sits through the laughs as a voyeur, watching the pleasure the actors give the audience without taking part himself.... Why, then, does the intellectual persist in trying to find some significance in a popular entertainment that has nothing to do with him?... Determined to avoid condescension, humbled by untutored achievement, he can only acknowledge some primeval vitality—and hope by absorbing it to rejuvenate energies that may be failing in his own declining culture.[6]

If critics are to understand and appreciate farce, they must try to do so on its own terms, or run the risk of distorting it to suit their prejudices. Yet while intellectuals may laud the work of *farceurs* of other times and other cultures (like the French film critics who revere Jerry Lewis), they are apt to be suspicious of their own creators of farce. Intellectuals can more easily admire the irresponsible gaiety of traditional farce from a distance than when the social and moral questions it treats so frivolously are of immediate concern. Shaw was right to be irritated by contemporary farce. It deliberately adopted an attitude of irresponsbility and acceptance toward institutions and beliefs that he was convinced must be examined and changed.[7] The mechanical situations to which he objected because they seemed to deny human will and thought are a prime symptom of the sense of fatality which has been discovered in Feydeau by later writers, but which is nothing more than the kind of common fatalism seen in ordinary people of any time or place: a passive acceptance or resignation to what is or is thought to be. It is not a concept that can be embraced in good conscience by the intellectual, particularly the intellectual reformer.

Je m'en foutisme: The Philosophy of Frivolous Disenchantment

If we are to accept Feydeau on his own terms, we must be willing to accept his irresponsibility. Having said that, it can be acknowledged that his irresponsibility is a crucial factor in his ability to outlive so many of his more serious contemporaries. The issues and problems that Feydeau used are not that different from those dealt with in varying degrees of gravity by his contemporaries. He may be directly indebted to them for some of his basic themes. The incompatible couple in Porto-Riche's *Amoureuse* (1891), for instance, might be the prototype of a number of Feydeau husbands and wives. Other writers treated adultery, cupidity, vanity, and cynicism, but Feydeau refused to weight his plays down with the moral judgments that many others could not resist.[8] When he once strayed from his usual practice (in *Le Bourgeon*) he produced what Lorcey is compelled to call a "frightful melodrama," although the play is not at all without its strong points.[9] The plays which have survived are those in which judgment is withheld, in which the vices of the characters and the situations in which they find themselves are regarded with a good-humored but total objectivity. It would be more accurate to say that Feydeau's longevity is dependent, not on skirting the social and moral questions of his age, but on his refusal to provide them with answers.

Feydeau was careful to avoid offending or shocking the prejudices of his audience, but he also took care not to affirm them.[10] His plays illustrate the negative viewpoint that Dobrée claims is inherent in comedy. Dobrée speaks of three types of comedy: "critical" comedy, which deflates or satirizes; "free" comedy, which is irresponsible; and a third category, which deals with the "disillusion of mankind" and "comes when the positive attitude has failed, when doubt is creeping in to undermine values, and men are . . . laughing in the face of it all." Feydeau might be said to combine the last two approaches. He never quite abandons the irresponsible clowning of his earliest plays even when his work more realistically reflects the attitudes of his time. He neither criticizes nor endorses, illustrating Dobrée's assertion that "comedy gives us the courage to face life without any standpoint," and allows us to observe without committing us to judgment.[11]

Does this mean that the value of Feydeau lies in the undercurrent of disillusionment and melancholy that many critics see beneath the gaiety and irresponsibility?[12] It is hard to deny that the melancholy is there, for Feydeau himself underlined it in remarks about himself and his work. He told Brisson in an interview: "Do not be surprised if I am moody [*triste*]. That, indeed, is my usual disposition. . . . I never laugh in the theatre. I rarely laugh in private. I am taciturn and rather unsociable."[13] He claimed that a good *vaudeville* should be based on a "tragic" situation, and added, "Moreover, that is why the authors you call comic are always sad. They think 'sad' first."[14] This underlying melancholy is seen by some to imply hidden depth. Shapiro, for instance, praises Feydeau by asserting that "one does not have to scratch far below the surface of a typical Feydeau comedy to find a fatalistic vision of the human condition and, along with it, an undercurrent of pessimism."[15]

But fatalism and pessimism do not make a good playwright. Perhaps the most significant thing about Feydeau's pessimism is that it is *not* obvious in his plays; it must be sought beneath the surface. It is inferred rather than experienced directly. What is manifest is a persistent refusal to take seriously the situations on which his plays are based no matter how "tragic" or "sad" he might have perceived them to be in life. Excepting always *Le Bourgeon*, there is no attempt to mingle tears with laughter, or even a strong indication of bitterness or heavy irony in his portraits. Feydeau's disillusionment and melancholy are of the kind suggested by Dobrée; they lead him to eschew positive or even definitive standpoints and to seek refuge in laughter. He refuses to take seriously even his own pessimism. His attitude toward the world and its troubles is no more complex than that expressed by Hortense in the title of his last play, an attitude endorsed by Follbraquet when his wife tells him of the maid's insolence:

Marcelle.   I reprimand her, and she says, "I don't give a damn."
Follbraquet.   Fine! Why don't you do the same?
Marcelle.   You permit it! You'll let her say "I don't give a damn" to me!
Follbraquet.   That proves that she's philosophical.[16]

This is the "philosophy" expressed in Feydeau's plays: *Je-m'en-foutisme* (I-don't-give-a-damnism); a deliberate comic indifference in the face of the assorted trials of living.

Feydeau and the Absurdists

His renunciation of positive values and attitudes does allow us to see a certain kinship, however distant, between Feydeau and the Absurdists. With hindsight we may see in his gaily anarchistic point of view a premonition of the collapse of traditional beliefs, a sense of a world in the process of disintegration. The sense of kinship is reinforced by the observation that the Absurdists often make use of the techniques of farce. The fact that Beckett uses clowns as the protagonists of *Waiting for Godot,* and Ionesco calls *Les Chaises* a "tragic farce" suggests that there is something inherent in the nature of farce that lends itself to their vision of futility and hopelessness. But if they use farce, they also radically alter it. To begin with, expressions such as "the human condition" are relevant to the discussion of the Absurdists in a way wholly inappropriate to Feydeau and the generations of traditional farce writers that preceded him. Feydeau's subject matter is nothing so sweeping or abstract as "mankind." His situations and characters are always specific, defined, and limited precisely where Beckett, Ionesco, and Pinter are abstract, inexplicable, and undefined. The Absurdists achieve universality through a lack of specificity. It is difficult to discuss their work without using broad, abstract terms because they often permit no more limited frame of reference. Feydeau's world is carefully limited to specific places, times, and circumstances. No matter how relentlessly foolish the characters that inhabit that world, or how absurdly terrifying the situations in which they inevitably find themselves, there is no reason to conclude that this is the only world possible, or that it represents anything so inescapable as human existence.

The abstract and undefined nature of the Absurdists' world also distinguishes it from that of Feydeau in the treatment of causal relationships, so central to the Absurdist modes. The situations that they portray are often "absurd" in the traditionally farcical sense of being ridiculous or ludicrous. Pinter, for example, often makes use of farcical misunderstandings (although not, like Feydeau, to sustain the plot) and occasionally employs ancient *lazzi,* such as the quarrel over the bag in the second act of *The Caretaker.* But by avoiding answers to questions of causality, he creates an absurdity that is not contingent on specific causes or motivations and is therefore absolute and unconditional. The vision of despair and the sense of menace derive in large part from our inability to define causes for the madness. It seems unavoidable because it is inexplicable and unpredictable. The opposite situation prevails in Feydeau's plays, in which everything that happens, no matter how bizarre, is explained, regulated, and made logical and comprehensible. Even events which in life are subject to chance are made to seem predictable through the logic of theatrical convention.[17] Feydeau's characters may seem to have little control over their respective destinies, but the world in which they exist is ordered and predictable. This contrasts with the worlds of Ionesco and Beckett, whose characters must submit to an unknowable and mindless universe.

The Value of Frivolous Objectivity

Order and clearly explained causal relationships are characteristics Feydeau shared with nearly all of his contemporaries. Like many of them, he presents a strictly defined world that reflects his urban bourgeois audience. He differs from them in his refusal to be taken seriously, in maintaining an atmosphere of frivolity even while treating subjects that others regarded with gravity. Frivolity had its uses, for it allowed him a kind of amoral objectivity that produced a more honest picture of his society than that of many more serious writers.[18] Feydeau's observation of people is exaggerated and extreme, but the distortions are easily recognized as such. They are not the result of attempts to interpret, explain, or philosophize. Beneath the extravagance his audience would recognize characteristics they could have seen in themselves or their neighbors. Only in that atmosphere of fantasy could they see themselves so honestly portrayed without offense. This is true not merely for Feydeau's favorite themes of marriage, love, and adultery. It can be seen even in an atypical play like *Cent millions qui tombent*. Feydeau's picture of a society that values money, particularly the lavish expenditure of money, as the principal criterion of worth and respectability might almost have been drawn from Thorstein Veblen's *The Theory of the Leisure Class*. As an observation of human society, *Cent millions qui tombent* compares most favorably with Mirbeau's *Les Affaires sont les affaires* and Becque's *Les Corbeaux,* the two best known plays of the period on the subject of greed. Both of the latter plays have their virtues, but each portrays greed in traditionally moralistic and melodramatic terms, pitting a cynical and consuming passion for money against a virtuous lack of concern with material profit. Respectability, it is implied, is on the side of virtue, and the desire for money corrupts both. Feydeau comes closer to the truth when he equates money with respectability and leaves virtue entirely out of the picture. For all his frivolity, Feydeau's portrayal of his society's attitudes toward money is actually more perceptive and honest.

Feydeau and Shaw

Interestingly, the moral objectivity of Feydeau brings him closer, in certain limited respects, to the purported optimist Shaw than to a pessimist such as Becque. Despite his objections to conventional farce, Shaw was not above occasionally indulging in what he called "tomfoolery," a practice he defended by saying that "irresponsible laughter is salutary in small quantities."[19] His clearest example of "irresponsible" foolishness is *Passion, Poison, and Petrifaction* (1905), a piece of extravagant buffoonery which is passed over in embarrassed silence by most Shaw authorities.[20] The farcical treatment of Edward III in *The Six of Calais* (1934) is less fantastic but equally free of Shaw's more serious concerns. *You Never Can Tell* (1896) employs themes and devices of conventional farcical comedy in unconventional ways, and *The Millionairess* (1935) is enlivened by scenes that verge on pure slapstick.[21]

Shaw also used farce for his own special ends, attempting to transform it and make it more responsible. Shaw's efforts to "humanize" farce are described by Meisel, who refers to the Shavian "Discussion Play" as a "kind of cerebral farce." According to Meisel, Shaw uses the fastpaced action of farce in order that plot might "keep pace with thought" and help "keep the intellectual pot bubbling."[22] Shaw's use of farce in this fashion is less unusual than it might seem, because even conventional farce uses action to dramatize "ideas," although such ideas are on a considerably lower plane than Shaw's and are not often actually discussed. Meisel himself cites *Divorçons!* by Sardou and Najac as an example of a conventional farce in which "discussion" plays an important role, and compares it to Shaw's *Getting Married*.[23]

Discussion has a part in the plays of Feydeau as well, but with Feydeau it is limited to the expression of ideas and attitudes which, however common, are at odds with conventional morality, and he never suggests that attitudes or institutions should be changed. The best example of this type of discussion in Feydeau is in the first act of *Le Dindon,* which is almost entirely devoted to a discussion of attitudes toward marriage, adultery, and the double standard of sexual morality.

In a limited way, and for his own serious ends, Shaw also takes advantage of the frivolity and consequent freedom from judgment that farce provides. In a review of an English adaptation of *L'Hôtel du Libre-Echange,* Shaw made note of the "fantastic atmosphere of moral irresponsibility" that is necessary to farce.[24] In a play like *Getting Married,* the fantastic atmosphere of farce that frees Feydeau's characters to commit outrageous acts permits those of Shaw to express outrageous ideas. The situations in *Getting Married* could provide plots for several farces if Shaw had his characters act out the difficulties they experience with marriage and divorce.[25] Instead, the various complications and dilemmas are described, and several unusual ways of resolving them are discussed. In accordance with the Bishop's belief that the devil must be given a fair hearing, even the most bizarre notions can be examined. Addressing an audience as easily shocked by ideas as by action, Shaw uses farce's immunity from judgment to forestall the outright condemnation of unusual proposals and thus permit a genuine dialogue to take place.

Limitations to the "Absolutely Comic"

Shaw, Pinter, and Ionesco, in their diverse uses of farce, demonstrate that it has greater versatility than is generally suspected of this slightly regarded form. They are serious writers, however, and in utilizing farce for their own ends, they must necessarily alter it drastically. They include farce in a larger vision that finally transcends farce. By contrast, Feydeau neither adds nor subtracts, but stays entirely within the boundaries of the farcical mode, devoting himself to developing to the fullest the possibilities contained within that circumscribed view of the world. The devotion to the narrow aims of farce gives Feydeau's work a kind of "purity" that has been noted by a number of critics. Yahiel, for example, feels that the essence of Feydeau's theatre is a "pure and objective idea of the comic."[26] And Versini writes that Feydeau's *vaudevilles* "belong to pure theatre." They operate, he says, in accordance with unchanging laws and have not aged because they are "outside of life and, because of that, outside of time."[27] Richard Hayes made a similar comment in a review of *Hotel Paradiso,* Peter Glenville's adaptation of *L'Hôtel du Libre-Echange.* Hayes refers to the distinction Baudelaire makes "between the 'significantly comic'—an imitation—and the 'absolutely comic, or grotesque'—a creation." He places *Hotel Paradiso* with the absolutely comic, for "it is a parody of nothing but itself; not even remotely does it suggest an ideal of the useful or the rational."[28]

The "absolute" or abstract side of Feydeau's art is only one part of his complex method, but it is one that may appear more obvious and important to us than it did to his contemporaries. The mechanical and abstract aspect of farce is but one side of a careful balancing of contrasting elements. Farce needs the constant reference to daily life, to life as it is seen and felt, in order to maintain its vitality. As the context in which they were written becomes increasingly remote, Feydeau's plays will probably appear even more dominated by their fantastic, grotesque, and mechanical side. In the process, they will lose a significant part of their power to amuse. Except as an exercise in a certain "style," the "absolutely comic" may turn out not to be very funny.

Feydeau's observations of the society in which he lived are less obvious to us than might be the case because the end result of his theatre is not observation of reality, but its distortion. He was not offering new insights or attempting to make his audience see what they had never seen before. He showed them an image of themselves with which they were already most familiar, but he presented it through a carnival mirror. He could rely on them to recognize their image beneath the distortions, but we, less familiar with the lines and colors of the original, might be tempted to dismiss Feydeau's extravagant rendering of it as sheer fantasy, unrelated to anything in reality. Our confusion could be increased if we do not realize that even many of the distortions themselves would have been recognized by Feydeau's public, for they often parallel the fears, anxieties, and frustrations that change the way the world is perceived. While it represents no "ideal of the useful or the rational," and exists for no purpose greater than or beyond itself, Feydeau's theatre is not created purely of imagination, but is based on a rather sophisticated form of "imitation."

The evaluation of Feydeau's work must rest finally on the fact that within the context of its determined frivolity, it represents a highly developed art, which, while avoiding serious ends, is nevertheless deeply relevant to an essential part of our human nature. His excellence lies in his ability to choreograph his ordinary characters in a dance of mathematical precision, and to set emotions and motivations worthy of the naturalists into patterns that seem as delightfully artificial as a Gilbert and Sullivan patter song. He did not set out to satirize the world in which he lived, to point out its foibles, but that may have been an indirect result of his efforts. He simply took advantage of what his age provided, of the outlandish foreigners who visited Paris, of the sensational *cocottes,* and above all of a society whose obsession with appearances and sexual scandal was ideal material for his sophisticated and highly civilized farce.

It is more difficult to say what the study of Feydeau reveals about the nature of farce in general. Feydeau represents a highly developed stage of the art and shows some of the complexity of which it is capable. But despite the complexity that can be seen beneath the surface, there is justification for the view that farce is simple if simplicity is understood to mean a lack of intellectual pretension. Although perpetually scorned by those who would confine our vision to loftier things, traditional farce has maintained its popularity by unashamedly exploiting our most basic and primitive emotions. It is not afraid to use simple and universal images to reach us at this most elemental of levels, where our responses are strong, automatic, and virtually instinctive. Pratfalls and sudden blows, frantic chases, and lost trousers are all images to which we react almost without the intervention of thought. They are among the most direct and universal symbols of violence, speed, and humiliation. Farce is not limited to such things, but because it is alone in its acceptance of them, they have become its most distinctive and obvious feature. They are basic to farce not because farce is crude and physical, but because it is shameless. It freely accepts all that we dislike, fear, and censor in ourselves. It includes our elementary responses to violence and sex, our basic bodily needs and functions, although it is capable of going well beyond them. It permits us to look at aspects of our lives that we cannot yet bear to view both seriously and honestly. It allows us to acknowledge the baser side of ourselves, our laws, and our institutions, and lets us admit how much lower than the angels we really are.

For the Love of Foolish Things

Farce can do this because it is irresponsible. It would be tempting to say, in defense of farce, that it presents a closer and franker look at ourselves under a cloak of irresponsibility, but that would not be quite accurate. The irresponsibility of farce is not a "cloak," an external covering that serves to conceal its true face. Irresponsibility is at the heart of farce, and it often conceals nothing more penetrating than playful silliness. Like the traditional court fool, farce is granted license to say what it pleases, not because it voices criticisms in a clever or amusing way, but because it *is* foolish and need never be taken seriously. Farce invites us to join in the foolishness, to expose, even to celebrate, our own folly. It resists all efforts at reform because to make it responsible would be to change its essential nature. Defiantly incorrigible, it perversely offers little assistance to those who would defend it. The defense of farce, like the defense of folly, can never be wholly serious. Erasmus, the most famous defender of folly, is still an excellent guide for those who would accept folly even while maintaining their own claims to seriousness. Although there is a great deal of ironic criticism in *The Praise of Folly,* Erasmus is not really a crusader against folly. He exploits the ambiguities inherent in the concept of folly, and, in the main, is "inspired by a wise humor that accepts folly as a necessary part of life."[29]

It is appropriate that Erasmus wrote *The Praise of Folly* during a visit to England, because the English have a long tradition of viewing folly and seriousness as part of an integrated whole. It is an attitude that can be seen in the combination of farcical and serious elements in the medieval cycle plays, in the plays of Shakespeare, and even in the fond tolerance that the English have always had for their eccentrics. Feydeau belongs to a different tradition, one that by segregating folly from the serious pursuits of life has allowed it the full and unhampered development that produced Pathelin, Pantagruel, and La Môme Crevette. The French decorum, their isolation of the foolish from the serious, has left them uneasy in the presence of their own rich comic inheritance. Trying to understand why his countrymen failed to fully appreciate Feydeau's talent, Nozière observed that the French have always been suspicious of those who make them laugh. "They adore gaiety, but they don't value it."[30] They fear that to value comics would imply taking them seriously, and the French are never so comfortable as the English with the notion that the love of foolish things is compatible with, even necessary to, a serious life. Yet the French segregation of the important from the trivial is more apparent than real. It is a matter of aesthetics and literature, not of life; a question of treatment rather than subject matter. If the French are disinclined to see life as simultaneously foolish and serious, they acknowledge the pervasiveness of folly in the unequaled thoroughness, scope, and richness of their greatest comic writers, who are allowed to range unhampered through every aspect of life. Although France could have never produced a Shakespeare, only she could have given birth to Rabelais. Like Rabelais, Feydeau also represents something unique to the French comic genius. The differences between the two, although vast, are in part a consequence of the ages in which they lived. Each encompassed the experience of his epoch in a world limited to folly and laughter. Each has frustrated serious admirers who recognize genius but cannot comprehend the refusal to be serious. Like the theorists who strive to enlist laughter in the service of reason, these sober critics sense wisdom and philosophy in the midst of the frivolity and conclude that there must also be seriousness and reason, if it could only be found. But the wisdom of laughter is that same wise humor of Erasmus, and its philosophy teaches one only to tolerate a world so often unreasonable and incomprehensible. The point is not that we should laugh at the folly of others, nor even that we should laugh at ourselves, but just that we should laugh.

Appendix A

On Performing Feydeau

In the preceding discussion of Feydeau and the nature of farce there has been little mention made of individual productions or the contribution of actors, directors, and designers to the final theatrical event. This might seem a surprising lack in view of the acknowledged theatrical and visual nature of farce. Had the discussion centered on the type of farce that is organized around the personality of the clown, such an omission, if possible, would have been inexcusable. But one can conduct a comprehensive discussion of Feydeau's plays primarily on the basis of the texts because they are remarkably detailed, and written so as to permit any intelligent reader, acquainted with the theatre and accustomed to reading plays, easily to imagine the effect intended by the author. The avoidance of the elements of production was made necessary, or at least highly desirable, by the ephemeral nature of the performing arts. The information that may be gleaned about past performances is sketchy at best. When one reads that a given actor was "very natural" or that a certain actress was "charming and vivacious," one probably learns little that could not have been guessed by reading the text. More importantly, the text can be studied and reexamined; the comments that any critic offers may be questioned or refuted on the basis of evidence to which all have access. The observations of the critic of a performance, once the performance is no more, must be accepted or rejected on little better evidence than the observer's word. For these reasons it was thought wise to keep the discussion of performance separate, even though it is too important a matter to ignore altogether.

One reason it may be assumed that the texts of Feydeau's plays closely reflect their actual performances is that Feydeau, like many *vaudevillistes*, was nearly always his own *metteur en scène*. It was a task he enjoyed. He was fascinated with the mechanics of theatrical production and took great pains over the smallest of details. The ample stage directions and notes in his published plays are aimed less at the general reader than at potential producers, and in his notes he attempts to anticipate all major problems of production. In addition to advice to actors and detailed instructions on how to achieve certain special effects, he provided contingency plans in the event that a desired effect failed to work or the theatre was not equipped to produce it properly. He was fond of stage tricks, but was well aware of the effect they had on an audience. In *Les Fiancés de Loches* he suggested that the bathtubs in the third act be equipped with practical faucets and wrote a section of dialogue which was to be eliminated if real running water could not be provided. The dialogue, he noted, "was written only to take up the time during which the audience, distracted by the effect of the water, cannot pay attention to what is being said."[1]

Feydeau enjoyed all aspects of production, not just the gimmicks and tricks. Louis Verneuil relates how Feydeau came to his rescue during the staging of Verneuil's first play. The young writer's play was being offered as a curtain raiser, but the director was busy with the main piece and had left Verneuil on his own. Feydeau, one of whose plays was also on the bill, chanced to come into the theatre, noticed his colleague's inexperience, and immediately took over the staging. By the time of the opening he had transformed the play, discovering things in it of which its author was unaware. Verneuil adds admiringly that "beside Victorien Sardou, certainly no other author could direct his own plays better than Georges Feydeau."[2] If we are to believe Feydeau's own protestations of laziness and distaste for writing, he was more enthusiastic about staging his plays than about preparing the manuscripts. Those who had never seen him in rehearsal, wrote Robert Dieudonné, "did not know at all a man transformed by the theatre. That indolent fellow inspired his actors with intense life, that sceptic brought to the final stages of rehearsal an unexpected perfectionism."[3]

Feydeau was intensely concerned with the production of his plays, but what did he demand of his performers, and what sort of style did he develop? These are much more difficult questions to answer. It is probable that his own style changed in keeping with theatrical fashion, and that he had the flexibility, necessary to all intelligent directors, to utilize the talents of his actors rather than to impose on them an interpretation for which they were not suited. Armande Cassive, the creator of the role of La Môme Crevette and thereafter Feydeau's favorite actress, described her reluctance to play the role of Léontine in *Monsieur chasse!*, which Berthe Cerny had originated eighteen years earlier. She had protested to Feydeau that her style was much different from that of Cerny, exclaiming:

> Now look... I could never be as sedate as she was.
> "Obviously," smiled *my* author, "but Cerny couldn't be as animated as you."
> Apparently, it is necessary to be very animated in the year of our Lord 1911. That is what Feydeau says, and he must be right. Eighteen years ago, when *Monsieur chasse* was given for the first time, everyone was crazy about quiet comedians. Raimond [who played Moricet] was a quiet comedian. Saint-Germain [who played Duchotel] was a quiet

comedian. In such company, Mme Cerny had it all set up for her. Today... if a play is called a comedy, it has got to be played at a diabolical pace."[4]

Feydeau himself may have been partly responsible for the popularity of that "diabolical pace"; it is in any case a characteristic for which his productions were noted. Even more than his concern with *le mouvement* (very roughly the equivalent of "pacing," but applicable to plot as well as to staging), Feydeau was known for his attention to detail and his demands for precision. Hervé Lauwick quotes Feydeau as saying, "I am insistent about... the precise expression of meanings, and about the intonation of the least remark. That is why I wrote down all the "oh's" and "ah's" musically.[5] The last statement, of course, is an exaggeration, but in one instance it was literally true. Not knowing how else to indicate the exact intonation he wanted for an important exchange, he wrote it out on a musical staff.[6] His emphasis on precision is echoed by Peter Glenville, writing about the performance of *Hotel Paradiso:* "However wildly pandemonium may reign in the play, the actors need the control and exactitude of tumblers and tightrope dancers.... This precision is a far cry indeed from the inner probings of the actor of the Stanislavski school."[7]

There is much more to playing farce than just precision and energetic pacing (as many amateurs have discovered, much to their chagrin). Unfortunately, Feydeau did not leave a complete analysis of the technique of presenting his plays, but a number of observers have made interesting and helpful comments since his time. Surprisingly perhaps, in view of Glenville's remark about the "Stanislavski school," Stanislavski himself was quite perceptive on the subject of the *vaudeville.* According to Gorchakov, Stanislavski said that a special "world of feelings" was involved in this particular type of acting.

> I intentionally use the word "world," because vaudeville is a world of its own, inhabited by creatures whom one does not meet in comedy, drama, or tragedy. There is an accepted notion that vaudeville is a very special kind of symbolic form, and that, as a result, you should not be guided by the laws of logic and psychology in directing vaudeville. The world of vaudeville is a perfectly realistic one but the most unusual incidents occur in it every step of the way. The life in vaudeville flows according to all laws of logic and psychology, but it is constantly interrupted by the unexpected. Characters in vaudeville are ordinary and realistic. One should not consider them strange creatures. On the contrary, they are most ordinary people. Their only strangeness is their absolute credulity about everything.[8]

Stanislavski was not referring to Feydeau, yet his remarks apply to the world Feydeau created: a special world which has its own laws and probabilities, inhabited by characters who, despite being quite ordinary and realistic, are disposed to automatically accept appearances as reality. Most important is his observation that the actors should never regard the characters they are playing as "strange," no matter how extraordinary the situations in which they find themselves, or how bizarre their behavior may seem. This cardinal rule of playing any form of comedy is almost second nature to the gifted comedian, but is often forgotten by the amateur, with inevitably disastrous results. Peter Glenville affirms the rule when he says that "the outrageousness of the characters in the play [*Hotel Paradiso*] requires the utmost sincerity in the playing."[9] And Cassive wrote of the art of playing *vaudeville:*

> Sobriety in gestures is indispensable. The *vaudeville* doesn't demand as much agitation as everyone thinks. The essential thing is to stay within the truth and to bring oneself as close as possible to life.
>   I believe it is necessary to play with great sincerity and that the audience should not feel that you are working at the role. For my part, I get great effects by speaking enormities with apparent naïveté. Apparent unconsciousness is a sure-fire effect. But I carefully avoid any coarse device. Vulgarity, ridiculous costumes, outrageous make-up: those are methods I hate to use, and which, in my opinion, are useless.[10]

Naïveté may seem a surprising quality to find in the actress who became famous as Amélie and La Môme Crevette, but it corresponds exactly to the credulity mentioned by Stanislavski. Both are instances of farcical oblivion, that blindness to enormities which would ordinarily evoke either skepticism or embarrassment. This oblivion is what makes sincerity especially important in playing farce. If the actress appears to be commenting on, or in any way emphasizing, the enormity, the effect is lost. The more outrageous the situation or behavior, and the greater the discrepancy between it and the performer's reaction, the more important it is that the actor "believe" in his role.

The need for "belief" in farce goes well beyond specific reactions to individual situations. It extends to all those involved in the production, including those who never appear on stage. It creates a particular problem for contemporary stagings of Feydeau, produced at a cultural remove from the climate in which the plays were written. The original production of *Look After Lulu,* Noël Coward's adaptation of *Occupe-toi d'Amélie,* provided an example of the major hazard Feydeau faces in the hands of modern directors. The critics were generally unfavorable, but Kenneth Tynan's remarks were particularly perceptive. He complained that Cyril Ritchard's direction and Cecil Beaton's costumes seemed based on the assumption that the play itself "is unactable, and must therefore be parodied.... We are encouraged to laugh not so much at the piece itself as at the period in which it was thought funny."[11] Compare Jacques Charon's comment on his successful production of *A Flea in Her Ear* for the National Theatre: "The aim ... is to be natural within the style; not to turn the style itself into a joke."[12]

Eric Bentley is another who stresses the importance of a sense of reality in the production of farce. In his essay on farce psychology he makes it clear that neglect of the reality of farce is often both more hurtful and obvious in the visual aspects of production (recall Cassive's advice against using ridiculous costumes and outrageous make-up). He makes his point by contrasting photographs of modern productions of Labiche (elegant but unreal) with a drawing made of the first production of *An Italian Straw-Hat*. In the drawing

> the clothes are clothes—a little drab, perhaps, as is proper to the period and the milieu, yet, with their high collars, their bulgy trousers, their bulbous bodices, full of drama. Here the associations would not be operetta, period charm, "stylization," but realistic plays, immediacy, forthrightness.[13]

The point could be made perhaps even more strongly with photographs of Feydeau's plays then and now.[14] It could reasonably be argued that praising the original productions of Feydeau's plays for their commonplace realism is a clear case of *faute de mieux*. There were then few alternatives to realistic scenery in the staging of contemporary plays. But such an objection would miss the point. The problem is that modern scenic and costume designers, faced with the receding reality of older comedies and farces, almost inevitably use their art to increase the cultural gap, emphasizing fantasy and unreality, rather than helping to give these plays a sense of immediacy.

It is, however, much easier to point out the common mistakes and pitfalls of producing farce than it is to prescribe a reliably correct formula. The best that can be done is to offer a few basic and somewhat obvious guidelines. It is obvious that the producer of Feydeau should emulate the contrapuntal techniques of the writer; he should balance the chaos of the situations with precision in his actors, match outrageousness and lunacy with sincerity and sobriety, and above all strive to weld a stark sense of felt reality onto all of the extravagant fantasy. The *vaudeville,* as Feydeau said simply, should be played like a tragedy.[15] It should also be added that the director and actors of farce must not ignore what Bentley calls the "inner experience," the intense reservoir of fundamental emotions from which farce derives so much of its force. But here a note of caution is needed. This is the area that demands the greatest skill and delicacy. Handling powerful emotions is like working with high explosives. Great skill is required to direct the explosive force into its proper channel—laughter—rather than allowing it to degenerate into unpleasant vulgarity and bad taste. It was this sort of mistake that was obviously feared by one critic of a Feydeau play in English when he noted with relief that the director had "managed to persuade an English cast to present embarrassing situations instead of identifying with embarrassed characters."[16] Skillful use of the indispensable tool of farcical oblivion is required to control, but not to defuse, the response to a charged situation. The importance of that magical oblivion might prompt one to hazard a final, somewhat riskier, suggestion. It is probable that the difference between the successful actor of Feydeau's kind of farce and the actor in other forms of drama lies less in what is *added* in performing Feydeau than in what is taken away. The special key to Feydeau's characterization, the thing that sets his people apart from the most ordinary run of humanity, lies in that curious blindness to emotional pain and moral guilt. It is this lack, this deficiency, that paradoxically permits these limited and ordinary creatures to convey the feeling of freedom and abandon that impelled one observer to exclaim: "The happy privilege to be mad with such extravagance!"[17]

Such a meager list of rules and suggestions will never guarantee a successful performance. Even if the list were expanded, the director must ultimately put his trust in the talents of the performers. Puzzling over what he felt to be the erratic nature of farce, Kierkegaard concluded that while the supporting players in farce achieve their effect "by means of that abstract category, 'the general,'" success depends upon two or three geniuses who abandon themselves confidently to the spirit of laughter.[18] This seems a very apt description of farce in the style of the Marx Brothers, but Feydeau too had a core of players on whose talent he relied. There were three in particular— Cassive, Germain, and his good friend Marcel Simon—whose work may well have given him almost as much inspiration as his writing gave to them. One should never underestimate the importance of a gifted clown in the performance of farce, even farce as disciplined as that of Feydeau. Kierkegaard's assessment needs to be amended in one important respect, however. A dancer may be originally inspired by the same vision of effortless grace that is finally communicated to the audience, but the means by which the appearance of light, graceful beauty is achieved in performance involves the straining of disciplined muscles to their limit. Just so the inspired *farceur* cannot obtain the necessary effect of effortless spontaneity by simply abandoning himself to the spirit of laughter. He conveys that spirit to his public through a medium that is as complex, varied, and exacting as any in art.

Appendix B

Feydeau and the French Theatre: A Chronology

Georges Feydeau was born on December 8, 1862, and died, June 5, 1921. Much of the thirty-nine year period from the production of his first play to his death was marked by intense theatrical activity in France. It was the time of Antoine and the Théâtre Libre, and of Lugné-Poë and the Théâtre de l'Oeuvre, a time of experimentation and apparent revitalization in French theatre. The decade of the 1870s had been one of transition. Other than Emile Zola (1840-1902), no major playwrights had appeared to challenge the dominance of Second Empire "Realists" like Alexandre Dumas *fils* (1824-95) and Emile Augier (1820-89). But between the production of Henry Becque's (1837-99) *Les Corbeaux (The Vultures)* in 1882 and the turn of the century, many young playwrights had emerged, both on the Boulevard and in the experimental houses, to give the theatre a sense of renewed life and innovation. Yet few of those writers are remembered today. Most of them were realists or naturalists who attempted to portray life more honestly than had been done before, but, with few exceptions, the playwrights who are read today did not produce realistic dramas. The best known play of the period is Edmond Rostand's (1868-1918) heroic comedy *Cyrano de Bergerac*. Alfred Jarry (1873-1907) and Maurice Maeterlinck (1862-1949) anticipated the nonrealistic trends of the twentieth century. Paul Claudel became a major figure in modern French drama, but his work went unrecognized during his most creative period. Of the many playwrights who were first produced by Antoine, only Georges Courteline (1858-1929) survives. Others who are still read and performed, at least in France, were thought inconsequential by their contemporaries: Jules Renard (1864-1910), Tristan Bernard (1866-1947), and, of course, Georges Feydeau.

The principal themes dealt with by the realistic playwrights of the time were those of Feydeau: love triangles, adultery, and divorce. The French playwrights at the turn of the century, as Maurice Coindreau has observed, seemed obsessed by the question of divorce.[1] Earlier authors had used the stage to argue for the establishment of a divorce law (e.g., in Dumas's *La*

Femme de Claude [1873] and Augier's *Mme Cavelet* [1876]), but the issue did not die when the law became a reality in 1883. Paul Hervieu (1857-1915), whose thesis plays were in the tradition of Dumas *fils*, raised the question of adultery and divorce in most of his works. His *Les Paroles restent (Words Remain)* is about the lasting effects of scandal. In *Les Tenailles, (The Pincers)* a couple finds their legal bond is too strong to break despite the divorce law, and *La Loi de l'homme (The Law of Man)* concerns the double standard of sexual morality. Many of his plays seem to show that divorce is an inadequate answer to adultery. In *Connais-toi, (Know Thyself)*, two men forgive rather than divorce their wives, despite their conviction that such a choice reveals moral weakness, and in *L'Enigme, (The Enigma)*, a husband decides that forcing his faithless wife to continue living with him will be a more severe punishment than killing her.

Less didactic than Hervieu, Georges de Porto-Riche (1849-1930) pictured adultery as the consequence of the different sexual natures of men and women. While men cannot be satisfied with one woman, women are fiercely possessive and become unfaithful in their search for a man whom they need not share. Maurice Donnay (1859-1945) followed the lead of Porto-Riche in creating plays of strong sexual passion. His *Amants (Lovers)* involves a triangle of a woman and her two lovers in which money wins out over love, and *L'Autre danger (The Other Danger)* is based on a rivalry between mother and daughter for the same man. Jules Lemaître's (1853-1914) best-known play, *Le Pardon*, ends when both husband and wife agree to forgive the other's infidelities. *Poliche* and *Le Scandale* by Henri Bataille (1872-1922) are also plays of adultery. In Renard's *Le Pain de ménage, (Household Bread)* two people are tempted by adultery, but finally reject it. The conflict between sexual passion and the bonds of marriage was not monopolized by the realists. Maeterlinck exploited the theme in both *Pélléas and Mélisande* and *Monna Vanna*, in each of which a woman is torn between a lover and her loyalty to a passionless marriage. Other plays took up the theme of Feydeau's *Un Fil à la patte* and *Les Pavés de l'ours:* a man leaving his mistress to gain respectability and money. In Bataille's *La Femme nue (Nude Woman)*, as well as in *La Veine (Luck)* by Alfred Capus (1858-1922), a man becomes successful with the help of his mistress, then leaves her when he finds she is an embarrassment to his newly-acquired respectability. Renard's *Le Plaisir de rompre (The Pleasure of Breaking Off)* is a scene of parting in which a man leaves his mistress for an advantageous marriage.

Some writers combined sex with other themes, particularly avarice. In *Le Prince d'Aurec* by Henri Lavedan (1859-1940), the portrait of a cynical, dissolute prince is complicated by the attempts of a Jewish banker to seduce the aristocrat's wife. In Capus's *Brignol et sa fille (Brignol and His Daughter)*, an opportunistic father seeks financial gain by exploiting a young man's lust for his daughter. Henry Bernstein's (1876-1953) *Le Voleur (The Thief)* is about a woman whose theft of a large sum of money causes her to be suspected of adultery when an admirer tries to protect her. In Lavedan's *Le Duel*, the quarrel of two brothers over a woman develops into a debate between science and religion. The writers least concerned with sexual mores and passions were François de Curel (1854-1902) and Eugène Brieux (1858-1932). Curel dealt with the role of the aristocracy in modern bourgeois society in *Les Fossiles (Fossils)* and *Le Repas du lion (The Lion's Share)*. He broached a number of other subjects, including atheism and the ethics of science in *La Nouvelle idol (The New Idol)* and the effects of guilt and self-punishment in *L'Envers d'une sainte (The Other Side of a Saint)*. Brieux, more than any other French playwright, was interested in the causes of social ills rather than their effects. In *Les Trois filles de M. Dupont (M. Dupont's Three Daughters)*, he blames the system of dowry marriages for producing the unhappy bonds whose consequences preoccupied other writers. Some of the many questions he examined were the effects of divorce on children *(Le Berceau* [The Cradle]), syphilis *(L'Avariés* [Damaged Goods]), and abortion and birth control *(Maternité)*.

The following chronology of the decades from 1880 to 1920 corresponds roughly to the span of Feydeau's career. It lists the premieres of all of Feydeau's plays as well as the important revivals in his lifetime. The list of important events in the French theatre during that time is selective, intended only to illustrate the background against which Feydeau was working. Unless otherwise noted, plays are listed under the date of their first presentation in France. The symbol *R* stands for revival; *NP* means "never published"; and *UF* designates those plays left unfinished at Feydeau's death.

	Feydeau		French Theatre
		1880	
			Zola, "Le Naturalisme au théâtre"
		6 Dec.	Sardou & Najac, *Divorçons!*
		1881	
		25 Apr.	Pailleron, *Le Monde où l'on s'ennui*
		1882	
1 June	*Par la fenêtre*		
		14 Sept.	Becque, *Les Corbeaux*
		11 Dec.	Sardou, *Fédora*
		1883	
28 Jan.	*Amour et piano*		
1 June	*Gibier de potence*		
5 July	*Par la fenêtre (R)*		

Appendix B

		1884	
23 Dec.	Gibier de potence (R)		
		26 Dec.	Sardou, *Théodora*
		1885	
		19 Jan.	Dumas *fils*, *Denise*
		7 Feb.	Becque, *La Parisienne*
20 Feb.	Gibier de potence (R)		
		1886	
29 Mar.	Fiancés en herb		
17 Dec.	Tailleur pour dames		
		1887	
		17 Jan.	Dumas *fils*, *Francillon*
		Mar.	Antoine founds Théâtre Libre
		24 Nov.	Sardou, *La Tosca*
23 Dec.	La Lycéenne		
		1888	
		10 Feb.	Tolstoy, *The Power of Darkness* (Théâtre Libre)
		3 Mar.	Bisson & Mars, *Les Surprises du divorce*
13 Apr.	Un Bain de ménage		
19 Sept.	Chat en poche		
27 Sept.	Les Fiancés de Loches		
		1889	
			Claudel, *Tête d'or* (date written)
12 Jan.	L'Affaire Edouard		
		1890	
10 Mar.	C'est une femme du monde		
10 Mar.	Le Mariage de Barillon		
25 Apr.	Mademoiselle Nounou (NP)		
		30 May	Ibsen, *Ghosts* (Théâtre Libre)
		1891	
		25 Apr.	Porto-Riche, *Amoureuse*
		21 May	Maeterlinck, *L'Intruse*
		1892	
		25 Jan.	Curel, *L'Envers d'une sainte*

Appendix B 127

23 Apr.	*Monsieur chasse!*		
		1 June	Lavedan, *Le Prince d'Aurec*
5 Nov.	*Champignol malgré lui*		
		17 Nov.	Hervieu, *Les Paroles restent*
		29 Nov.	Curel, *Les Fossiles*
30 Nov.	*Le Système Ribadier*		

1893

27 Apr.	Courteline, *Boubouroche*
17 May	Lugné-Poë opens Théâtre de l'Oeuvre
22 May	Maeterlinck, *Pélléas et Mélisande*
27 Oct.	Sardou & Moreau, *Madame Sans-Gêne*

1894

9 Jan.	*Un Fil à patte*		
11 Feb.	*Notre futur*		
24 Feb.	*Le Ruban*		
		26 Feb.	Villiers de l'Isle-Adam, *Axël*
2 May	*Champignol malgré lui (R)*		
		23 Nov.	Capus, *Brignol et sa fille*
24 Nov.	*Monsieur chasse! (R)*		
5 Dec.	*L'Hôtel du Libre-Echange*		

1895

11 Feb.	Lemaître, *Le Pardon*
28 Sept.	Hervieu, *Les Tenailles*
5 Nov.	Donnay, *Amants*

1896

8 Feb.	*Le Dindon*
26 Sept.	*Les Pavés de l'ours*

10 Dec.	Jarry, *Ubu roi*

1897

6 Feb.	Richepin, *Le Chemineau*
15 Feb.	Hervieu, *La Loi de l'homme*
16 Mar.	Renard, *Le Plaisir de rompre*

128   Appendix B

29 Mar.	*Séance de nuit*		
29 Apr.	*Dormez, je le veux!*		
10 May	*Le Dindon (R)*		
		Sept.	Antoine opens Théâtre Antoine
		8 Oct.	Brieux, *Les Trois filles de M. Dupont*
		26 Nov.	Curel, *Le Repas du lion*
		28 Dec.	Rostand, *Cyrano de Bergerac*
		30 Dec.	Porto-Riche, *Le Passé*

1898

		16 Mar.	Renard, *Le Pain de ménage*
11 May	*La Bulle d'amour* (ballet scenario, *NP*)		
		19 Dec.	Brieux, *Le Berceau*

1899

17 Jan.	*La Dame de chez Maxim*		
		28 Feb.	Bernard, *L'Anglais tel qu'on le parle*
		11 Mar.	Curel, *La Nouvelle idol*
1 Apr.	*Un Fil à la patte (R)*		
5 Dec.	*L'Hôtel du Libre-Echange (R)*		
11 Dec.	*La Dame de chez Maxim (R)*		
		16 Dec.	Courteline, *Le Commissaire est bon enfant*

1900

		2 Mar.	Renard, *Poil de carotte*
		15 Mar.	Rostand, *L'Aiglon*
		15 Mar.	Brieux, *La Robe rouge*
8 May	*Champignol malgré lui (R)*		
26 July	*Le Dindon (R)*		
14 Nov.	*Séance de nuit (R)*		
14 Nov.	*Tailleur pour dames (R)*		
		12 Dec.	Courteline, *L'Article 330*

Appendix B 129

		1901	
		2 Apr.	Capus, *La Veine*
		17 Apr.	Hervieu, *La Course du flambeau*
		5 Nov.	Hervieu, *L'Enigme*
		1902	
23 Feb.	*Le Billet de Josephine (NP)*		
3 Apr.	*Dormez, je le veux! (R)*		
		17 May,	Maeterlinck, *Monna Vanna*
30 Aug.	*Un Fil à la patte (R)*		
3 Dec.	*La Duchesse des Folies-Bergère*		
		22 Dec.	Donnay, *L'Autre danger*
		1903	
2 Apr.	*L'Hôtel du Libre-Echange (R)*		
		20 Apr.	Mirbeau, *Les Affaires sont les affaires*
		25 Nov.	Courteline, *La Paix chez soi*
		1904	
1 Mar.	*La Main passe!*		
		9 Dec.	Brieux, *Maternité*
		1905	
			Claudel, *Partage de midi* (date written)
		22 Feb.	Brieux, *Les Avariés* (perf. at Liège in 1902)
		17 Apr.	Lavedan, *Le Duel*
1 May	*L'Age d'or*		
5 June	*Champignol malgré lui (R)*		
		1906	
1 Mar.	*Le Bourgeon*		
21 Mar.	*La Dame de chez Maxim (R)*		
11 May	*L'Hôtel du Libre-Echange (R)*		
27 June	*Un Fil à la patte (R)*		
		7 Dec.	Bernstein, *Le Voleur*
		10 Dec.	Bataille, *Poliche*

1907

2 Mar.	La Puce à l'oreille	17 Oct.	Bernard, *Monsieur Codomat*

1908

15 Mar.	Occupe-toi d'Amélie	27 Feb.	Bataille, *La femme nue*
15 Nov.	Feu la mère de Madame	7 Apr.	Flers & Caillavet, *Le Roi*

1909

		29 Mar.	Hervieu, *Connais-toi*
29 Oct.	Le Circuit	30 Mar.	Bataille, *Le Scandale*

1910

	Cent millions qui tombent (date written, *UF*)		
28 Jan.	Feu la mère de Madame (R)		
12 Apr.	On purge Bébé!		
27 June	La Dame de chez Maxim (R)		

1911

20 Jan.	Monsieur chasse! (R)		
29 Apr.	Champignol malgré lui (R)		
10 May	Un Fil à la patte (R)		
10 May	Feu la mère de Madame (R)		
		12 Oct.	Bernard, *Le Petit café*
23 Oct.	Monsieur chasse! (R)		
25 Nov.	"Mais n'te promène donc pas toute nue!"		
9 Dec.	Léonie est en avance		

1912

26 Apr.	On purge Bébé! (R)		
17 June	Le Dindon (R)		
8 Oct.	Séance de nuit (R)		
		20 Dec.	Claudel, *L'Annonce faite à Marie*

1913

Feb.	On va faire la cocotte (date written, *UF*)		

30 May	Le Bourgeon (R)		
1 June	La Dame de chez Maxim (R)		
15 July	Un fil à la patte (R)		
15 July	"Mais n'te promène donc pas toute nue!" (R)		
		Oct.	Copeau opens Théâtre du Vieux Colombier

1914

17 Feb.	Je ne trompe pas mon mari		
		5 June	Claudel, L'Otage
			July, Theatres closed (until Mar. 1915)

1915

		8 Apr.	Guitry, La Jalousie
8 May	Un fil à la patte (R)		
18 June	Monsieur chasse! (R)		
10 Oct.	Séance de nuit (R)		
19 Nov.	La Puce à l'oreille (R)		

1916

14 Mar.	Le Dindon (R)		
16 Apr.	La Dame de chez Maxim (R)		
30 May	L'Hôtel du Libre-Echange (R)		
14 June	Hortense a dit: "Je m'en fous!"		
9 Sept.	Un Fil à la patte (R)		
26 Oct.	La Dame de chez Maxim (R)		
9 Dec.	Je ne trompe pas mon mari (R)		

1917

			Claudel, L'Ours et la lune (date written)
19 Feb.	Champignol malgré lui (R)		
		24 June	Apollinaire, Les Mamelles de Tirésias
30 Oct.	Occupe-toi d'Amélie (R)		
		9 Nov.	Bataille, L'Amazone

1919

17 Jan.	Champignol malgré lui (R)		
16 Apr.	La Dame de chez Maxim (R)	15 Apr.	Bataille, Le Soeurs d'amour
		2 Dec.	Lenormand, Le Temps est un songe
		22 Dec.	Curel, L'Ame en folie

1920

		2 Feb.	Cocteau, Le Boeuf sur le toit
16 Apr.	"Mais n'te promène donc pas toute nue!" (R)		
		22 May	Lenormand, Ratés
28 May	L'Hôtel du Libre-Echange (R)		
13 Aug.	Champignol malgré lui (R)		
27 Aug.	L'Hôtel du Libre-Echange (R)		
25 Nov.	La Dame de chez Maxim (R)		
		20 Dec.	Crommelynck, Le Cocu magnifique

Notes

Chapter 1

1. Sören Kierkegaard, "Farce is Far More Serious," *Yale French Studies* 14 (Winter, 1954-55):3.
2. "Notes on Comedy," in *Comedy: Meaning and Form*, ed. Robert W. Corrigan (San Francisco: Chandler Publishing Co., 1965), pp. 181-83. Samuel Johnson made a similar observation in *The Rambler* (no. 125, May 28, 1751), reproduced in Paul Lauter, *Theories of Comedy* (Garden City, N.Y.: Doubleday & Co., 1964), pp. 253-58. Johnson discussed the hazards of defining or prescriptive criticism in two other *Rambler* essays (no. 156, September 14, 1751, and no. 158, September 21, 1751).
3. "Farce is Far More Serious," p. 3.
4. John Dryden, Preface to *An Evening's Love,* in Bernard F. Dukore, *Dramatic Theory and Criticism: Greeks to Grotowski* (New York: Holt, Rinehart and Winston, 1974), p. 334.
5. Kathleen Marguerite Lea, *Italian Popular Comedy,* 2 vols. (New York: Russell & Russell, 1962), 1:185.
6. Leo Hughes, *A Century of English Farce* (Princeton: Princeton University Press, 1956), p. 24.
7. Robert C. Stephenson, "Farce as Method," in Corrigan, *Comedy: Meaning and Form,* pp. 318, 321.
8. Albert C. Bermel, "Farce," in *The Reader's Encyclopedia of World Drama,* ed. John Gassner and Edward Quinn (New York: Thomas Crowell Co., 1969), p. 263.
9. Ibid., pp. 263-65.
10. George Bernard Shaw, *Our Theatres in the Nineties,* Standard ed., 3 vols. (London: Constable and Co., 1932), 2:118-19.
11. Eric Bentley, "The Psychology of Farce," in *"Let's Get a Divorce!" and Other Plays,* ed. Eric Bentley (New York: Hill and Wang, 1958), p. xiii.
12. See chap. 5, note 4.
13. C.L. Barber, *Shakespeare's Festive Comedy* (Princeton: Princeton University Press, 1959); Erich Segal, *Roman Laughter: The Comedy of Plautus* (Cambridge: Harvard University Press, 1968); Mikhail Bakhtin, *Rabelais and His World,* trans. Hélène Iswolsky (Cambridge: M.I.T. Press, 1968).
14. *Rabelais and His World,* p. 66.

15. Ibid., p. 12.
16. *De partibus animalium* 3. 10. 673^{a}28.
17. Bakhtin, *Rabelais and His World,* p. 68.
18. See N.R.F. Maier, "A Gestalt Theory of Humor," *British Journal of Psychology* 23 (1932):69-74, and D.E. Berlyne, *Conflict, Arousal, and Curiosity* (New York: McGraw-Hill Book Co., 1960), pp. 253-61.
19. On the relationship between humor and play and the function of play in the adaptive and learning processes of higher mammals, see N.J. Ellis, *Why People Play* (Englewood Cliffs, N.J.: Prentice-Hall, 1973), pp. 83-100.
20. *Rabelais and His World,* p. 10.
21. Sigmund Freud, *Jokes and Their Relation to the Unconscious,* trans. James Strachey (New York: W.W. Norton & Co., 1960), pp. 128-33. These are the situations Freud classifies as "humor," as opposed to "jokes" or the "comic."
22. Arthur Koestler, *Insight and Outlook* (New York: Macmillan Co., 1949), pp. 69-70.
23. Albert Rapp, *The Origins of Wit and Humor* (New York: E.P. Dutton & Co., 1951), p. 21. Italics in the original.
24. Cited by Max Eastman, *Enjoyment of Laughter* (New York: Simon and Schuster, 1936), p. 31.
25. Eric Bentley, *The Life of the Drama* (New York: Atheneum, 1967), p. 222. Bentley, however, feels that the abstractness of the violence is symptomatic of farce's cruelty.
26. "Farce," p. 265.
27. Ibid.
28. Ian Maxwell, *French Farce & John Heywood* (Melbourne: Melbourne University Press, 1946), p. 47.
29. Walter Kerr, *The Silent Clowns* (New York: Alfred A. Knopf, 1975), p. 64.
30. Elizabeth Sewell, *The Field of Nonsense* (London: Chatto and Windus, 1952, reprint ed., Folcroft, Pa.: Folcroft Library Editions, 1973), p. 163.
31. Feydeau, for example, spoke of controlling his characters as a chess player does his pieces. Adolphe Brisson, *Portraits intimes,* 5 vols. (Paris: Armand Colin, 1894-1901), 5 (1901):15.
32. Francisque Sarcey, *Quarante ans de théâtre,* 8 vols. (Paris: Bibliothèque des Annales, 1900-02), 4:402. See chapter 2, note 25.
33. Henri Bergson, *Le Rire* (Paris: Presses Universitaires de France, 1940), pp. 53-63, 78.
34. Sewell, *The Field of Nonsense,* pp. 36-7.
35. Bermel, "Farce," p. 264.
36. This is not to imply that fantasy is in any way inferior to farce. Fantasy might also be regarded as a game, but its rules would be quite different.
37. This is the term used by George E. Duckworth in *The Nature of Roman Comedy* (Princeton: Princeton University Press, 1952), pp. 132-36. K.J. Dover refers to the same device as "rupture of dramatic illusion." *Aristophanic Comedy* (Berkeley: University of California Press, 1972), pp. 55-59.

38. Like other devices of farce, the frank admission of theatrical pretense may be used for serious purposes, as it is at the end of *The Beggar's Opera*.
39. Kerr, *The Silent Clowns*, p. 131.
40. Introduction to *Four Farces by Georges Feydeau*, trans. Norman Shapiro (Chicago: University of Chicago Press, 1970), p. xvii.
41. Although Feydeau respected the "dramatic illusion," he sometimes called attention to the stage and its artifice in more subtle ways. Twice in *La Puce à l'oreille* and once in *Occupe-toi d'Amélie*, for example, characters explain their present situations with examples drawn from the theatre, indirectly reminding the audience that they are watching a play. In *Occupe-toi d'Amélie*, an earlier play by Feydeau is specifically mentioned, and in *La Puce à l'oreille*, the example comes from a play that had been presented in the same theatre as *La Puce à l'oreille* only a few months before. Georges Feydeau, *Théâtre complet*, 9 vols. (Paris: Editions du Bélier, 1948-56), vol. 1: *Occupe-toi d'Amélie*, act 3, 2nd tableau, sc. 4, p. 149; vol. 4: *La Puce à l'oreille*, act 1, sc. 4, p. 131; sc. 8, p. 140.
42. Cf. Bentley, *The Life of the Drama*, p. 247.
43. For a discussion of the theatrical nature of the mask and its relation to farce, see Vsevolod Meyerhold, "Farce," trans. Nora Beeson, in Corrigan, *Comedy: Meaning and Form*, pp. 313-16.
44. Enid Welsford, *The Fool* (London: Faber and Faber, 1968), p. 318.
45. Ibid., p. 319.
46. Lionel Abel, *Metatheatre* (New York: Hill and Wang, 1963), p. 61.
47. Recall Harpo Marx's trick of extending his knee in such a way that another person would grab it in an automatic, unthinking gesture.
48. *The Silent Clowns*, p. 72.
49. Ibid., p. 117.
50. Lea, *Italian Popular Comedy*, 1:196.
51. Grace Frank, *The Medieval French Drama* (Oxford: Clarendon Press, 1954), p. 244.
52. *French Farce & John Heywood*, p. 19.
53. Frank, *The Medieval French Drama*, p. 244; Maxwell, *French Farce & John Heywood*, pp. 18-19.
54. Maxwell, *French Farce & John Heywood*, p. 19.
55. Ibid., p. 38. *Le Cuvier (The Washtub)*, one of the better known farces, provides a good example of these characteristics. The "point" about which the action revolves is the *rollet*, or list of household chores, dictated to the husband by the domineering wife in the first phase of the action. The second begins when the wife falls into the washtub and is in danger of drowning. The husband answers her frantic pleas for help by reading the list aloud and interjecting variations of the phrase, "That's not on my list!" Part of the sense of balance comes from the fact that only material circumstances have altered their relationship in the second half. Until the closing lines, the wife is aggressive even in her distress, and the husband is passive in victory.
56. "It is in the nature of farce to weave itself round some concrete thing" (Ibid., p. 38).

57. Ibid., p. 46. Maxwell lists some of the artificial devices used by farce writers: "sequences... of single-word speeches or split lines in which the close answers or completes the opening, comic litanies, monosyllabic answers falling on the rhyme word, and the like" (pp. 43-44). Another favorite device was the triolet. Maxwell gives an example from the *Farce de arquemination* in which the rigidity and artifice of the verse form serve as counterpoint to the frantic sense of disorder.

58. Stark Young, *Immortal Shadows* (New York: Hill and Wang, 1959), p. 177.

59. H.B. Charlton, *Shakespearian Comedy* (New York: Barnes and Noble, 1938), p. 66.

60. Maxwell describes medieval farce as concerned "rather with the accidents of a moment than with permanent relations and matters of weight" *(French Farce & John Heywood,* p. 17).

61. Daniel C. Gerould, "The Well-Made Play and Its Heritage" (Manuscript in the possession of the author), pp. 43-44.

62. Ibid., p. 55.

63. Ibid., p. 57.

64. See William Archer, *Play-Making: A Manual of Craftsmanship* (New York: Dover Publications, 1960): p. 119.

65. Gerould, "The Well-Made Play and Its Heritage," pp. 53-54.

Chapter 2

1. *Théâtre complet*, vol. 2: *Le Système Ribadier*, act 1, sc. 4, p. 72. Subsequent references to the plays contained in the *Théâtre complet* will give only the volume number followed by the name of the play and act, scene, and page numbers. Unless otherwise noted, the translations are my own.

2. *Hypnotisé*, by Emile de Najac and Albert Milland. A hypnotist is hypnotised by the husband of the woman he was pursuing and is given a desire to be deceived by his own wife. Described in Edouard Noël and Edmond Stoullig, eds., *Les Annales du théâtre et de la musique*, 41 vols. (Paris: Charpentier et Cie, 1875-1916), année 14, 1888, pp. 245-46.

3. Martin Meisel describes the English farcical comedy—mostly adaptations of French originals—as following this basic pattern in *Shaw and the Nineteenth-Century Theatre* (Princeton: Princeton University Press, 1963), pp. 256-57.

4. There are virtually no standard translations of Feydeau's titles. Since the titles of published English versions of his plays often bear little or no resemblance to the original titles, I have supplied literal translations for the names of the plays. Titles of particularly well-known English versions (e.g. *Hotel Paradiso*) are mentioned, but the reader interested in available English translations should refer to the bibliography.

5. A word-for-word rendering of this virtually untranslatable phrase would be "a string on the paw." It refers to someone so subjugated to the will of another that he can be led about like a puppy with only a string tied to its paw.

6. E.g., vol. 3, *La Main passe!*, act 2, sc. 2, p. 73; and vol. 7, *La Dame de chez Maxim*, act 2, sc. 8, p. 175.

7. *Un Monsieur qui est condamné à mort* (Paris: Ollendorff, 1899).

Notes to Chapter 2

8. For a thorough treatment of this aspect of Feydeau's work, see Norman Richard Shapiro, "Suffering and Punishment in the Theatre of Georges Feydeau," *Tulane Drama Review* 5 (September 1960):117-26.

9. Neil Cole Arvin describes the historical development of the *vaudeville* in *Eugene Scribe and the French Theatre, 1815-1860* (Cambridge: Harvard University Press, 1924; reprint ed., New York: Benjamin Blom, 1967). pp. 33-37.

10. *The Nature of Roman Comedy*, pp. 140-41.

11. Hugh Allison Smith, *Main Currents of Modern French Drama* (New York: H. Holt and Co., 1925; reprint ed., Freeport, N.Y.: Books for Libraries Press, 1968), p. 117.

12. William Archer devotes two pages to defending the plausibility of just one such exit in *Playmaking* (pp. 78-79). See also Gerould, "The Well-Made Play and Its Heritage," p. 37.

13. See Stephan S. Stanton, ed., *"Camille" and Other Plays* (New York: Hill and Wang, 1957), p. xxviii.

14. Jacques Lorcey, *Georges Feydeau* (Paris: La Table Ronde, 1972), pp. 92-94, 96-98, 100-101, 105-6.

15. *Figaro*, 24 December 1887, p. 3.

16. Noël and Stoullig, eds., *Les Annales du théâtre et de la musique*, année 14, 1888, pp. 300-301, 363.

17. Francisque Sarcey, *Quarante ans de théâtre*, 8 vols. (Paris: Bibliothèque des Annales, 1900-1902), 8 (1902):180-83.

18. See pp. 21-22 above.

19. The best known use of this device is in Pailleron's *Le Monde où l'on s'ennui*. The plot hinges on the numerous interpretations given to an unaddressed, unsigned note.

20. No one exploited this theme in a serious vein more than Porto-Riche. Frank Chandler observed that "deception... is the normal expectancy of every man or woman in the plays of Porto-Riche." *Modern Continental Playwrights* (New York: Harper & Row, 1931), p. 171.

21. Vol. 4, act 1, sc. 8, p. 155.

22. Ibid., act 3, sc. 14, p. 226.

23. Vol. 4, *L'Hôtel du Libre-Echange*, act 3, sc. 5, p. 103.

24. Vol. 4, act 2, sc. 4, p. 166; act 3, sc. 12, p. 221.

25. Sarcey felt that it was a great advantage to the modern writers of comedies to have established "between the *vaudevillistes* and the audience an agreed upon strategy of devices and effects... We comprehend everything at half a word, because we know the game." *Quarante ans de théâtre*, 4:402.

26. Quoted in Michel Georges-Michel, *Un Demi-siècle de gloires théâtrales* (Paris: Editions André Bonne, 1950), p. 124.

27. Gerould compares the construction of a well-made play to "building an entire house for the sake of the roof." "The Well-Made Play and Its Heritage," p. 35.

28. Feydeau was not original even in this inversion of popular dramatic theory. Labiche had used the same technique in *Un Chapeau de paille d'Italie*.

29. Feydeau often portrays women as quite cavalier in their attitudes toward *les convenances*. A characteristic shared by the ingénues, wives, and *cocottes* of Feydeau's world is a willingness to use scandal as a weapon. Bois d'Enghien's fiancée uses essentially the same trick employed earlier by Finette in *La Lycéenne* (vol. 8, act 3, sc. 7). On scandal used as a weapon by wives, see p. 67.

30. The first act illustrates this "looseness" of construction. The opening scene with the phonograph, the argument between Amélie and her brother, and several other scenes are there for their own comic sake, not to provide exposition or preparation for later events. These scenes are not irrelevant to the play, for they reveal the nature of Amélie's world and the people who inhabit it, but they do not provide preparation comparable to that of the well-made play. The only hint Feydeau gives that Amélie and Marcel will be discovered together in bed when the curtain rises on the second act is Etienne's admonition to "look after Amélie." The hint is effective only because the audience already knows what kind of people they are.

31. Emile Faguet, *Journal des débats*, 12 December 1902, p. 1128, quoted in Norman Richard Shapiro, Introduction to *Four Farces by Georges Feydeau*, trans. Norman Richard Shapiro (Chicago: University of Chicago Press, 1970), p. xxxvii. Lorcey makes a similar comment in *Georges Feydeau*, p. 166.

32. George Bernard Shaw, *Complete Plays with Prefaces*, 6 vols. (New York: Dodd, Mead & Co., 1963), 6:343.

33. Their punishment contrasts with the harsh fate which awaited most adulteresses in drama. See p. 68.

34. Unlike Feydeau, Courteline does not limit his use of this basic method to domestic conflict. In *Le Commissaire est bon enfant*, one of the antagonists is an actual lunatic. In others (e.g., *La Paix chez soi, L'Article 330*), one combatant seems to have made a conscious decision to use irrationality as a weapon against a mad world.

35. Vol. 6, act 1, sc. 1, p. 215.

36. Vol. 7, act 1, sc. 6, p. 282.

37. Lorcey, *Georges Feydeau*, p. 251.

38. *Overruled*. Shaw details his objections to the lies, evasions, and stratagems of farcical comedy in the preface to this play. *Complete Plays with Prefaces*, 6:343-44.

Chapter 3

1. André Roussin, "Le Cas Feydeau," *World Premières Mondiales*, February 1963, p. 4.

2. Quoted in Lorcey, *Georges Feydeau*, p. 198. Adolphe Brisson reports a conversation in which Feydeau told him: "My plays are entirely improvised; the overall effect and the details, the ground work and the structure; everything comes into place just as I write it. And I've never made a blueprint for a single one of them" *Portraits intimes*, 5:14.

3. *The Theory of Comedy* (Bloomington: Indiana University Press, 1968), p. 63.

4. Vol. 6, act 1, sc. 8, p. 123; act 2, sc. 14, p. 168; act 3, sc. 4, p. 182.

5. Vol. 6, act 1, sc. 15, p. 50; act 3, sc. 5, p. 98.

6. Vol. 2, act 1, sc. 8, p. 135.

7. Quoted in Georges-Michel, *Un Demi-siècle de gloires théâtrales*, p. 124.
8. Ibid. Cf. Bermel, "Farce," p. 265 (quoted on p. 7 above).
9. Vol. 6, *Champignol malgré lui*.
10. Vol. 6, act 1, sc. 20, p. 145.
11. Vol. 4, act 2, sc. 8, p. 182.
12. *Italian Popular Comedy*, p. 195.
13. Vol. 6, *Un Fil à la patte*, act 3, sc. 8, p. 194.
14. This is also true of the unfinished *On va faire la cocotte* (vol. 7). The conflicting attitudes of the protagonists regarding sex and marriage are brought into direct, explosive confrontation.
15. *Enjoyment of Laughter*, p. 150.
16. Jacques Feydeau, quoted in Lorcey, *Georges Feydeau*, p. 203.
17. Vol. 6, sc. 5, p. 13.
18. "The Psychology of Farce," p. xv.
19. Vol. 3, act 3, sc. 4-5, pp. 280-83.
20. Vol. 5, act 2, sc. 10, p. 44.
21. Vol. 7, sc. 3, p. 259.
22. Vol. 5, *Le Mariage de Barillon*, act 2, sc. 8, p. 41.
23. Vol. 2, act 1, sc. 2, p. 123.
24. Ibid., act 2, sc. 12, pp. 173-74. In addition to material indicated by ellipses, all stage directions have been deleted, as they will be in subsequent quotations of dialogue unless essential to the meaning or the point being illustrated.
25. E.g., Sarcey, *Quarante ans de théâtre*, 8:179; Léon Treich, "Le dixième anniversaire de la mort de Georges Feydeau," *Les Nouvelles littéraires* (Paris), 30 May 1931, p. 5; Marcel Achard, Introduction to *Théâtre complet* by Georges Feydeau, 1:14.
26. Vol. 5, *Le Mariage de Barillon*, act 3, sc. 5, p. 58.
27. Bentley, *The Life of the Drama*, p. 245.
28. Jean-Louis Barrault, *Une Troupe et ses auteurs* (Paris: Vautrain, 1950), p. 52.
29. Vol. 4, act 1, sc. 11, p. 55.
30. Welsford, *The Fool*, p. 66.
31. Ibid.
32. Feydeau was not unique in using this kind of comic fatalism. The hero of another vaudeville escapes his despised mother-in-law through divorce only to acquire two mothers-in-law when his ex-wife marries the father of his new wife. When the discovery is made, the former mother-in-law declares triumphantly, "It's the finger of God!" Alexandre Bisson and Anthony Mars, *Les Surprises du divorce* (Paris: Editions Stock, 1947), act 2, sc. 15, p. 105.
33. Vol. 3, act 1, sc. 2, p. 40.

34. Vol. 4, *L'Hôtel du Libre-Echange,* act 2, sc. 5, p. 71.
35. Vol. 3, *On purge Bébé,* sc. 4, p. 183; vol. 5, *Le Mariage de Barillon,* act 1, sc. 4, p. 15.
36. Vol. 5, *Monsieur chasse!,* act 3, sc. 4, p. 135.
37. Fernand Weyl [Nozière], "Georges Feydeau," *Gil Blas* (Paris), 4 June 1913, p. 1.
38. Cf. James Kern Feibleman, *In Praise of Comedy: A Study of Its Theory and Practice* (New York: Russell & Russell, 1939), p. 180: "Comedy is always illustrative of the principle.... that chance begets order. It is indeed a principle upon which instinctively the great comedians depend."
39. E.g., Scribe's *Le Verre d'eau* (act 2, sc. 7-8), in which one of the characters dramatically appears the moment he is declared safely out of the country.
40. Many critics have noted similarities between dreams and extreme or farcical forms of comedy. K.J. Dover discusses the dream-like quality of Aristophanes' plays in *Aristophanic Comedy,* pp. 41-45. Bermel says that the atmosphere of farce often "approximates the condition of a dream world or, rather, of a nightmare:. . . ", "Farce," p. 264.
41. Cf. Bermel, "Farce," p. 265: "Dream fears [such as those realized in farce] are familiar to audiences. As they recognize them, consciously or unconsciously, they laugh; they are relieved witnesses of somebody else's nightmare." Léon Treich quotes Feydeau as saying that a *vaudeville* should be based on a situation "as tragic as possible, a situation that would give the shivers to a night watchman at the morgue, and you try to bring out the burlesque side of it." "Le dixième anniversaire de la mort de Georges Feydeau," p. 5.
42. Vol. 6, act 2, sc. 7, p. 160; act 3, sc. 6, p. 189.
43. *The Life of the Drama,* p. 241.
44. Vol. 5, act 2, sc. 17, p. 125.
45. Vol. 7, act 1, sc. 8.
46. Vol. 5, *Monsieur chasse!,* act 3, sc. 4, p. 134.
47. Vol. 4, *La Puce à l'oreille,* act 2, sc. 7, pp. 176-77.
48. Vol. 8, *La Duchesse des Folies-Bergère,* act 4, sc. 9, pp. 219-20.
49. Vol. 1, *L'Affaire Edouard,* act 3, sc. 9, p. 201.
50. Vol. 2, act 3, sc. 3, p. 49.
51. Evidence of the importance of the aside in this function is the fact that it continued to play a large role even as Feydeau's work became more "realistic," and as he ceased using other conventional devices such as the opening monologue to the audience. In the late one-act plays, in which misunderstandings play a very minor role, the use of the aside is minimal.
52. Vol. 1, act 1, sc. 2-5.
53. Vol. 7, act 3, sc. 7, p. 204.
54. An example of Feydeau's use of ancient theatrical devices in more elaborate form. This one is essentially the same as the tunnel between the houses in the *Miles Gloriosus* of Plautus.
55. Vol. 5, *Le Circuit,* act 2, sc. 17, p. 207; vol. 2, *Le Dindon,* act 2, sc. 15, pp. 179-80.
56. Raymond Rudorff describes many manifestations of this interest in *The Belle Epoque* (New York: Saturday Review Press, 1973), pp. 185-205.

57. Lorcey, *Georges Feydeau*, p. 200.

58. Claude Berton, "Georges Feydeau et l'âme de chez Maxim's," *Les Nouvelles littéraires* (Paris), 5 April 1924, p. 4.

59. Jules Huret, *Loges et coulisses* (Paris: Editions de la Revue Blanche, 1901), pp. 289-90.

60. See pp. 100-101.

61. Its reliance on the familiar and the everyday tends to make farce dependent for its effects on the specific culture which engendered it, making translation difficult. The importance of the familiar seems to have been instinctively understood by British and American adaptors of French farces who usually transplanted the action to London or New York.

62. There has been a recent increase in this type of farce. The technique is used extensively by Mel Brooks, notably in his television series "When Things Were Rotten" and the film *History of the World, Part 1*.

63. *The Life of the Drama*, p. 229.

64. A pointed moral or lesson was not uncommon in the *vaudeville*. *Divorçons*, by Victorien Sardou and Emile de Najac, is an example of a farcical play which delivers an obvious lesson in conventional morality.

65. Vol. 4, *L'Hôtel du Libre-Echange*, act 2, sc. 1, p. 67.

66. Vol. 5, *Le Mariage de Barillon*, act 2, sc. 6, p. 39.

67. Ibid., sc. 7, p. 40.

68. Vol. 7, *La Dame de chez Maxim*, act 1, sc. 17, p. 120.

69. Ibid.

70. Ibid., act 1, sc. 15, p. 118.

71. Vol. 2, *Le Dindon*, act 2, sc. 4, p. 157.

72. Vol. 8, *La Lycéenne*, act 1, sc. 6, p. 18.

73. E.g., vol. 6, *Un Fil à la patte*, act 2, sc. 2, pp. 149-50; and vol. 6, *Notre futur*, sc. 2, p. 207.

74. Vol. 3, *La Main passe!*, act 1, sc. 1, p. 39.

75. Ibid., act 1, sc. 11, p. 60.

76. Vol. 6, act 1, sc. 1, p. 31.

77. Vol. 4, act 1, sc. 8, p. 53.

78. Vol. 2, *Le Dindon*, act 1, sc. 10, p. 140.

79. There were exceptions to this rule, the most notable of which was *Le Plus heureux des trois*, mentioned above. Labiche avoids the prohibition by stressing (as the title indicates) the difficulties and embarrassments of the wife and her lover, but the play was still considered unusual. During Feydeau's career the Naturalists and others were breaking such conventions in plays like Becque's *La Parisienne* and Courteline's *Boubouroche*. But the majority opinion, and certainly that which prevailed on the Boulevard, was not far from that expressed by Brander Matthews. Matthews criticizes the death of the heroine of *Frou-Frou* as inappropriate to the overall tone of the play, but concedes that the authors had little choice: "To say what fate shall be meted out to the woman taken in adultery is always a hard task for a dramatist." *French Dramatists of the Nineteenth Century*, 3rd ed. (New York: Charles Scribner's Sons, 1901; reprint ed., New York: Benjamin Blom, 1968), p. 263.

80. Vol. 3, *Je ne trompe pas mon mari.*
81. Even in this case the pardon is not genuine, as the husband is merely afraid of what the scandal would do to his business affairs. Vol. 2, *Le Système Ribadier,* act 3, sc. 5, p. 110.
82. Vol. 4, *L'Hôtel du Libre-Echange,* act 1, sc. 4, p. 45.
83. Vol. 2, act 1, sc. 4, p. 129.
84. Lorcey, *Georges Feydeau,* p. 141.
85. Vol. 6, act 1, sc. 19, p. 144.
86. Vol. 4, act 3, sc. 14, p. 224.
87. Vol. 8, act 4, sc. 4, p. 210.
88. Vol. 2, act 2, sc. 10, pp. 168-69.
89. Vol. 3, act 1, sc. 3, p. 42.
90. Vol. 4, *L'Hôtel du Libre-Echange,* act 2, sc. 21, p. 91.
91. Vol. 5, *Le Mariage de Barillon,* act 1, sc. 3, p. 13.
92. Vol. 2, *Le Système Ribadier,* act 2, sc. 3, pp. 92-93.
93. Vol. 7, *La Dame de chez Maxim,* act 3, sc. 17, p. 223.
94. Vol. 2, *Le Système Ribadier,* act 3, sc 3, p. 105.
95. Vol. 3, *On purge Bébé!* and vol. 1, *Hortense a dit: "Je m'en fous!"* His full-length play, *Je ne trompe pas mon mari,* is the only one in which a duel actually takes place during the course of the play.
96. Penelope Gilliatt, *Unholy Fools: Wits, Comics, Disturbers of the Peace: Film and Theatre* (New York: Viking Press, 1973), p. 175.
97. Vol. 9, Epilogue, p. 198.

Chapter 4

1. E.g., vol. 2, *Le Dindon,* and vol. 4, *La Puce à l'oreille.*
2. "The contest of the *eiron* and *alazon* forms the basis of the comic action,...." Northrup Frye, *Anatomy of Criticism: Four Essays* (Princeton: Princeton University Press, 1957), p. 172. Cf. Duckworth, "Since persons usually make themselves out better than they are and only rarely does a person pretend to be worse than he is, the imposter and the braggart are far more frequent in comedy than the ironical person who feigns stupidity." *The Nature of Roman Comedy,* p. 322.
3. Vol. 2, sc. 2, p. 230.
4. Vol. 4, act 1, sc. 9, p. 146.
5. Vol. 2, act 1, sc. 1, p. 9.
6. Vol. 4, *Léonie est en avance,* sc. 7, pp. 255-56; vol. 3, *La Main passe!,* act 3, sc. 4, p. 96.
7. Vol. 5, act 2, sc. 17, p. 126; act 3, sc. 11, p. 148.
8. Vol. 6, *Cent millions qui tombent,* act 1, sc. 9, p. 224; act 2, sc. 2-3, pp. 246-48.

Notes to Chapter 4   143

9. Vol. 2, act 2, sc. 3, p. 93.
10. Vol. 4, act 1, sc. 3, p. 43.
11. Ibid., sc. 6, pp. 47-49.
12. Chandebise is unusual in his lack of self confidence, an exceptional characteristic for a figure in farce. This may be why he becomes identified in the second act with Poche, who is the opposite of Chandebise both in lacking any trace of pride and in being completely unaware of his deficiencies. See pp. 79-80.
13. E.g., Pierre Voltz, "This *vaudevilliste* ... has ... no sense of the life of his characters, which he deliberately sacrifices to the most mechanical gaiety." *La Comédie* (Paris: Librairie Armand Colin, 1964), p. 159.
14. "The Society of the Incomplete: The Psychology and Structure of Farce" (Ph.D. dissertation, University of Michigan, 1969).
15. Vol. 5, act 1, sc. 2, p. 12.
16. Vol. 6, *Gibier de potence,* sc. 1, p. 10 See p. 49 above.
17. Feydeau described his attitude toward his characters and his work as extremely objective. While working on a play, he said, "I am not amused by it; I maintain my gravity, the sangfroid of a chemist preparing a prescription." Quoted in Adolphe Brisson, *Portraits intimes,* 5:16.
18. *Unholy Fools: Wits, Comics, Disturbers of the Peace: Film and Theater,* p. 184.
19. Oblivion in farce (blindness to what should be obvious) is not limited to personal defects. Chambers notes a "singular kind of oblivion" in *The Comedy of Errors* which allows the characters to be unaware of their twins and to so readily accept appearances for reality. *Shakespeare: A Survey,* p. 30. There is the same kind of oblivion in Shakespeare's source, especially in the final scene when the brothers, although face to face, require a lengthy argument to convince them of the obvious.
20. Vol. 9, act 3, sc. 12, p. 61.
21. Vol. 6, act 1, sc. 16, p. 138.
22. Vol. 2, act 2, sc. 2, p. 87.
23. Vol. 8, sc. 2, p. 246.
24. Vol. 5, act 3, sc. 6, p. 137.
25. Ibid., sc. 7, p. 141.
26. Vol. 4, *La Puce à l'oreille,* act 2, sc. 1, p. 160.
27. Vol. 7, act 1, sc. 2, p. 89.
28. Vol. 9, act 1, sc. 8, p. 16.
29. Vol. 8, *"Mais n'te promène donc pas toute nue!",* sc. 2, p. 245.
30. Vol. 7, act 1, sc. 1, pp. 27-29.
31. Vol. 4, act 1, sc. 5, p. 135.
32. Vol. 2, act 1, sc. 17, p. 150.
33. Vol. 3, act 4, sc. 7, p. 148.

34. Vol. 4, sc. 4, p. 26.
35. Vol. 6, act 1, sc. 1, p. 32.
36. Vol. 9, act 2, sc. 2, p. 32.
37. Vol. 5, act 2, sc. 4, p. 103; sc. 6, p. 108.
38. Vol. 4, act 2, sc. 6, p. 172.
39. Vol. 7, sc. 1, p. 10.
40. Vol. 8, *"Mais n'te promène donc pas toute nue!",* sc. 5, p. 255.
41. Vol. 2, act 1, sc. 2, pp. 125-26.
42. Vol. 6, *Cent millions qui tombent,* act 1, sc. 14, p. 236.
43. Ibid., sc. 11, p. 228.
44. Ibid., act 2, sc. 10, p. 267.
45. Ibid., sc. 4, p. 251.
46. Vol. 6, act 1, sc. 1, p. 32.
47. Feydeau's characters reach their heights of eloquence when describing the only possible true love as that of a lover for his mistress. See vol. 5, *Monsieur chasse!,* act 2, sc. 4, p. 103; and vol. 2, *Le Dindon,* act 1, sc. 4, p. 130.
48. Vol. 5, act 1, sc. 3, p. 80.
49. Vol. 2, *Le Dindon,* act 1, sc. 2, p. 127.
50. Ibid., p. 125.
51. Vol. 6, *Un Fil à la patte,* act 2, sc. 3, p. 151.
52. Ibid., act 1, sc. 8, p. 124.
53. See p. 46.
54. Lucienne's first reaction upon meeting Camille is to assume that he is a foreigner. Vol. 4, *La Puce à l'oreille,* act 1, sc. 3, p. 126.
55. Vol. 4, act 1, sc. 13, p. 57.
56. Vol. 3, act 3, sc. 5, p. 99.
57. Ibid., act 1, sc. 7, p. 54.
58. The retired doctor and his deaf wife in *Le Dindon* (vol. 2) are exceptions.
59. Vol. 8, act 1, sc. 6, pp. 16-18.
60. Vol. 2, act 2, sc. 3, p. 91; sc. 6, p. 98.
61. E.g., vol. 2, *Séance de nuit,* sc. 10, p. 242; vol. 7, *La Dame de chez Maxim,* act 3, sc. 19, pp. 225-26; vol. 2, *Chat en poche,* act 1, sc. 6, p. 20.
62. E.g., Général Petypon in vol. 7, *La Dame de chez Maxim,* act 3, sc. 17, pp. 219-23, and Capitaine Camaret in vol. 6, *Champignol malgré lui,* act 2, sc. 3, p. 56.
63. Erich Segal argues that the comedy of Plautus should be understood as taking place in a festival or Saturnalian atmosphere, in which the triumph of the slave represents a holiday

reversal of normal values and standards. *Roman Laughter: The Comedy of Plautus*, pp. 99-169.

64. Francis de Croisset (who collaborated with Feydeau on *Le Circuit*) considered the sentimentality of Pailleron and the gaiety of Meilhac and Halévy to be related to the number of young girls in the plays of the former and their absence in those of the latter. *La Vie parisienne au théâtre* (Paris: Bernard Grasset, 1929), pp. 58-59.

65. Adrienne, in *Champignol malgré lui* (vol. 6), is exceptional. The most conventional of the ingénues, her romantic scene with Célestin in the third act is the only such love scene in Feydeau's theatre.

66. Norman Shapiro discusses the satiric undercurrent in the play and its relevance to the controversy in "Topical Allusions in the Theatre of Georges Feydeau" (Ph.D. dissertation, Harvard University, 1958), pp. 215-24.

67. Ibid., p. 216. Note also that La Môme Crevette was a *lycéenne* and lost her innocence while in the pursuit of higher learning. Vol. 7, *La Dame de chez Maxim*, act 1, sc. 6, p. 98.

68. Vol. 8, *La Lycéenne*, act 1, sc. 6, p. 17.

69. Ibid., sc. 13, p. 30.

70. For example, see Bouzin's rationalization for a similar song in vol. 6, *Un Fil à la patte*, act 1, sc. 8, p. 124.

71. Auguste Vitu, *Figaro* (Paris), 24 December 1887, p. 3.

72. Vol. 6, act 2, sc. 1, pp. 147-48.

73. Ibid., sc. 2, pp. 150-51.

74. Ibid., act 3, sc. 8, pp. 196-97.

75. Vol. 8, *Le Ruban*, act 1, sc. 2, pp. 71-72.

76. Ibid., act 3, sc. 12, p. 122.

77. Vol. 4, sc. 1, p. 9.

78. Vol. 8, *"Mais n'te promène donc pas toute nue!"*, sc. 2, p. 247; vol. 1, *Hortense a dit: "Je m'en fous!"*, sc. 8, p. 247.

79. Vol. 2, *Le Système Ribadier*, act 1, sc. 4, p. 72.

80. Vol. 5, act 3, sc. 14, p. 152.

81. Vol. 2, act 3, sc. 6, p. 111.

82. Vol. 3, act 4, sc. 4, p. 135.

83. Vol. 7, *On va faire la cocotte*, act 1, sc. 1, p. 264.

84. "Marriage is popular because it combines the maximum of temptation with the maximum of opportunity." "Maxims for Revolutionists," *Complete Plays with Prefaces*, 3:733.

85. Vol. 3, *Je ne trompe pas mon mari*, act 1, sc. 18, p. 232.

86. Vol. 7, *On va faire la cocotte*, act 1, sc. 2, p. 274.

87. Vol. 4, *L'Hôtel du Libre-Echange*, act 2, sc. 6, pp. 73-74.

88. Vol. 2, act 3, sc. 9.

89. Vol. 7, sc. 2, p. 242.
90. Ibid., sc. 3, p. 249.
91. Vol. 1, sc. 2, p. 234.
92. Vol. 1, act 1, sc. 2, 14.
93. Vol. 3, *La Main passe!*, act 4, sc. 8.
94. Vol. 1, act 1, sc. 3, p. 159. This was a jibe at Fernand Samuel, Feydeau's former employer and director of the Théâtre de la Renaissance, who changed his name from Adolphe Louveau when his family objected to having their name associated with the theatre. See Lorcey, *Georges Feydeau*, p. 65.
95. Vol. 8, act 1, sc. 4, p. 142. Another example is John in vol. 6, *Cent millions qui tombent*, act 1, sc. 1, p. 215.
96. Vol. 2, act 2, sc. 1, p. 27.
97. Vol. 8, act 1, sc. 1, p. 11.
98. Vol. 2, act 3, sc. 1, 9.
99. Vol. 6, act 1, sc. 1, p. 215.
100. See p. 69.
101. Vol. 2, act 1, sc. 15, p. 148. The word is also used to describe Homenidès. Vol. 4, *La Puce à l'oreille*, act 1, sc. 13, p. 154.
102. Vol. 2, act 2, sc. 10, pp. 168-69.
103. Vol. 4, act 2, sc. 7-8.
104. Vol. 3, *La Main passe!*, act 2.
105. Vol. 3, *Je ne trompe pas mon mari*, act 1, sc. 16, p. 230.
106. See Rudorff, *The Belle Epoque*, pp. 62-65.
107. Vol. 2, *Le Dindon*, act 2, sc. 4, p. 158.
108. Lorcey, *Georges Feydeau*, p. 106. Vol. 6, *Un Fil à la patte*, act 1, sc. 16, p. 137. Another foreigner based on a real person is Soldignac, the Englishman from Marseille, who was drawn in part from the actor Max Dearly. See Edwin Daniel Yahiel, "Georges Feydeau et son oeuvre" (Ph.D. dissertation, University of Michigan, 1955)., p. 149.
109. Vol. 3, *Je ne trompe pas mon mari*, act 1, sc. 3, p. 211.
110. Anne Manson, "Quand les trois grandes régnaient sur Paris," in *La Belle Epoque*, ed. Gilbert Guilleminault (Paris: Editions Denoël, 1957), p. 165.
111. Vol. 1, *Occupe-toi d'Amélie*, act 2, sc. 6, pp. 94-95.
112. Ibid., sc. 10-11, pp. 102-103.
113. Manson, "Quand les trois grandes régnaient sur Paris," p. 163.
114. Vol. 8, act 1, sc. 9, pp. 78-81. According to Lorcey, Feydeau was obliged for reasons of casting to cut two such unnecessary roles—in this case female circus performers—from the cast of *L'Affaire Edouard*. *Georges Feydeau*, p. 100.

115. Vol. 4, act 2, sc. 4. It is probably more than coincidence that the initials of her nickname are identical with those of Cora Pearl, the Second Empire *cocotte*. Mlle Pearl once wagered her guests that she could serve them some meat that none would dare cut. Then she had herself borne in on a large silver salver, unadorned but for a garnish of parsley. Joanna Richardson, *The Courtesans* (New York: World Publishing Company, 1967), pp. 53-54.

116. Vol. 1, sc. 1, p. 233.

117. Quoted in Lorcey, *Georges Feydeau*, p. 229.

118. Vol. 9, act 3, sc. 10, p. 303.

119. See p. 52.

120. See Segal's discussion of the limited nature of the Plautine slave's misrule and his apparent acceptance of the fact that it must end. *Roman Laughter: The Comedy of Plautus*, pp. 137-69.

121. Vol. 3, act 3, sc. 5-6, pp. 283-87.

122. "Quand les trois grandes régnaient sur Paris," pp. 182-86.

123. Lorcey, *Georges Feydeau*, p. 199.

Chapter 5

1. Voltz, *La Comédie*, p. 159; Jean Morgan, "Georges Feydeau et Francis de Croisset," *Le Gaulois* (Paris), 28 October 1909, p. 1.

2. *French Dramatists of the Nineteenth Century*.

3. *Quarante ans de théâtre*, 8 (1902):179-80.

4. Paul Morand, "Champignol parle au nom des dieux," *La Parisienne* 10 (October 1953):1424-25. The critics who have compared Feydeau to various avant-garde playwrights include Gérard Bauer, *"Occupe-toi d'Amélie," La Revue de Paris*, April 1948, p. 149; Claude Damiens, "Georges Feydeau, le maître du naturalisme absurde," *Paris-Théâtre*, no. 150 (1959), p. 3; Gilles Sandier, "Un faux Stendal, un vrai Feydeau," *Arts*, 13 (22-28 December 1965):39; Renée Saurel "Une bonne soirée Feydeau," *Les Lettres françaises*, no. 1197 (31 August-6 September 1967), p. 24; Robert Kemp, *La Vie du Théâtre* (Paris: Albin Michel, 1956), p. 140.

5. Roger J. Steiner, "The Perennial Georges Feydeau," *Symposium* 15 (Spring 1961):53; Shapiro, "Topical Allusions in the Theatre of Georges Feydeau," pp. 148-50, 224, 263; Lorcey, *Georges Feydeau*, p. 199.

6. "Forms of Shock Treatment for a World Out of Plumb," *Times Literary Supplement*, 18 June 1971, p. 689.

7. Shaw's principal objection to farcical comedy was its lack of sympathy and humanity. But he also disliked its refusal to deal honestly with the moral and social questions it seemed to be raising. He felt that the "paradoxical wit" of W.S. Gilbert was "morally unjustifiable." Gilbert had to "depend for the piquancy of his ridicule on the general assumption of the validity of the very thing ridiculed" (*London Music in 1888-89* [New York: Vienna House, 1973], p. 283; *Music in London* 2 vols. [New York: Vienna House, 1973], 1:238). He later clarified this point of view:

"The worst thing that can happen in a play is that the people with whom the audience makes friends at first should disappoint it afterwards. Mr. Gilbert carried this disappointment further: he would put forward a paradox which at first promised to be one of those humane truths which so many modern men . . . have worded so as to flash out their contradiction of some weighty rule of our systematized morality, and would then let it slip through his fingers, leaving nothing but a mechanical topsy-turvitude. Farcical comedy combines the two disappointments. Its philosophy is as much a sham as its humanity" (*Our Theatres in the Nineties*, 2:230).

8. For a brief survey of contemporary playwrights, see Appendix B.

9. Lorcey, *Georges Feydeau*, p. 188.

10. Although Feydeau attempted to keep his plays just within the limits of good taste, there were times when critics and audiences felt he had strayed over the boundary. The most notable of these instances was the secret chamber scene in *Le Circuit*, which several commentators found offensive (see Lorcey, *Georges Feydeau*, pp. 205-208). Another was the climactic scene in the second act of *La Dame de chez Maxim*, which was amended because it had displeased certain members of the audience. Among those offended by the scene was the Duchesse d'Uzès, at whose request it was altered (Lorcey, *Georges Feydeau*, pp. 148-50). There may have been a more personal reason, unconnected with that scene, for the Duchesse's displeasure with the play, but she wisely refrained from mentioning it in her letter to Feydeau. Ten years earlier, her son, Duc Jacques d'Uzès, was financially ruined through his attentions to Emilienne d'Alençon, one of the most famous *cocottes* of the era. His mother broke up the liaison by sending Jacques to the Congo (Manson, "Quand les trois grandes régnaient sur Paris," pp. 166-67). She may have felt that Feydeau's portrait of a duchess whose obsession was to protect her young and susceptible son from courtesans, and La Môme's announcement, at the end of the play, of her coming trip to Africa, were allusions to her family's scandal.

11. Bonamy Dobrée, *Restoration Comedy: 1660-1720* (London: Oxford University Press, 1924, pp. 15-16.

12. Thierry Maulnier offers one of the most extreme statements of this point of view, claiming that the message of Feydeau's characters is that "before a world in which absurdity is man himself, man experiences in the depths of his soul 'the horror of being conscious!'" "La Querelle du *Dindon*," *Combat* (Paris) 9 March 1951, p. 2.

13. *Portraits intimes*, 5:11.

14. Quoted in Treich, "Le Dixième anniversaire de la mort de Georges Feydeau," p. 5.

15. "Topical Allusions in the Theatre of Georges Feydeau," p. 375.

16. Vol. 1, *Hortense a dit: "Je m'en fous!"*, sc. 2, p. 234.

17. See pp. 53-54.

18. Jacques Charon has commented that "there is more observation, more sense of reality, in an extravagance like *Un Fil à la Patte* than in a heavy, pseudo-philosophical melodrama like *La Course au flambeau* [*The Torch Race* by Paul Hervieu]." "Le Théâtre de Georges Feydeau," *Les Annales*, July 1962, p. 26.

19. "Preface: Trifles and Tomfooleries," *Complete Plays with Prefaces*, 4:723.

20. Arthur H. Nethercot, one of the few to mention the play, dismisses it as "the worst farce Shaw ever wrote." *Men and Supermen: The Shavian Portrait Gallery* (New York: Benjamin Blom, 1966), p. 36.

Notes to Appendix A 149

21. On *You Never Can Tell* as a farcical comedy, see Meisel, *Shaw and the Nineteenth-Century Theater*, pp. 253-56, and Charles A. Carpenter, *Bernard Shaw & the Art of Destroying Ideals: The Early Plays* (Madison: University of Wisconsin Press, 1969), pp. 127-31.
22. *Shaw and the Nineteenth-Century Theater*, pp. xii, 264.
23. Ibid., pp. 265-66.
24. *Our Theatres in the Nineties*, 2:121.
25. For example, a situation comparable to the triangle in Shaw's play involving Sinjon, Leo, and Reginald provides the plot of *Divorçons!* The Sinjon—Mrs. George—George Collins triangle is a Shavian version of the happy cuckold theme that is the basis of numerous plays, including Labiche's *Le Plus heureux des trois* and Becque's *La Parisienne*. The difficulties that Cecil anticipates if he marries Edith and becomes responsible for her actions are realized in Feydeau's *Hortense a dit: "Je m'en fous!"*
26. "Georges Feydeau et son oeuvre," p. 215.
27. Georges Versini, *Le Théâtre français depuis 1900* (Paris: Presses Universitaires de France, 1970), p. 13.
28. "The Mathematics of Farce," *Commonweal*, 10 May 1957, p. 154. Baudelaire describes an English pantomime in which Pierrot, an incorrigible thief, is guillotined, and true to his thieving nature, steals his own head and stuffs it into his pocket. "The pantomime is the refinement, the quintessence of comedy; it is the pure comic element, purged and concentrated." "On the Essence of Laughter, and, in General, on the Comic in the Plastic Arts," trans. Jonathan Mayne in *Comedy: Meaning and Form*, ed. Robert W. Corrigan, p. 462.
29. Willard Farnham, "The Medieval Comic Spirit in the English Renaissance," in *Joseph Quincy Adams Memorial Studies*, ed. James G. McManaway, Giles E. Dawson, and Edwin E. Willoughby (Washington: Folger Shakespeare Library, 1948), p. 429.
30. Fernand Weyl [Nozière], "Georges Feydeau," p. 1.

Appendix A

1. Vol. 7, act 3, sc. 3, p. 72.
2. Louis Verneuil, *Rideau à neuf heures* (New York: Editions de la Maison Française, 1944), p. 92.
3. Quoted by Lorcey, *Georges Feydeau*, p. 177.
4. Ibid., p. 212.
5. "Georges Feydeau, distrait, souriant et melancolique," in *D'Alphonse Allais à Sacha Guitry* (Paris: Plon, 1963), pp. 90-91.
6. Vol. 1, *Occupe-toi-d'Amélie*, act 3, 1st tableau, sc. 7, p. 134.
7. "Feydeau: Father of Pure Farce," *Theatre Arts*, April 1957, p. 87.
8. Nikolai M. Gorchakov, *Stanislavski Directs*, trans. Miriam Golding (New York: Funk & Wagnalls Co., 1954), pp. 204-5.
9. "Feydeau: Father of Pure Farce," p. 87.

10. Quoted by Lorcey, *Georges Feydeau,* pp. 253-54.
11. "Putting on the Style," *New Yorker,* 14 March 1959, p. 80.
12. Quoted (in English) by Michael Billington, *"A Flea in Her Ear," The Listener,* 3 March 1966, p. 315.
13. "The Psychology of Farce," p. xviii.
14. See the photographs reproduced in the *Théâtre complet,* esp. vol. 3, *La Main passe!,* pp. 64, 80. These could be compared to photographs of a 1965 production of *La Dame de chez Maxim* in Arlette Shenkan, *Georges Feydeau* (Paris: Editions Seghers, 1972), p. 97.
15. Michel Perrin, "Feydeau, l'impitoyable," *La Revue de Paris,* July 1963, p. 91.
16. "Buoyant French Farce," *Times* (London), 11 January 1966, p. 12.
17. Jean Morgan, "Georges Feydeau et Francis de Croisset," *Le Gaulois* (Paris), 28 October 1909, p. 1.
18. Sören Kierkegaard, "Farce is Far More Serious," p. 6.

Appendix B

1. Maurice Edgar Coindreau, *La Farce est jouée: Vingtcing ans de théâtre français: 1900-1925* (New York: Editions de la Maison Française, 1942), p. 24.

Bibliography

Works by Feydeau: Plays

All of Feydeau's published plays are included in his *Théâtre complet*. 9 Vols. Paris: Editions du Bélier, 1948-56. For the convenience of the reader, they are listed alphabetically below:

Affaire Edouard, L'. Comédie-vaudeville in 3 acts. With Maurice Desvallières. Vol. 1.
Age d'or, L'. Musical comedy in 3 acts and 9 tableaux. With Maurice Desvallières. Vol. 9.
Amour et piano. Comedy in 1 act. Vol. 1.
Bain de menage, Un. Vaudeville in 1 act. Vol. 7.
Bourgeon, Le. Comedy in 3 acts. Vol. 9.
Cent millions qui tombent. Play in 3 acts. Vol. 6.
C'est une femme du monde. Comedy in 1 act,. With Maurice Desvallières. Vol. 4.
Champignol malgré lui. Play in 3 acts. With Maurice Desvallières. Vol. 6.
Chat en poche. Vaudeville in 3 acts. Vol. 2.
Circuit, Le. Comedy in 3 acts and 4 tableaux. With Francis de Croisset. Vol. 5.
Dame de chez Maxim, La. Play in 3 acts. Vol. 7.
Dindon, Le. Play in 3 acts. Vol. 2.
Dormez, je le veux! Vaudeville in 1 act. Vol. 3.
Duchessse des Folies-Bergère, La. Play in 5 acts. Vol. 8.
Feu la mère de Madame. Play in 1 act. Vol. 7.
Fiancés de Loches, Les. Vaudeville in 3 acts. With Maurice Desvallières. Vol. 7.
Fiancés en herbe. Comédie enfantine in 1 act. Vol. 1.
Fil à la patte, Un. Comedy in 3 acts. Vol. 6.
Gibier de potence. Comédie-bouffe in 1 act. Vol. 6.
Hortense a dit: "Je m'en fous!" Play in 1 act. Vol. 1.
Hôtel du Libre-Echange, L'. Play in 3 acts. With Maurice Desvallières. Vol. 4.
Je ne trompe pas mon mari. Comedy in 3 acts. With René Peter. Vol. 3.
Léonie est en avance, or *Le Mal joli.* Play in 1 act. Vol. 4.
Lycéenne, La. Vaudeville-opérette in 3 acts. Vol. 8.
Main passe!, La. Play in 4 acts. Vol. 3.
"Mais n'te promène donc pas toute nue!" Comedy in 1 act. Vol. 8.
Mariage de Barillon, Le. Vaudeville in 3 acts. With Maurice Desvallières. Vol. 5.
Monsieur chasse! Comedy in 3 acts. Vol. 5.
Notre futur. Play in 1 act. Vol. 6.
Occupe-toi d'Amélie. Play in 3 acts and 4 tableaux. Vol. 1.
On purge Bébé! Play in 1 act. Vol. 3.
On va faire la cocotte. Play in 2 acts. Vol. 7.

Par la fenêtre. Play in 1 act. Vol. 4.
Pavés de l'ours, Les. Comedy in 1 act. Vol. 2.
Puce à l'oreille, La. Play in 3 acts. Vol. 4.
Ruban, Le. Comedy in 3 acts. With Maurice Desvallières. Vol. 8.
Séance de nuit. Comedy in 1 act. Vol. 2.
Système Ribadier, Le. Comedy in 3 acts. With Maurice Hennequin. Vol. 2.
Tailleur pour dames. Comedy in 3 acts. Vol. 9.

Monologues

Aux Antipodes. Paris: Ollendorff, 1883.
Billet de mille, Le. Paris: Ollendorff, 1885.
Célèbres, Les. Paris: Ollendorff, 1884.
Colis, Le. Paris: Ollendorff, 1885.
Complainte du pauv' propriétaire, La. Paris: Librairie Théâtrale, 1915.
Coup de tête, Un. Paris: Librairie Théâtrale, 1882.
Enfants, Les. Paris: Ollendorff, 1887.
Homme économe, L'. Paris: Ollendorff, 1885.
Homme intègre, L'. Paris: Ollendorff, 1886.
J'ai mal aux dents. Paris: Michaud, 1882.
Juré, Le. Paris: Librairie Théâtrale, 1898.
Monsieur qui est condamné à mort, Un. Paris: Librairie Théâtrale, 1899.
Monsieur qui n'aime pas les monologues, Un. Paris: Ollendorff, 1882.
Mouchoir, Le. Paris: Ollendorff, 1881.
Patte-en-l'air. Paris: Michaud, 1883.
Petit ménage, Le. Paris: Ollendorff, 1883.
Petite révoltée, La. Paris: Ollendorff, 1880.
Potache, Le. Paris, Michaud, 1883.
Réformés, Les. Paris: Librairie Théâtrale, 1885.
Trop vieux. Paris: Ollendorff, 1882.
Tout à Brown-Sequard. Paris: Ollendorff, 1890.
Volontaire, Le. Paris: Ollendorff, 1884.

Feydeau's Plays in English

(Plays are listed alphabetically by the French title, followed by the English title used in this book.)

Amour et piano. (Love and Piano).
    Call Me Maestro, in *Ooh! La-la!*. Translated by Caryl Brahms and Ned Sherrin. London: W. H. Allen, 1973.
Champignol malgré lui. (Champignol in Spite of Himself).
    A Close Shave. Translated by Peter Meyer. London: British Broadcasting Corp., 1974.
Dame de chez Maxim, La. (The Lady from Maxim's).
    The Lady from Maxim's. Translated by John Mortimer. London: Heineman, 1977.
    St. Shrimp, in *Ooh! La-la!*. Translated by Caryl Brahms and Ned Sherrin. London: W. H. Allen, 1973.
    The Lady from Maxim's. Translated by Gene Feist. New York: Samuel French, 1971.
Dindon, Le. (The Sucker).
    Paying the Piper. Translated by Caryl Brahms and Ned Sherrin. London: Davis-Poynter, 1972.
    Sauce for the Goose. Translated by Peter Meyer. London: British Broadcasting Corp., 1974.

Feu la mère de Madame. (Madam's Late Mother).
   A Good Night's Sleep, in *Ooh! La-la!*. Translated by Caryl Brahms and Ned Sherrin. London: W. H. Allen, 1973.
   Better Late. Translated by Peter Meyer. London: Samuel French, 1976.
Fiancés en herbe. (Budding Fiancés).
   Budding Lovers. Translated by Barnett Shaw. New York: Samuel French, 1969.
Fil à la patte, Un. (Tied by a String).
   Cat Among the Pigeons. Translated by John Mortimer. New York: Samuel French, 1970.
   Not by Bed Alone. Translated by Norman Shapiro, in *Four Farces by Georges Feydeau*. Chicago: Univ. of Chicago Press, 1970.
   Get Out of My Hair! Translated by Frederick Davies, in *Three French Farces*. Baltimore: Penguin, 1973.
Gibier de potence. (Gallows-Bird).
   Before We Were So Rudely Interrupted. Translated by Caryl Brahms and Ned Sherrin, in *Ooh! La-la!*. London: W. H. Allen, 1973.
Hortense a dit: "Je m'en fous!". (Hortense Said: "I Don't Give A Damn!"
   Hortense Said: "No Skin Off My Ass!" Translated by Norman Shapiro. *Comedy: New Perspectives, New York Literary Forum* 1 (Spring, 1975): 281-311.
Hôtel du Libre-Echange. (Hotel Paradiso).
   Hotel Paradiso. Translated by Peter Glenville. New York: Samuel French, 1958.
La Main passe!. (Pass The Deal!).
   Chemin de fer. Translated by Suzanne Grossmann and Paxton Whitehead. New York: Samuel French, 1968.
Mariage de Barillon, Le. (Barillon's Marriage).
   On The Marry-Go-Wrong. Translated by Norman R. Shapiro, in *Four Farces by Georges Feydeau*. Chicago: Univ. of Chicago Press, 1970.
Monsieur chasse! (Monsieur Has Gone Hunting!).
   A 'hunting We Will Go. Translated by R. Barron. London: New Playwrights' Network, 1976.
   The Happy Hunter. Translated by Barnett Shaw. London: Samuel French, 1972.
Occupe-toi d'Amélie. (Keep an Eye on Amélie).
   Keep an Eye on Amélie. Translated by Brainard Duffield, in *Let's Get a Divorce! and Other Plays*. New York: Hill and Wang, 1958.
   Keep An Eye on Amélie. Translated by Caryl Brahms and Ned Sherrin, in *Ooh! La-la!* London: W. H. Allen, 1973.
   Look After Lulu. Translated by Noel Coward. New York: Samuel French, 1959.
On purge Bébé. (Junior Gets A Laxative).
   Going to Pot. Translated by Norman R. Shapiro, in *Four Farces by Georges Feydeau*. Chicago: Univ. of Chicago Press, 1970.
   The Purging. Translated by Peter Barnes, in *Frontiers of Farce*. By Peter Barnes. London: Heineman, 1977.
Par la fenêtre. (Through the Window).
   Wooed and Viewed. Translated by Norman R. Shapiro, in *Four Farces by Georges Feydeau*. Chicago: Univ. of Chicago Press, 1970.
Pavés de l'ours, Les. (The Bear's Embrace).
   A Little Bit to Fall Back On. Translated by Caryl Brahms and Ned Sherrin, in *Ooh! La-la!* London: W. H. Allen, 1973.
Puce à l'oreille, La. (A Flea in Her Ear).
   A Flea in Her Ear. Translated by Carol Johnson. Dramatic Publishing Company, 1968.
   A Flea in Her Ear. Translated by John Mortimer. London: Samuel French, 1968.
   A Flea in Her Ear. Translated by Barnett Shaw. New York: Samuel French, 1966.

Tailleur pour dames. (Ladies' Dressmaker).
Fitting for Ladies. Translated by Peter Meyer. London: British Broadcasting Corp., 1974.
A Gown for His Mistress. Translated by Barnett Shaw. New York: Samuel French, 1969.

On Feydeau, His Plays, and His Age

Achard, Marcel. "Georges Feydeau, notre grand comique." *Conférencia, Journal de l'Université des Annales* 37 (15 April 1948):133-49, and 37 (15 May 1948): 214-20.
Arban, Dominique. "Nostalgie de 1900?" *Combat* (Paris), 10 March 1948.
Baldy, Claude. "Ingénieur du rire, Feydeau avait trouvé les formules qui font rire aujourd'hui comme hier." *Arts,* 10-16 March 1954, pp. 2-3.
Barrault, Jean-Louis. *Une Troupe et ses auteurs.* Paris: Vautrain, 1950.
Bauer, Gerard. *"Occupe-toi d'Amélie."* *La Revue de Paris,* April 1948, p. 149.
Berton, Claude. "Georges Feydeau et l'âme de chez Maxim's." *Les Nouvelles littéraires,* 5 April 1924, p. 4.
Billington, Michael. "A Flea in Her Ear." *The Listener,* 3 March 1966, p. 315.
Brisson, Adolphe. *Portraits intimes.* 5 Vols. Paris: Armand Colin, 1894-1901.
"Buoyant French Farce." *Times* (London), 11 January 1966, p. 12.
Cahiers de la Compagnie Madeleine Renaud—Jean-Louis Barrault: La Question Feydeau, no. 32, December 1960.
Cassou, Jean, "Le Génie systématique de Feydeau." *Cahiers de la Compagnie Madeleine Renaud—Jean-Louis Barrault,* no. 15, January 1956, pp. 55-61.
Chandler, Frank Wadleigh. *The Contemporary Drama of France.* Boston: Little, Brown and Co., 1920.
———. *Modern Continental Playwrights.* New York: Harper & Brothers, 1931.
Charon, Jacques. "Le Théâtre de Georges Feydeau." *Les Annales,* July 1962, pp. 23-34.
Clurman, Harold. "Theatre." *Nation,* 21 March 1959, pp. 262-63.
Cocteau, Jean. "C'était Feydeau..." *Cahiers de la Compagnie Madeleine Renaud—Jean-Louis Barrault,* no. 15, January 1956, pp. 53-54.
Coindreau, Maurice Edgar. *La Farce est jouée: Vingt-cinq ans de théâtre français: 1900-1925.* New York: Editions de la Maison Française, 1942.
Croisset, Francis de. *La Vie parisienne au théâtre.* Paris; Bernard Grasset, 1929.
Damiens, Claude. "Georges Feydeau, le maître du naturalisme absurde." *Paris-Théâtre,* no. 150 (1959), pp. 2-3.
Daniels, May. *The French Drama of the Unspoken.* Edinburgh: Edinburgh University Press, 1953.
Dumur, Guy. "Des pantins et des monstres." *Le Nouvel observateur,* 29 November-5 December 1967, pp. 43-44.
Dussane, Beatrix. *Notes de théâtre, 1940-1950.* Lyons: Lardanchet, 1951.
Feydeau, Michel. "Mon père, auteur gai." *L'Intransigeant* (Paris), 3 December 1937.
Flers, Robert de. *"La Dame de chez Maxim."* *Revue d'art dramatique,* 5 February 1899, pp. 206-8.
"Forms of Shock Treatment for a World out of Plumb." *Times Literary Supplement,* 18 June 1971, pp. 689-90.
Fouquier, Henry. "Le Krach du théâtre." *Figaro* (Paris), 18 November 1891, p. 1.
Georges-Michel, Michel. *Un Demi-siècle de gloires théâtrales.* Paris: Editions André Bonne, 1950.
Glenville, Peter. "Feydeau: Father of Pure Farce." *Theatre Arts,* April 1957, pp. 66, 86-87.
Hayes, Richard. "The Mathematics of Farce." *Commonweal* 66 (10 May 1957):154.
Huret, Jules. *Loges et coulisses.* Paris: Editions de la Revue Blanche, 1901.

Jeanson, Henri. "Notes sur Georges Feydeau." *Cahiers de la Compagnie Madeleine Renaud—Jean-Louis Barrault,* no. 15, January 1956, pp. 62-70.
Kemp, Robert. *La Vie du théâtre.* Paris: Albin Michel, 1956.
Lalou, René. *Le Théâtre en France depuis 1900.* Paris: Presses Universitaires de France, 1951.
Lauwick, Hervé. "Georges Feydeau, distrait, souriant et melancolique," In *D'Alphonse Allais à Sacha Guitry,* pp. 79-96. Paris: Plon, 1963.
"Look After Lulu." *Theatre Arts,* May 1959, pp. 24, 65.
Lorcey, Jacques. *Georges Feydeau.* Paris: La Table Ronde, 1972.
Manson, Anne. "Quand les trois grandes régnaient sur Paris." In *La Belle Epoque,* pp. 163-93. Edited by Gilbert Guilleminault. Paris: Editions Denoël, 1957.
Martin, Jules. *Nos auteurs et compositeurs dramatique.* Paris: Flammarion, 1897.
Matthews, Brander. *French Dramatists of the Nineteenth Century.* 3rd ed. New York: Charles Scribner's Sons, 1901; reprint ed., New York: Benjamin Blom, 1968.
_____. *The Theatres of Paris.* London: Sampson Low, Marston, Searle and Rivington, 1880.
Maulnier, Thierry. "La Querelle du *Dindon."* *Combat* (Paris), 9 March 1951, p. 2.
Mignon, Paul-Louis. "L'Accessoire, deus ex machina, ou la fatalité dans le théâtre de Feydeau." *Cahiers de la Compagnie Madeleine Renaud—Jean-Louis Barrault,* no. 15, January 1956, pp. 72-78.
Morand, Paul. "Champignol parle au nom des dieux." *La Parisienne* 10 (October 1953):1424-25.
Morgan, Jean. "Georges Feydeau et Francis de Croisset." *Le Gaulois* (Paris), 28 October 1909, p. 1.
Moynet, Georges. *La Machinerie théâtrale: Trucs et decors.* Paris: Librairie Illustrée, 1893.
Noël, Edouard, and Stoullig, Edmond, eds. *Les Annales du théâtre et de la musique.* 41 Vols. Paris: Bibliothèque Charpentier, 1895-94; Berger-Levrault, 1895; Ollendorff, 1896-1916.
Perrin, Michel. "Feydeau l'impitoyable." *La Revue de Paris,* July 1963, pp. 85-92.
_____. "Trois quarts d'heure avec M. Feydeau." *Les Nouvelles littéraires,* 6 December 1962, p. 12.
Peter, René. *Le Théâtre et la vie sous la Troisième République, première époque.* Paris: Editions Littéraires de France, 1945.
Pronko, Leonard C. *Georges Feydeau.* World Dramatists Series. New York: Frederick Ungar Publishing Co., 1975.
Reney, George Richard. "The Dramatic Technique of the Comic Playwright Georges Feydeau." Ph.D. dissertation, University of Missouri, 1973.
Richardson, Joanna. *The Courtesans.* New York: World Publishing Co., 1967.
Roussin, André. "Le Cas Feydeau." *World Premières Mondiales,* New Series, February 1963, pp. 1, 4.
Rudorff, Raymond. *The Belle Epoque.* New York: Saturday Review Press, 1973.
Sandier, Gilles. "Un faux Stendhal, un vrai Feydeau." *Arts,* 22-28 December 1965, p. 39.
Sarcey, Francisque. *Quarante ans de théâtre.* 8 Vols. Paris: Bibliothèque des Annales Politiques et Littéraires, 1900-1902.
Saurel, Renée. "Une bonne soirée Feydeau." *Les Lettres françaises,* 31 August-6 September 1967, p. 24.
Sée, Edmond. "Le Bourgeon." *Gil Blas* (Paris), 31 May 1913, p. 4.
Shapiro, Norman Richard. "Georges Feydeau et le fauteuil extatique." *Revue d'histoire littéraire de la France* 60 (October-December 1960):557-59.
_____. Introduction to *Four Farces by Georges Feydeau.* Translated by Norman Richard Shapiro. Chicago: University of Chicago Press, 1970.
_____. "Suffering and Punishment in the Theatre of Georges Feydeau." *Tulane Drama Review* 5 (September 1960): 117-26.
_____. "Topical Allusions in the Theatre of Georges Feydeau." Ph.D. dissertation, Harvard University, 1958.

Shenkan, Arlette. *Georges Feydeau*. Paris: Editions Seghers, 1972.
Smith, Hugh Allison. *Main Currents of Modern French Drama*. New York: H. Holt and Co., 1925; reprint ed., Freeport, N. Y.: Books for Libraries Press, 1968.
Steiner, Roger J. "The Perennial Georges Feydeau." *Symposium* 15 (Spring 1961):49-54
Thibaudet, Albert. *Histoire de la littérature française de 1789 à nos jours*. Paris: Stock, 1936.
Touchard, Pierre-Aimé. *Grandes heures de théâtre à Paris*. Paris: Librairie Académique Perrin, 1965.
──────. *Six années de Comédie-Française*. Paris: Seuil, 1953.
Treich, Léon. "Le dixième anniversaire de la mort de Georges Feydeau." *Les Nouvelles littéraires*, 30 May 1931, p. 5.
Tynan, Kenneth. "Putting on the Style." *New Yorker*, 14 March 1959, pp. 80-83.
Van Druten, John. "A Gem from the French Crown." *Theatre Arts*, March 1958, pp. 19-21.
Verneuil, Louis. *Rideau à neuf heures*. New York: Editions de la Maison Française, 1944.
Versini, Georges. *Le Théâtre français depuis 1900*. Paris: Presses Universitaires de France, 1970.
Vitu, Auguste. *"La Lycéenne." Figaro* (Paris), 24 December 1887, p. 3.
Weyl, Fernand [Nozière]. "Georges Feydeau." *Gil Blas* (Paris), 4 June 1913, p. 1.
Weightman, J. G. "What Price 'la Gloire'?" *Observer* (London), 22 March 1959, p. 23.
Yahiel, Edwin Daniel. "Georges Feydeau et son oeuvre." Ph.D. dissertation, University of Michigan, 1955.

Works Related to the Theory and Technique of Farce

Archer, William. *Play-making: A Manual of Craftsmanship*. New York: Dover Publications, 1960.
Arvin, Neil Cole. *Eugène Scribe and the French Theatre, 1815-1860*. Cambridge: Harvard University Press, 1924; reprint ed., New York: Benjamin Blom, 1967.
Bakhtin, Mikhail. *Rabelais and His World*. Translated by Hélène Iswolsky. Cambridge: M.I.T. Press, 1968.
Barber, C. L. *Shakespeare's Festive Comedy*. Princeton: Princeton University Press, 1959.
Baudelaire, Charles. "On the Essence of Laughter, and, in General, on the Comic in the Plastic Arts." Translated by Jonathan Mayne. In *Comedy: Meaning and Form*, pp. 448-65. Edited by Robert W. Corrigan. San Francisco: Chandler Publishing Co., 1965.
Bentley, Eric. *The Life of the Drama*. New York: Atheneum, 1967.
──────. "The Psychology of Farce." In *"Let's Get a Divorce!" and Other Plays*. Edited by Eric Bentley. New York: Hill and Wang, 1958.
Bergson, Henri. *Le Rire*. Paris: Presses Universitaires de France, 1940.
Berlyne, D. E. *Conflict, Arousal, and Curiosity*. New York: McGraw-Hill Book Co., 1960.
──────. "Laughter, Humor, and Play." In *The Handbook of Social Psychology*, 3:795-852. 3rd ed. 5 Vols. Edited by Gardner Lindzey and Elliot Aronson. Reading, Mass.: Addison-Wesley Publishing Co., 1968.
Bermel, Albert C. "Farce." In *The Reader's Encyclopedia of World Drama*. Edited by John Gassner and Edward Quinn. New York: Thomas Crowell Co., 1969.
Blistein, Elmer. *Comedy in Action*. Durham, N. C.: Duke University Press, 1964.
Cornford, Francis Macdonald. *The Origins of Attic Comedy*. Cambridge: Cambridge University Press, 1934; reprint ed., Gloucester, Mass.: Peter Smith, 1968.
Corrigan, Robert W., ed. *Comedy: Meaning and Form*. San Francisco: Chandler Publishing Co., 1965.
Cox, Harvey. *The Feast of Fools*. Cambridge: Harvard University Press, 1969.
Davis, Jessica Milner. *Farce*. London: Methuen, 1978.
Dobrée, Bonamy. *Restoration Comedy: 1660-1720*. London: Oxford University Press, 1924.
Dover, K. J. *Aristophanic Comedy*. Berkley: University of California Press, 1972.

Duckworth, George E. *The Nature of Roman Comedy*. Princeton: Princeton University Press, 1952.
Dukore, Bernard F. *Dramatic Theory and Criticism: Greeks to Grotowski*. New York: Holt, Rinehart and Winston, 1974.
Eastman, Max. *Enjoyment of Laughter*. New York: Simon and Schuster, 1936.
———. *The Sense of Humor*. New York: Charles Scribner's Sons, 1921.
Ellis, M. J. *Why People Play*. Englewood Cliffs, N. J.: Prentice-Hall, 1973.
Farnham, Willard. "The Medieval Comic Spirit in the English Renaissance." In *Joseph Quincy Adams Memorial Studies*, pp. 429-37. Edited by James G. McManaway, Giles E. Dawson, and Edwin E. Willoughby. Washington: Folger Shakespeare Library, 1948.
Feibleman, James Kern. *In Praise of Comedy: A Study of Its Theory and Practice*. New York: Russell & Russell, 1962.
Fleming, Rudd. "Of Contrast between Tragedy and Comedy." *Journal of Philosophy* 36 (January-December 1939): 543-53.
Frank, Grace. *The Medieval French Drama*. Oxford, England: Clarendon Press, 1954.
Freud, Sigmund. *Jokes and Their Relation to the Unconscious*. Translated by James Strachey. New York: W. W. Norton & Co., 1960.
Frye, Northrup. *Anatomy of Criticism: Four Essays*. Princeton: Princeton University Press, 1957.
Gilliatt, Penelope. *Unholy Fools: Wits, Comics, Disturbers of the Peace: Film & Theater*. New York: Viking Press, 1973.
Godfrey, F. La T. "The Aesthetics of Laughter." *Hermathena* 50 (1937):126-138.
Gorchakov, Nikolai M. *Stanislovski Directs*. Translated by Miriam Goldina. New York: Funk & Wagnalls Co., 1954.
Greig, John Young Thompson. *The Psychology of Laughter and Comedy*. London: George Allen & Unwin, 1923.
Grotjahn, Martin. *Beyond Laughter*. New York: McGraw-Hill, 1957.
Hughes, Leo. *A Century of English Farce*. Princeton: Princeton University Press, 1956.
Jensen, Ruth. "Quid rides?" *Classical Journal* 16 (1920-21): 207-19.
Kerr, Walter. *The Silent Clowns*. New York: Alfred A. Knopf, 1975.
Kierkegaard, Sören. "Farce is Far More Serious." *Yale French Studies* 14 (Winter 1954-55):3-9.
Koestler, Arthur. *Insight and Outlook*. New York: Macmillan Co., 1949.
Langer, Susanne. *Feeling and Form*. New York: Scribner, 1953.
Lanson, Gustave. "Molière et la farce." *La Revue de Paris* 8 (1901):129-53.
Lauter, Paul, ed. *Theories of Comedy*. Garden City, N. Y.: Doubleday & Co., 1964.
Lea, Kathleen Marguerite. *Italian Popular Comedy*. 2 Vols. New York: Russell & Russell, 1962.
Maier, N. R. F. "A Gestalt Theory of Humour." *British Journal of Psychology* 23 (1932):69-74.
Mast, Gerald. *The Comic Mind: Comedy and the Movies*. New York: Bobbs-Merrill Co., 1973.
Maxwell, Ian. *French Farce & John Heywood*. Melbourne: Melbourne University Press, 1946.
Meisel, Martin. *Shaw and the Nineteenth-Century Theater*. Princeton: Princeton University Press, 1963.
Merchant, W. Moelwyn. *Comedy*. London: Methuen, 1972.
Meyerhold, Vsevolod. "Farce." Translated by Nora Beeson. *Tulane Drama Review* 4 (September 1959):139-49.
Olson, Elder. *The Theory of Comedy*. Bloomington: Indiana University Press, 1968.
Oreglia, Giacomo. *The Commedia dell'Arte*. Translated by Lovett F. Edwards. New York: Hill and Wang, 1968.
Perry, Henry Ten Eyck. *Masters of Dramatic Comedy and Their Social Themes*. Cambridge: Harvard University Press, 1939.
Prescott, Henry W. "The Comedy of Errors," *Classical Philology* 24 (January 1929):32-41.
Rapp, Albert. *The Origins of Wit and Humor*. New York: E. P. Dutton & Co., 1951.

Segal, Erich. *Roman Laughter: The Comedy of Plautus.* Cambridge: Harvard University Press, 1968.
Sewell, Elizabeth. *The Field of Nonsense.* London: Chatto and Windus, 1952; reprint ed., Folcroft, Pa., Folcroft Library Editions, 1973.
Shaw, George Bernard. *Our Theatres in the Nineties.* Standard edition. 3 Vols. London: Constable and Co., 1932.
Smith, Elizabeth Nusbaum. "The Society of the Incomplete: The Psychology and Structure of Farce." Ph.D. dissertation, University of Michigan, 1969.
Smith, Willard M. *The Nature of Comedy.* Boston: Richard G. Badger, 1930.
Smith, Winifred. *The Commedia dell'Arte.* New York: Benjamin Blom, 1964.
Spector, Jack J. *The Aesthetics of Freud.* New York: Praeger Publishers, 1973.
Stanton, Stephen S., ed. *"Camille" and Other Plays.* New York: Hill and Wang, 1957.
Stephenson, Robert C. "Farce as Method." *Tulane Drama Review* 5 (1961):85-93.
Stern, Alfred. *Philosophie du rire et des pleurs.* Paris: Presses Universitaires de France, 1949.
Sully, James. *An Essay on Laughter.* New York: Longmans, Green, and Co., 1902.
Swain, Barbara. *Fools and Folly During the Middle Ages and the Renaissance.* New York: Columbia University Press, 1932.
Taylor, John Russell. *The Rise and Fall of the Well-Made Play.* New York: Hill and Wang, 1969.
Voltz, Pierre. *La Comédie.* Paris: Librairie Armand Colin, 1964.
Welsford, Enid. *The Fool.* London: Faber and Faber, 1968.
Willeford, William. *The Fool and His Scepter.* Evanston, Ill.: Northwestern University Press, 1969.
Willmann, J. M. "An Analysis of Humor and Laughter." *American Journal of Psychology* 53 (1940):70-85.
Wimsatt, W. K. *Hateful Contraries.* Lexington: University of Kentucky Press, 1965.
_____. *The Idea of Comedy.* Englewood Cliffs, N. J.: Prentice-Hall, 1969.
Worcester, David. *The Art of Satire.* New York: Russell & Russell, 1960.
Young, Stark. *Immortal Shadows.* New York: Hill and Wang, 1959.

Index

Absurdists, 110-11
Actors in farce, 10-11, 12-18, 117-22
Adultery: in Feydeau's plays, 34, 38, 41, 67-69, 92-94, 96; in 19th-century drama, 68, 104. *See also* Cuckolds, Philanderers
Age, treatment of, 86
Age D'Or, L', 27, 41, 60, 61, 72; historical setting of, 62-63
Aggression: laughter and, 5, 6; in farce, 7, 49
Affaire Edouard, L', 26, 57, 77, 78, 97, 103
Alazon, 76, 87
Alençon, Emilienne, d', 102
Amants (Donnay), 124
Amorality in farce, 3, 14-15, 67, 80-81
Amour et Piano, 31, 90, 102
Appearances, importance of, 34-35, 37, 82-84
Aristocrats in Feydeau's plays, 101-2
Augier, Emile, 123
Avariés, L' (Brieux), 125
Autre danger, L' (Donnay), 124

Bain de ménage, un, 82-83, 102
Bakhtin, Mikhail, 5
Barber, C. L., 5
Barillon's Marriage. See Mariage de Barillon, Le
Barrault, Jean-Louis, 51
Bataille, Henri, 124
Bear's Embrace, The. See Pavés de l'ours, Les
Beaton, Cecil, 120
Beckett, Samuel, 110-11
Becque, Henry, 123, 141 n.79

Bentley, Eric, 3, 49, 51, 63, 120-21; on farce dialectic, 58; on violence in farce, 7
Berceau, Le (Brieux), 125
Bergson, Henri, 5, 10, 134 n.33
Bermel, Albert, 2-3, 7-8, 9, 139 n.8, 140 notes 40, 41
Bernard, Tristan, 123
Bernstein, Henry, 125
Berton, Claude, 61-62
Bisson, Alexandre, 139 n.32
Bourgeon, Le, 27, 41, 41-42, 75, 90, 103, 105, 109, 110
Brieux, Eugene, 125
Brignol et sa fille (Capus), 124-25
Brooks, Mel, 141 n.62
Budding Fiancés. See Fiancés en herbe

Capus, Alfred, 124-25
Carroll, Lewis. *See* Dodgson, Charles Lutwidge
Cassive, Armande, 118-19, 120, 122
Cent millions qui tombent, 42, 77, 98, 102-3, 104, 112; money in, 83-84
Cerny, Berthe, 118-19
C'est une femme du monde, 38, 82
Chaises, Les (Ionesco), 10
Champignol in Spite of Himself. See Champignol malgré lui
Champignol malgré lui, 26, 39, 46, 67, 78, 82, 84, 97
Chaplin, Charlie, 16-17
Characters: in farce, 12-18, 22; in Feydeau's plays, 37, 46, 55, 72-105
Charlton, H. B., on Shakespeare, 20
Charon, Jacques, 120, 148 n.18
Chat en Poche, 27, 32, 34, 47, 77, 78, 97;

160   Index

misunderstanding in, 39, 57, 58
Chess and farce, 21, 33
Circuit, Le, 60
Claudel, Paul, 123
Clothing in farce, 35, 55
Clowns, 13-18
Cocottes, 40-41, 56, 59, 62, 65, 86-87, 93, 98-99, 101, 102-5
Coincidence, 51-54
Coindreau, Maurice, 123
Comedy: literary, 3-5, 7; of intrigue, 30
Commedia dell'arte, 12, 13, 16, 18, 23, 47
Conflicts, integrated, in farce, 71-73
Connais-toi (Hervieu), 124
Contemporary settings in Feydeau, 62
Contradiction in farce, 14, 54-59, 120, 121
Corbeaux, Les (Becque), 112
Courteline, Georges, 42, 123, 141 n.79
Coward, Noel, 120
Cuckolds, 49, 51, 52-53, 65, 67, 92. *See also* Adultery
Curel, François de, 125

Dadaism, 107
Dame aux Camélias, La (Dumas), 104
Dame de chez Maxim, La, 26, 39, 40, 56, 59-60, 61, 71, 73, 81, 94; *cocotte* in, 103, 105; hypnotism in, 61; sexual conflict in, 66
Deception, 26, 37, 40. *See also* Deception formula plays
Deception formula plays, 26, 38, 39, 45, 47-48
Decoration, The. See Ruban, Le
Defects, physical, 84-86
Desvallières, Maurice, 32
Dieudonné, Robert, 118
Dindon, Le, 26, 39, 47, 50, 61, 66, 69, 83, 94, 97; adultery in, 46, 67, 68, 82; discussion in, 113; foreigners in, 70, 99, 100; love and money in, 84
Dobrée, Bonamy, 109
Doctors, 77, 81
Dodgson, Charles Lutwidge [pseud. Lewis Carroll], 8, 57
Donnay, Maurice, 124
Do Not Parade Around Stark Naked! See "Mais n'te promène donc pas toute nue!"
Dormez, Je le Veux!, 25, 27, 61, 97-98
Dramatic illusion, breaking of, 10-11
Dreams, 8-10, 54, 64. *See also* Nightmares
Dryden, John, 2, 6
Duchesse des Folies-Bergère, La, 41, 57, 60, 98; foreigners in, 70, 101; servants in, 97
Duchess from the Folies-Bergère, The. See Duchesse des Folies-Bergère, La
Duckworth, George E., 29
Duel, Le (Lavedan), 125
Dumas *fils,* Alexandre, 123
Dumas *père,* Alexandre, 63

Eastman, Max, 48
Ecole des femmes, L' (Molière), 64-65
Edward Affair, The. See Affaire Edouard, L'
Eiron, 76, 87
Endings in Feydeau's plays, 47-48
Enigme, L' (Hervieu), 124
Envers d'une sainte, L' (Curel), 125
Erasmus, 115-16
Evil eye, 52
Exaggeration, 46, 48-51
Exotic, Feydeau's use of the, 62-63

Familiar, Feydeau's use of the, 62-63
Fantasy in farce, 7-8, 10, 14, 15, 57-58, 59
Farce: characters of, 7; disturbing aspects of, 3; games and, 8-23; irresponsibility of, 44, 115-16; judged by standard of comedy, 1, 2, 4-5; magic in, 60-62; medieval French, 8, 18; melodrama and, 72; modes of, 12-23; opposing forces in, 9-11, 14, 17; and pornography, 3; reality in, 9-11, 49-52; theatrical nature of, 13-14, 17; tragedy and, 121; silent film, 8; violence in, 3, 8
Fatalism, 51-54
Femme de Claude, La (Dumas), 123-24
Feu la Mère de Madame, 27, 50, 94
Feydeau, Georges-Leon-Jules-Marie: on character probability, 46; conservative attitudes in plays of, 72-73; critical reaction to, 5, 32-33, 107; as director, 117-18; early plays of, 32, 57; on farce and tragedy, 140 n.41; film versions of plays, 11; lack of originality of, 25; as magician, 60-62; on melancholy in his work, 109; and mysticism, 60-61; on playing farce, 121; purity of, 113-14; on scenarios, 45; and Shaw, 112-13; and Simpson, 10; stage farce and, 11-12; on violence in his plays, 69. *See also* titles
Feydeau, Jacques, 49
Fiancés de Loches, Les, 46, 81, 118; misunderstanding in, 27, 39, 57
Fiancés en herbe, 27, 38-39
Fiancés from Loche, The. See Fiancés de Loches, Les
Fil à la patte, Un, 46, 47, 50, 55, 78, 80, 124; as deception formula play, 26, 39-40, 48; foreigners in, 69, 100; ingénue

in, 90; love and money in, 84; objects in, 34, 35
Flea in Her Ear, A. See Puce à l'oreille, La
Fleurs, Robert de, 103
Fools, 14-15, 115; tragic heroes and, 52
Foreigners, 50, 62, 69, 85, 86, 98-102
Form in farce, 12, 13, 18-21, 37-38
Fossiles, Les (Curel), 125
Freud, Sigmund, 6, 49
Frou-Frou (Meilhac and Halevy), 141 n.79

Gallows-Bird. See Gibier de potence
Games and farce, 8-22
Gerould, Daniel, 20-21, 137 n.27
Gibier de potence, 31-32, 46-47, 49, 79
Gilliatt, Penelope, 71-72, 79-80
Glenville, Peter, 119, 120
Going to Play the Courtesan. See On va faire la cocotte
Golden Age, The. See Age d'or, L'
Gorchakov, Nikolai M., 119

Hayes, Richard, 113-14
Hervieu, Paul, 124
Historical subjects, 63
Hortense a dit: "Je m'en fous!", 27, 77-78, 91, 95, 102, 110
Hortense Said: "I Don't Give a Damn!". See Hortense a dit: "Je m'en fous!"
Hôtel du Libre-Echange, L', 32, 33, 38, 61, 70, 77, 78, 85, 86, 94; adultery in, 41, 67; coincidence in, 51, 52; as deception formula play, 26-27, 38, 39, 48; film of, 11; objects in, 34, 36; sexual conflict in, 64, 69; Shaw on, 113
Hotel Paradiso. See Hôtel du Libre-Echange, L'
Household Bath. See Bain de ménage
Hughes, Leo, 2
Hypnotism, 25, 61, 62, 97

I Don't Cheat on My Husband. See Je ne trompe pas mon mari
Ingénue, Feydeau's treatment of, 27, 88-90
Intellectuals and farce, 108
Inverted pyramid in Feydeau, 36-37, 45
Ionesco, Eugene, 10, 107, 110
Irony in Feydeau's plays, 89

Jarry, Alfred, 107, 123
"Je m'en foutisme," 108
Je ne trompe pas mon mari, 49, 78, 93, 103; foreigners in, 70, 100, 101
Junior Gets a Laxative. See On purge Bébé

Keaton, Buster, 11, 17

Keep an Eye on Amélie. See Occupe-toi d'Amélie
Kerr, Walter, 8, 11, 16, 17
Kierkegaard, Sören, 1, 122
Knight, L. C., 1, 23
Koestler, Arthur, 6

Labiche, Eugène, 5, 35, 75-76; *The Italian Straw Hat,* 21; *Le Plus heureux des trois,* 68; *Le Voyage de Monsieur Perichon,* 75
Ladies' Dressmaker. See Tailleur pour dames
Lady From Maxim's, The. See Dame de chez Maxim, La
Laughter, 3-7; carnival, 5; creative thinking and, 5; emotional element in, 6-7
Lauwick, Hervé, 119
Lavedan, Henri, 124-25
Lea, Kathleen Marguerite, 2, 18, 47
Lear, Edward, 8
Lemaître, Jules, 124
Léonie est en avance, 27, 77, 78, 79, 95
Léonie is Premature. See Léonie est en avance
Leopold II of Belgium, 102
Logic in farce, 9-10, 21-22, 31-33, 47
Loi de l'homme, La (Hervieu), 124
Lorcey, Jacques, 108, 109
Love and Piano. See Amour et piano
Lycéenne, La, 32, 78, 86, 97, 102; as ingénue play, 27, 89-90

Madam's Late Mother. See Feu la mère de Madame
Maeterlinck, Maurice, 265-66
Main Passe!, La, 27, 41, 52, 61, 66-67, 77, 85, 96; adultery in, 68, 82, 92, 96; violence in, 35, 70
"Mais n'te promène donc pas toute nue!", 27, 78, 80, 81, 82-83, 91, 95
Mariage de Barillon, Le, 50, 51, 64-65, 70, 79; fatalism in, 52; as ingénue play, 27
Marriage, 63, 91-95
Mars, Anthony, 139 n.32
Marx brothers, 17-18, 122
Masks, 13-14
Maternité (Brieux), 125
Matthews, Brander, 107, 141 n.79
Maxwell, Ian, 7-8, 19
Meisel, Martin, 112
Melodrama and farce, 72
Military characters, 87
Mirbeau, Octave, 112
Misapprehension, 27, 28, 32, 34, 38-39, 42, 43, 56. *See also Quiproquo*

Mme. Cavelet (Augier), 124
Molière, 30, 64-65
Money in Feydeau's plays, 42, 82-84
Monna Vanna (Maeterlinck), 124
Monsieur chasse!, 32, 55, 57, 77, 81, 82, 84, 118; adultery in, 43, 68-69, 92; as deception formula play, 26-27, 43, 56, 175; fatalism in, 53; objects in, 34, 35
Monsieur Has Gone Hunting! See *Monsieur chasse!*
Morality, double standard of, 81-82
Morand, Paul, 107
Morgan, Jean, 107
Morton, J. M., 20
Mothers-in-law, 65, 92
Mysticism, 60

Najac, Emile de, 112, 136 n.2, 141 n.64
Names, comic, 78
Naturalism, 19, 123-25
New Comedy, 29-30, 37
Nightmares, 54. See also Dreams
Night Session. See *Séance de nuit*
Nonsense, 8-10
"Normative" characters, 75-76
Notre Futur, 27
Nouvelle idol, La (Curel), 125
Nozière. See Weyl, Fernand

Objects in farce, 19, 21, 22, 34, 35, 50, 55
Oblivion, farcical, 79-82, 95
Occupe-toi d'Amélie, 35, 59, 61, 68, 84, 90, 135 n.41; cocotte in, 104, 105; as deception formula play, 26-27, 39-40, 56; foreign aristocrats in, 101
Olson, Elder, 45
One-act plays, late, 27, 42, 48. See also titles
One Hundred Million Windfall. See *Cent millions qui tombent*
On va faire la cocotte, 43, 92-93, 95
Opéra-comique, 29
Order in farce, 8, 14
Otéro, Caroline, 102, 103-4
Our Intended. See *Notre futur*

Pailleron, Edouard, 137 n.19
Pain, 14, 54, 72
Pain de ménage, Le (Renard), 124
Par la fenêtre, 27, 31, 91
Pardon, Le (Lemaître), 124
Paroles restent, Les (Hervieu), 124
Pass the Deal! See *Main passe!, La*
Pavés de l'ours, Les, 97-98, 124
Pélléas et Mélisande (Maeterlinck), 124
Pierre Pathelin, 5

Pig in a Poke. See *Chat en poche*
Philanderers, 91, 94. See also Adultery
Physicality in farce, 49-50, 64
Pinter, Harold, 111
Pirandello, Luigi, 107
Plaisir de rompre, Le (Renard), 124
Plautus, 30, 87
Play and creative thinking, 5
Playwright as player of farce, 12-13, 18
Plus heureux des trois, Le (Labiche), 68
Poliche (Bataille), 124
Porto-Riche, Georges de, 109, 124, 137 n.20
Prince d'Aurec, Le (Lavedan), 124
Probabilities in farce, 45-46, 48
Professional humor in Feydeau, 77, 81
Psychologists, motivational, 5
Puce à l'oreille, La, 12, 36, 47, 56, 60, 76, 77, 78, 81, 82, 94, 102, 135 n.41; as deception play, 26-27, 38, 47; disabilities in, 85; foreigners in, 99; oblivion in, 80, 81; violence in, 70. 71
On Purge Bébé, 27, 49, 52, 78, 95
Pyramid, inverted. See Inverted pyramid

Quiproquo, 29, 55, 57-59. See also Misapprehension

Rabelais, François, 5, 116
Racine, Jean, 19-20
Rapp, Albert, 16
Reality in comedy and farce, 8, 9, 10, 11, 14, 15, 28, 114
Renard, Jules, 123-24
Repas du lion, Le (Curel), 125
Ribadier System, The. See *Système Ribadier, Le*
Rigidity and laughter, 6
Ritchard, Cyril, 120
Road Race, The. See *Circuit, Le*
Rostand, Edmond, 123
Ruban, Le, 27, 76, 90, 102

Sarcey, Francisque, 8, 32-33, 36, 41, 108
Sardou, Victorien, 35, 112, 141 n.64
Scandal, 35, 37, 40, 62
Scandale, Le (Bataille), 124
Schoolgirl, The. See *Lycéenne, La*
Science in Feydeau's plays, 61-62
Scribe, Eugène, 29-31, 36, 54
Séance de nuit, 38, 76, 78
Segal, Erich, 5
Sennett, Mack, 22
Servants, 96-98
Sewell, Elizabeth, 8-9
Sexual fantasy in Feydeau, 63-69

Shakespeare, William, 20, 30
Shapiro, Norman, 108, 109, 145 n.66
Shaw, George Bernard, 3, 41, 43-44, 107, 108, 112-13
She's a Respectable Woman. See *C'est une femme du monde*
Simon, Marcel, 122
Simpson, N. F., 10
Sleep! I Command You! See *Dormez, je le veux!*
Smith, Elizabeth Nusbaum, 79
Smith, H. A., 30
Sottie, 182
Spiritualism, 62
Spontaneity in Feydeau's plays, 45
Sprout, The. See *Bourgeon, Le*
Stanislavski, Constantin, 119
Steiner, Roger, 108
Stephenson, Robert C., 2
Stoullig, Edmond, 32
Sucker, The. See *Dindon, Le*
Suffering in farce, 7, 54
Surprises du divorce, Les (Bisson and Mars), 139 n.32
Surrealism, 107
Système Ribadier, Le, 35, 70-71, 77, 78, 80, 86; adultery in, 92, 96; as deception formula play, 26-27, 39; hypnotism in, 25, 61

Tailleur pour dames, 32, 77, 80, 81, 82; as deception formula play, 26-27, 32, 48, 56, 57; philanderers in, 91-92
Tenailles, Les (Hervieu), 124

Through the Window. See *Par la fenêtre*
Tied by a String. See *Fil à la patte, Un*
Tragedy and farce, 54, 109
Transformations, 54-59
Treich, Leon, 139 n.25
Trickery, 56
Trois filles de M. Dupont, Les (Brieux), 125
Tynan, Kenneth, 120

Unselfishness in Feydeau, 103

Vaudeville, 8, 21, 25, 28-29, 31, 32-33, 46
Veblen, Thorstein, 112
Verne, Jules, 61
Verneuil, Louis, 118
Verse in farce, 19
Versini, Georges, 113
Violence in Feydeau's plays, 69-72
Vitu, Auguste, 32, 89-90
Voleur, Le (Bernstein), 125
Voltz, Pierre, 107, 143 n.13
Voyage de Monsieur Perichon, Le (Labiche), 75

Well-made play, 20-22, 31, 36, 46
Welsford, Enid, 14, 52, 53
Weyl, Fernand [pseud. Nozière], 53, 116
Women in Feydeau's plays, 87-93, 94

Xenophobia in Feydeau's plays, 62

Yahiel, Edwin Daniel, 113

Zola, Emile, 123